The Art of Peace Formation

The Art of Peace Formation

Arts-Based Social Movements, Opportunities
and Blockages

BIRTE VOGEL, STEFANIE KAPPLER AND
OLIVER P. RICHMOND

EDINBURGH
University Press

Edinburgh University Press is one of the leading university presses in the UK. We publish academic books and journals in our selected subject areas across the humanities and social sciences, combining cutting-edge scholarship with high editorial and production values to produce academic works of lasting importance. For more information visit our website: edinburghuniversitypress.com

Edinburgh University Press Ltd
13 Infirmary Street
Edinburgh EH1 1LT

First published in hardback by Edinburgh University Press 2024

Typeset in 10/13 Giovanni
by Cheshire Typesetting Ltd, Cuddington, Cheshire

A CIP record for this book is available from the British Library

ISBN 978 1 3995 1953 3 (hardback)
ISBN 978 1 3995 1954 0 (paperback)
ISBN 978 1 3995 1954 0 (webready PDF)
ISBN 978 1 3995 1956 4 (epub)

CONTENTS

ILLUSTRATIONS

Figures

Tables

About the Editors

Stefanie Kappler is Professor in Conflict Resolution and Peacebuilding at the School of Government and International Affairs at Durham University. Her research interests include spatial approaches to peace, memory politics and the role of the arts in peace processes. Stefanie has recently been working on research projects investigating the role of memory politics in peacebuilding (funded by The Swedish Foundation for Humanities and Social Sciences), the cultural heritage of conflict (funded by The Swedish Research Council), the impact of the arts on peace formation and decolonial approaches to peace education (both funded by the Arts and Humanities Research Council).

Oliver P. Richmond is Research Professor in IR and Peace and Conflict Studies at the University of Manchester, UK. He is also International Professor at Dublin City University, Distinguished Visiting Professor at Ewha University, Seoul, Korea, and Honorary Professor in the School of International Relations, University of St Andrews, UK. He received a Distinguished Scholar award from the ISA Peace Studies Section in 2019. His publications include *The Grand Design: The Evolution of the International Peace Architecture* (2022), *Peace Formation and Political Order in Conflict Affected Societies* (2016), and *Failed Statebuilding* (2014). He is co-editor of the book series *Rethinking Peace and Conflict Studies*, and co-editor of the journal *Peacebuilding*.

Birte Vogel is Senior Lecturer in Humanitarianism, Peace and Conflict Studies at the Humanitarian and Conflict Response Institute (HCRI), University of Manchester, UK. She was a Co-Investigator on the Arts and Humanities Research Council project *The Art of Peace* looking at the role of the arts in peace processes and is a co-founder of the International Consortium for Conflict Graffiti (ICCG). She is the PI of a British Academy Knowledge

Frontiers grant on knowledge production and research ethics. Her co-edited books reflect her other research interest in the intersection of economics and peace and conflict studies (*Economies of Peace*, 2019), as well as her interest in research ethics and methodologies (*The Companion to Peace and Conflict Fieldwork*, 2021). She is the editor of the *HCRI Policy Brief Series*.

Contributors

Teresa Ó Brádaigh Bean is head of research and learning at In Place of War, a global charity that works to support grassroots arts-based social change processes in sites of conflict. Her research and practice have focused on hip hop as a social movement, grassroots arts education, creative entrepreneurship and community arts-based peacebuilding knowledge networks. She is an Honorary Research Fellow at the University of Manchester, a member of The Global Coalition on Youth, Peace and Security (GCYPS), a UN Inter-Agency Network, and interim Director for Education at the European Institute of Innovation & Technology Culture and Creativity.

Lydia C. Cole is a Lecturer in International Relations at the University of Sussex. Her research is situated at the intersection of aesthetic politics and critical peace and conflict studies, with a particular focus on activist curating in contested sites of memory in Bosnia and Herzegovina. Her research has been published in journals such as *International Political Sociology* and *Journal of Intervention and Statebuilding*.

Zingisa Nkosinkulu, is a curator, art historian and visual/graffiti artist. His areas of study and practice include contemporary African art, black radical tradition, decolonial aesthetics/aesthesis, Hip Hop, Free Jazz, Blockchain NFTs and indigenous Xhosa tradition in art. He acquired his diploma in Fine Art at NMMU, his B-Tech at WSU, his Master of Visual Art at Unisa, and his PhD at Unisa. Dr Nkosinkulu is a former research Post-Doctoral Fellow at Unisa and is currently a lecturer in the Faculty of Arts and Design at the Tshwane University of Technology. His research focus is on the relationship between art and the politics of decolonisation. His artworks can be viewed at www.drzingisankosinkulu.com.

Primitivo III Cabanes Ragandang is a Political Science Assistant Professor at Mindanao State University-Iligan in the Philippines. He earned his PhD at The Australian National University, exploring the intergenerational intersect of collective memory and community resilience in (post) conflict areas. His regional expertise is Mindanao in the Southern Philippines. He is the founder of BHOLI Youth Centre, a youth-led organisation that offers after school programmes to students pre-K-12 in Northern Mindanao in the Philippines. In 2021, he completed his co-edited book on youth, peacebuilding, and sustainability, published through the Young Southeast Asia Leaders Program of the United States Mission to ASEAN.

Peer Schouten is a Senior Researcher at the Danish Institute for International Studies and Associate Researcher at the International Peace Information Service (Antwerp). Peer is interested in the intersections of state formation and the political economy of conflict, with an empirical commitment to Central Africa.

Azadeh Sobout is a post-doctoral scholar with particular interest in artivism, geographies of displacement, post-conflict peacebuilding, (re)construction and justice. During the past eight years she has created visual and ethnographic accounts into the exploration of urbicide, war memoryscapes and narratives of displacement, bringing a new paradigmatic shift to the study of post-war reconstruction and transitional justice. With a commitment to solidarity scholarship, she has been practising, conceiving and researching an idea of 'justice' that reflects on the complexity of working through responsibility and ethics, while building long-term relationships and situated solidarities with specific struggles.

Aly Verjee is a non-resident Senior Advisor at the United States Institute of Peace and a Fellow of the Rift Valley Institute. He lived and worked in Sudan and South Sudan from 2005 to 2011, was a member of the secretariat of the Intergovernmental Authority on Development (IGAD)-led mediation of the South Sudan conflict from 2014 to 2015, and was subsequently Deputy and acting Chief of Staff of the Joint Monitoring and Evaluation Commission overseeing the 2015 peace agreement in South Sudan until 2016. In 2019, he received the Oslo Forum *PeaceWriter* Prize 'for bold and innovative responses to today's peacemaking challenges'.

ACKNOWLEDGEMENTS

This edited volume is related to 'The Art of Peace' project funded by the Arts and Humanities Research Council (AHRC, grant No: AH/S001484/1). We are also grateful to all participating artists and academics, in particular our project manager and creative brain Ruth Daniel from In Place of War. The book's cover picture was created by artist Barney Ibbotson. We also acknowledge language editing support from Patrick Tom.

ABBREVIATIONS

AHRC	Arts and Humanities Research Council
BiH	Bosnia and Herzegovina
CND	Campaign for Nuclear Disarmament
DRC	Democratic Republic of Congo
EU	European Union
EUAM	European Union Administration of Mostar
FARC	Fuerzas Armadas Revolucionarias de Colombia
ISIS	Islamic State of Iraq and Syria
NGO	Non-governmental organisation
PoA	Peace of Art
SAFMO	Street Arts Festival Mostar
SSTO	South Sudan Theatre Organisation
SSWE	South Sudan Wrestling Entertainment
UN	United Nations
UNESCO	United Nations Educational, Scientific and Cultural Organisation
WWI	World War One
WWII	World War Two

Artpeace: Arts-Based Social Movements, Peace Formation and Curation

Stefanie Kappler, Oliver P. Richmond and Birte Vogel

The arts have long been a visible instrument used to communicate political agendas, articulate dissent, or mobilise for change. Peace art, for instance, has been around for centuries, spanning Lorenzetti's painting *The Effects of Good Government on Town and Country* (1338–40) and Picasso's *Guernica* (1937), capturing the contrast between peace and war. Today, political graffiti appears in urban landscapes across the globe in times of social and political transitions and contestation, both in support of progressive political agendas and authoritarian regimes (Lennon 2021, 2). Music, in various forms, has brought dissident and alternative voices to local and global audiences, especially where freedom of speech is limited and political opposition silenced, as with the prominent political activism of Pussy Riot in Russia. This is by no means unique though. The picture below captures some of the creative resistance during the 2019 Hong Kong protests near Tsuen Wan MTR station. This anonymous Lennon Wall engaged commuters on their daily journeys with the political discourse of the time in an increasingly censored media landscape, and provided the opportunity to participate by adding messages via sticky notes. Thus, with the potential of art to connect to local communities and capture international (media) attention, it is not surprising that, over the past decades, funding for arts-based approaches to peace has been integrated into international and national peacebuilding agendas in the hope that the arts can be a vehicle for peace and peacebuilding. But what does the journey from the arts to politics look like? And how successful are arts-based interventions, funded and unfunded, local or international, in transforming social, political and economic realities at the national and international level? Can they really contribute to peace and political change? The contributions in this edited volume seek to explore and understand the arts' transformational potential, how their impact is mitigated by power and political structures, and what type of peace emerges as a result. In doing so, the book unpacks the complex factors that block or enable the assumed radical or hybrid potential of the arts.

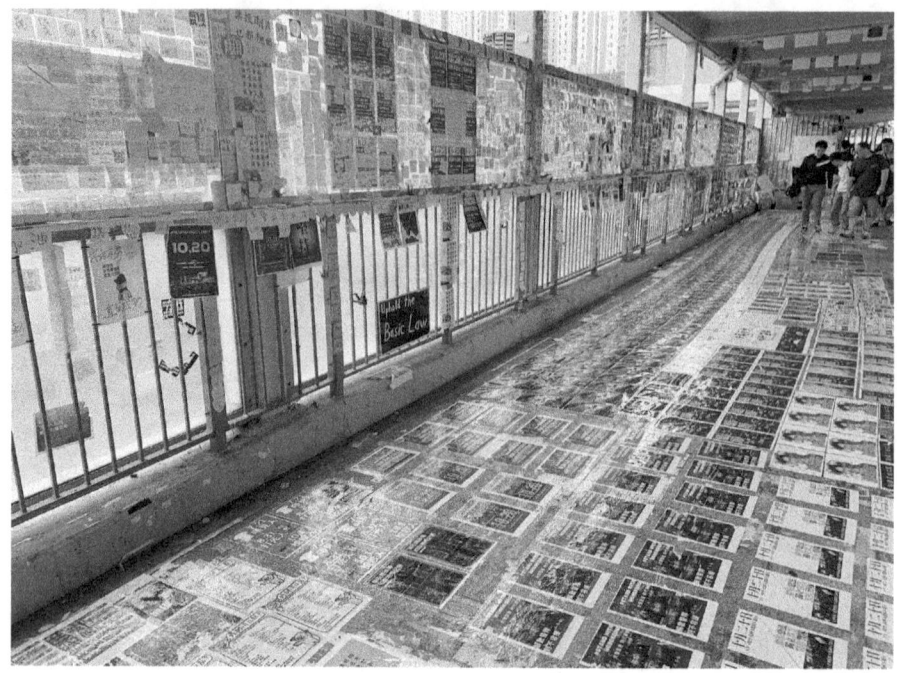

Figure 0.1 Lennon Wall in Hong Kong during the 2019 protests. Photo: Sherwin, 2019.

This book has emerged from the Arts and Humanities Research Council (AHRC) funded project *The Art of Peace*, which, over the course of four years (2018–22), engaged with the question of what type of political claims about peace are made by arts-based social movements, and whether or not these claims translate into political, cultural or social change. The outcome of the melange of arts-based activism, political response and resulting change is something we will refer to as *artpeace* throughout this book. *Artpeace* investigates the nature of emancipatory claims and related blockages, spanning urban infrastructures at the micro-level, to colonial legacies and practices at the micro- and macro-level. The *Art of Peace* project developed a range of collaborations with international and national researchers, non-governmental organisations (NGOs), community arts-groups and local artists who have tried to bridge the gap between the arts and politics, or navigate around the blockages that limit artistic impact. As such, this book is an attempt to bring into conversation the literature on global aesthetics (cf. Bleiker 2017, 2018; Baker 2021) on the one hand, and grassroots-driven arts activism on the other hand (cf. Bergh and Sloboda 2010; Ryan 2016; Mitchell et al. 2020). In this book, we deliberately understand the arts in very broad terms as any locally grounded artistic or cultural activity, ranging from hip hop, graffiti projects and traditional ballads to more established and formalised arts projects such as theatre performances, exhibitions and cultural festivals. Such a broad understanding helps to move the project beyond a Eurocentric understanding of what 'art' and 'culture' are, and, consequently does not limit the possibilities to which cultural activities may engage in peacemaking. This is reflected in the selection of case studies and authors from within and beyond the project, ranging from academics to those engaged in arts-based activism and some in between those worlds. Collectively, we investigate what *artpeace* means in different contexts in relation to formal and informal peace processes, both empirically and conceptually, ranging from more traditional practices of reconciliation to revolutionary, frictional politics that subverts the status quo. As such, the book takes the reader on various different journeys from the arts to politics.

The Journey of the Arts into Peacebuilding Debates

Our starting point in this introduction is to explore how the arts have become an area of interest for peace and conflict scholars and peacebuilders. Throughout the book, we explore arts-based approaches to peace and social change in the context of longstanding criticism of international peace interventions for their failure to connect to the societies they try to intervene in: in particular we explore the apparent inability of actors in power to reach out and connect with local communities and leaders who are key in transforming societies and enabling a lasting peace (Mac Ginty and Richmond 2013). While peacebuilding was initially thought to be focused on local agency, it was later co-opted by United Nations (UN) practice as well as connected with a range of local elites (Boutros-Ghali 1992; Lederach 1995). By the late 1990s peacebuilding had become thoroughly institutionalised and internationalised. Thus, peacebuilding processes have been theorised mainly in terms of improving security, extending law and rights, institutional development, and promoting civil society—often through top-down forms of intervention designed to align these areas with a liberal framework of politics. There has been little understanding of localised systems of governance, of peacemaking or of the related development of hybrid political order and forms of peace (Boege et al. 2008; Richmond 2011). For this reason, a 'local turn' in peace and conflict studies sought to understand the potential of local peace agency, including arts-based social movements and arts-based approaches to peace, in the broad context of conflict as well as international practices of peacebuilding and development (Kappler 2014; Richmond 2016). The local turn has investigated, through critical and in particular feminist or intersectional theories (Sylvester 2009; Crenshaw 1991) as well as post-colonial theory (Spivak 1988), the possibilities for alternative sites of peacemaking at everyday levels of society, citing their potential to resist injustice, or their tendency to be co-opted by elite power structures or international policies for peace and development (Richmond 2011). These dynamics help determine the legitimacy of both the peace process and any agreed reforms to the state from below. Yet there remains an ambivalent understanding of local peace agency, which has not been investigated fully.

As such, we deliberately shift our focus from *peacebuilding* to *peace formation* when thinking about *artpeace*, referring to localised peace practices and their political consequences for the state and international order. Peace formation emphasises localised peace practices over internationally driven ones and attempts to look beyond the often-artificial construction of a civil society (Keane 2005; Paffenholz 2015; Vogel 2016), instead emphasising more grounded everyday practices in a mundane sense (de Certeau 1985; Mac Ginty 2014) and customary forms of political authority (Boege et al. 2008; Richmond 2011). Richmond (2016, 2019), specifically, has argued that the concept of peace formation offers a view of the otherwise hidden subaltern political claims that influence, if only indirectly, the path of peace processes and the reform of the state. Focusing on peace formation also enables an understanding of local and everyday approaches to peace as discursive political claims, and relational and networked attempts to check and balance power structures.

Existing work on peace formation emphasises the need to examine peace not as an externally imposed, but as an organically forming concept raising cultural and art-based issues in a political context. In this sense, peace may be formed in a grammar that exists outside of the existing modes of power politics in an existing conflict-affected society (Lederach 1995; Richmond 2011). Local agency, utilising alternative methods that transcend the existing, formal, public, hierarchy of the state and the international system, raises everyday, subaltern issues through a form of intersectionality (Crenshaw 1991) and seeks to incorporate them into politics (Spivak 1988; Kappler and Lemay-Hébert 2019; Mac Ginty 2011). This often means that processes of resistance and multiple encounters between unexpected political agencies and hegemonic power structures lead to the production of hybrid political orders (Boege 2008), connecting matters of gender, race, class, representation, and political order. Peace formation agency is transversal, transnational, and scalar, exercising a dexterity the sphere of politics and power cannot match, even if the latter has far more weight. Its aim is to shape the state and the international, or at least to make an intervention in state formation and international political processes (Richmond 2019). International peace and development strategies may provide a platform for this circumnavigation of the politics of violence, but they may be challenged as well. They raise questions relating to shifting conceptions of legitimacy, and the expansion of rights (Arendt 1951; DeGooyer 2018; Richmond 2019). Instead of privileging institutional and formal agency as dominant forces in the formation of peace, they suggest that 'subaltern' agency can shape politics in different, creative ways. The negotiations between the various actors engaged in and having a stake in the formation of a peace regime in turn result in a negotiated outcome, or, in other words, in forms of hybrid peace which may be negative (the cessation of violence) or positive (the presence of human rights and economic well-being) in nature (Galtung 1969).

It is against the background of an attempt to centre local agency that arts-based approaches to supporting peace have gained some traction as an emerging area of research and practice. Scholars are interested in the question of whether the arts can overcome the gap between local, national and international actors, help to engage better with everyday issues in the political, cultural and social environment in which peace interventions take place, or act as a medium through which to read local responses to political events (for example, Kappler 2014; Shank and Schirch 2009; Tellidis and Glomm 2018; Vogel et al. 2020). Following this logic, the arts can be seen as a site of knowledge as much as practice. As such, they are an area of creativity and political innovation in terms of offering alternative perspectives on violence and those elements not easily identifiable from a Western-centric rationality, as well as creating alternative frameworks for a solution. The arts may offer new approaches that help solve power deadlocks, build legitimacy and contribute to peace formation processes, potentially influencing the nature of the state, good life and international political order by promoting positive forms of peace, highlighting unseen and structural violence and supporting the proscription of violence across the scales of analysis. They could offer a grounded, resonant, alternative grammar of representation, which utilises transnational and transversal networks for peace-oriented communication, advocacy reconciliation, reform and non-violence. In this book, we specifically read how communities perform hip hop, produce graffiti, host festivals or make music to communicate and engage in the midst of political turmoil and crisis. Art-based engagement, here, is part and parcel of transversal engagements with the formalities of institutional peace, and may act as a catalyst through which social ideas of peace can be imagined, rejected or modified, and may encounter state and international versions in a plausible dialogue (as opposed to being ignored).

And indeed, as Schouten describes in the context of the DRC where arts-based projects have increasingly become professionalised, (international) NGOs have increased the number of arts-based peacebuilding projects in recent years. However, this creative approach has often been pursued with a focus on individual healing or inter-group contact, while, sometimes, it has been accused of a deliberate attempt to de-politicise artistic activities as Sobout's case study hints at: in other words, within the liberal peace frame, the arts are becoming more therapeutic than emancipatory. This illustrates the tensions between understanding the arts as a radical force of political change within the frame of peace formation on the one hand, and the arts as a peacebuilding tool on the other. In the latter case, the arts should align and support already pre-defined peacebuilding objectives rather than challenging them. Current debates sometimes also gloss over the potential of the arts as a tool of powerful propaganda for the state, empire and ideology that sits in contrast to its supposed progressive potential. Artists often depend on funding, which can give them a degree of independence from local power-holders, but also renders them vulnerable to obtaining funding from (state or business) institutions, who in turn will want to use art to legitimise their own positions. Many wars have indeed been validated through posters and other art forms that serve to create an aesthetics of violence making resistance against warfare less likely. As such, it is worth first having a close look at the literature around arts and peace so far.

Disconnected? The Micro and Macro Perspective on the Arts and Peace

Arts-based approaches to peace as an area of study and practice remain under-researched, partly because of disciplinary hierarchies since the 1960s, which have placed a premium on econometric rationalities. There is a tendency to view the arts in binary ways, as a representation of power and authority, or alternatively a demonstration of resistance. Accordingly, the current literature paints a rather apolitical, therapeutic and pragmatic picture of the role of the arts in peacebuilding, and a significant proportion of current approaches to peace in the field via arts leave little room for radical and political artistic potential, being focused on policy-driven issues. The literature in fact holds a rather functional view of the marginal role of the arts within the liberal peace framework. It is mainly seen as a localised tool for reconciliation, conflict resolution and individual trauma therapy or connected to debates about memorialisation and identity representation. It supports the broader political transformation determined by top-down actors, rather than being a source of creative epistemology on peace from deep within a conflict-affected context and emerging to challenge injustice and authoritarian power, or inconsistent international intervention with limited legitimacy. It is thus much more interested in peacebuilding than peace formation.

For instance, most of the research has focused on the ability of the arts to effect change at the local level while remaining a top-down tool of the state or international community rather than identifying what, through the arts, peace might look like from local perspectives. To that end, different art forms have been co-opted into peacebuilding interventions. For example, community theatre (for its participants) has been associated with peacebuilding, dialogue and reconciliation (Sternberg and Barnett 1998). The underlying assumptions are that community theatre supports peace at the community level through contact between former conflict parties. It mainly relies on contact theory and the idea that engaging with 'the other' breaks down social stereotypes (Allport 1954) from before and during violent conflict. Second, theatre is expected to improve dialogue and lead to reconciliation as it offers a safe space shielded from high-level politics, allowing for engagement with contested issues under the umbrella of a fictional narrative. It allows participants to engage with the 'others'' perspective without the need to accept or contest it instantly. These assumptions largely build on Boal's (1979) idea of the 'Theatre of the Oppressed', where the audience is acknowledged as an active part of the performance. Street and community performances are also seen as an efficient way of reaching local populations by top-down actors, especially in rural areas. At the same time, and connected to the previous point, theatre is expected to have an educational function for its audience created by directors or sponsors. Grassroots actors may also use theatre to reach their opponents in society, as well as to challenge the state and elites or engage with the international community. Such strategies are not without risks for them, however. Humanitarian and development actors have been using this technique for over two decades to disseminate information about health-related issues, substance abuse or gender relations, in particular to low-income and highly oral and visual cultures (cf. Thompson 2007; Pelto and Singh 2010).

Similar processes have been applied through music as a tool for peace, such as the West-Eastern Divan Orchestra with regard to the Israel-Palestine conflict (founded in 1999 by Edward Said and Daniel Barenboim, both famed for breaking down boundaries within and between disciplines and practices). Again, the related literatures assume there might be improvement in inter-communal relations stemming from such cooperation, for example through joint orchestras, inter-faith choirs or bands, in order to engage with 'the other' (Lance 2012; Pruitt 2013; Bergh and Sloboda 2010). Street art and graffiti, on the other hand, are often seen as elements of space- and place-making or political communication, or as resistance against elite and state narratives or actions (Björkdahl and Kappler 2017; Ryan 2016; Vogel et al. 2020). Graffiti may represent new attempts to determine boundaries and establish informal authority in a given territory in defiance of political and economic elites.

What those micro arts-based approaches share, though, is the belief that diverse art projects and genres are best able to make a difference at the local level, to give voice to otherwise unheard actors, and help the healing of the individual or community. The literature is close to a consensus about the value and effectiveness of art initiatives in effecting local change, for the better or worse, though there is some controversy about how politically significant they may be. Scholarly inquiries make use of a range of creative and new methods to capture these micro-dynamics. These include, among others, photovoice (Reimers 2016), sound-based approaches (Chandola 2013; Cole and Kappler 2022) or the use of documentary films for peacebuilding (Premaratna 2021). Such approaches have indeed suggested that art-based projects can lead to meaningful change at community-level, but hard evidence remains limited. They have also largely refrained from explaining why changes in local constituencies are so rarely built into national or international peace processes, suggesting that beyond the local scale, political exclusions are resistant to arts-based, and indeed socially oriented strategies and dynamics.

Nevertheless, formal peacebuilding actors have started to consider art as a potential inroad into local peacebuilding. This endeavour tends to be conceived in problematic ways, however, representing their top-down view of the conflict and also often overloads civil society with the responsibility to resolve conflicts that may not be of their making with little in the way of plausible political resource. External peacebuilders have attempted to integrate culture in a broad sense, but this has often been linked to a somewhat simplistic understanding of culture as a static structure underpinning the ways in which international policies are received. Richmond (2009) calls this the 'romanticisation of the local', which refers to an indirect erasure of local agency, and the fact that international peacebuilding discourses often imagine culture as something discrete, bounded and unique (Handler 1986, 2). This ties in with how the literature depicts the arts in peacebuilding interventions—aimed from a top-down perspective involving a certain degree of functionalism in the arts as a peace methodology for state or international actors, NGOs as implementors and local actors as recipients. The use of art initiatives is thus often less a matter of enabling meaningful connections between external peacebuilders and those at the receiving end of peacebuilding, and instead rather an attempt to create structures of legitimacy for existing peacebuilding policies (cf. Kappler 2014). Political reform at the state and international level through arts-based initiatives remains rare.

This is contrasted by an emerging body of literature that investigates aesthetic regimes as a global phenomenon (Bleiker 2017, 2018; Baker 2021). While this literature has, importantly, highlighted the need to consider aesthetic practices as globally connected, it has so far not facilitated clear conclusions about how these practices can help us understand peace formation in political and social communities, nor broader political or international reforms. A current strand of theorising international relations has started to pay attention to the global dynamics, not only of art projects, but of aesthetics more generally. These approaches have tended to focus on visual aesthetics and are often labelled as 'visual global politics' (Bleiker 2018), attempting to make sense of the ways in which aesthetic impressions, such as images, shape our understanding of politics. Such approaches include the transnational movement of images (Bleiker 2018, 11) and take a dynamic perspective of aesthetics as a moving target. This scholarship remains somewhat vague in terms of the implications of aesthetic regimes for local communities and their political struggles. What it does though, is provide methodological inroads into capturing the connections between local and global dynamics. Examples are Lisle and Johnson's (2019) visual analysis of the traces of migration on the Greek island Kos; Shepherd's (2017) reflections on the ethics of aesthetics and visuality in a digital age; participatory art as a means to access youth knowledge (Mkwananzi et al. 2021); or Chouliaraki's (2005, 2006) work on the representation of war and humanitarian issues. This scholarship is starting to conceptualise in more depth the ways in which seemingly localised aesthetic manifestations (icons, symbols, sounds) are produced by, and themselves produce, larger patterns of politics. It helps us consider the circulatory trajectory of art and culture, which is no longer seen as parochially contained in isolated communities, but instead deeply entangled with the politics of violence and peace alike.

What does this then mean then for understanding the qualitative relationship between the arts and peace at large? Can the existing work on visual global politics suggest a way in which we can understand the translation of local aesthetics into political struggles, and even into global regimes, or the blockages preventing those local dynamics from turning into groundbreaking peace agendas? Why is it that, given the richness of local political and art initiatives, these so rarely affect the ways in which peace is designed at a national, regional or global level?

Our answer so far would be that the broader liberal peace project is too limited or conservative to incorporate creative challenges because it tends to maintain existing epistemological and methodological categories, which relate to class, gender, identity, the state and international actors. Such categories are often based on war-related divisions and translated into the peace process, but—as we will illustrate in this volume—tend not to draw together much beyond a micro-critique and small-scale mobilisation, nor impact on the transversal operation of politics. This is the case even though creative challenges tend to be closely aligned to contemporary scientific and ethical knowledge on peace, justice and sustainability, and about civil society strategies to disseminate their claims. This points to active and structural blockages against what are effectively subaltern signals for peacemaking which act as weathervanes for the legitimacy of the process, solution and the polity itself.

We argue that entrenched elite, state, security and internationally-based actors have an interest in stabilising political power rather than reconfiguring it. This helps us understand why they block the reach of arts-based approaches, explaining why we see such a clear disconnect between local arts-based ideas of peace, and the development of a national and/or global synthesis. To be inclusive and sustainable, peace processes would instead include ethics, aesthetics and practices associated with subaltern visions of political progress. Hence there is very substantial opposition to it, which conveniently can make the claim that subaltern, artistic expressions are 'agitprop' rather than meditations which carry political weight.

Organisation of the book

Our chapters are testimony to arts-based local knowledge and the diverse understandings of peace that would result if taken seriously. The authors trace what artistic intervention in each locale can and cannot do to change the political landscape they are operating in. In Chapter 1, Oliver P. Richmond lays some historical foundations by tracing back the relationship between peace, art, power and resistance. The chapter also makes the Eurocentric understanding of art that clouds much of the analysis and engagement with the arts today visible. In Chapter 2, the editors outline the theoretical framework underpinning the *Art of Peace* project, and this volume specifically, by exploring what *artpeace* means. This chapter maps out the journey from art to politics and the blockages and challenges this frictional relationship encounters along its way. It provides an analytical framework for the empirical chapters to follow.

In Chapter 3, Aly Verjee picks up the idea of what constitutes art by looking at 'high' and 'low' art in South Sudan. Verjee addresses how art is used across different levels, from the local to the national, to address the web of conflicts in South Sudan and finds that wrestling and theatre can both contribute to peacebuilding. At all levels, subaltern agency is ultimately working along a local-national-international spectrum, meaning many events might have started out locally but later contributed to the broader peace process.

In Chapter 4 and Chapter 5, Lydia Cole and Teresa Ó Brádaigh Bean look at the transformative potential of street art and hip hop culture, respectively. Cole's chapter investigates the relationship between street art and processes of peace formation in Mostar, focusing particularly on the aesthetic and spatial aspects of peace and its potential to transform urban landscapes. Ó Brádaigh Bean, in Chapter 5, discusses how hip hop culture has become a strong feature of peace formation in Medellín. In the absence of a state strategy, and with governance power still divided between illicit and state actors, she highlights how hip hop culture has spun its own networks across the city, transforming infrastructures and economic opportunities, and serving as a counter-weight to the dominant culture of violence.

Peer Schouten and Azadeh Sobout both grapple with the idea of *artivism* in their respective chapters. Schouten, in Chapter 6, explores the complex and sometimes competing processes of popular art in the Democratic Republic of Congo. Schouten highlights how art and activism merge and create alternative spaces in conflict-affected societies. He also analyses the fraught relations between Congolese artivism and international peacebuilding efforts, by exploring the influence of NGOs seeking to deploy art as a 'weapon of peace'. Sobout, in Chapter 7, focuses on the artivism of Syrian refugees in Lebanon who formed their own microcosm—a society in exile—leading to the creation of new temporalities and new forms of social and political imagination for a post-war order. Understanding artivism both as an artistic and political practice, this chapter explores whether the arts have the possibility to produce a kind of politics different from that promoted by state elites.

Chapters 8 and 9 zoom in on the role of art in societies with colonial legacies and the arts' ability to challenge and engage with them. In Chapter 8, Nkosinkulu explores graffiti as resistance against colonial realities drawing on his own graffiti project in a South African township. He frames the streets as a living and changing counterweight to established political systems that embody colonial legacies. By raising awareness about African thinkers he highlights local over colonial knowledge, arguing that peace can only be achieved if it embodies the decoloniality of knowledge, decoloniality of being and decoloniality of power. In his chapter, graffiti becomes a peace formation process articulated by the streets. In the final chapter of this book, Primitivo III Cabanes Ragandang engages with how the colonial past is remembered in traditional ballads in the Philippines. He argues that, through their music, local populations clearly point to societal issues peacebuilding interventions could engage with—in this case the unhealed wounds of the past—if national and international actors were both able and willing to listen.

Reflections

Throughout the chapters, we observe a non-linear, intricate relationship between art and politics. While it is clear that art has historically often sought to replicate political power structures, whether it was to obtain access to funding, power or other forms of privilege, we also realise the potential of arts-based approaches to make a meaningful, and potentially transformative, contribution to the status-quo-oriented politics of peace. It is then not a question of *whether artpeace* impacts politics, but a question of *how* it does so in the face of the clear power asymmetries between those who hold

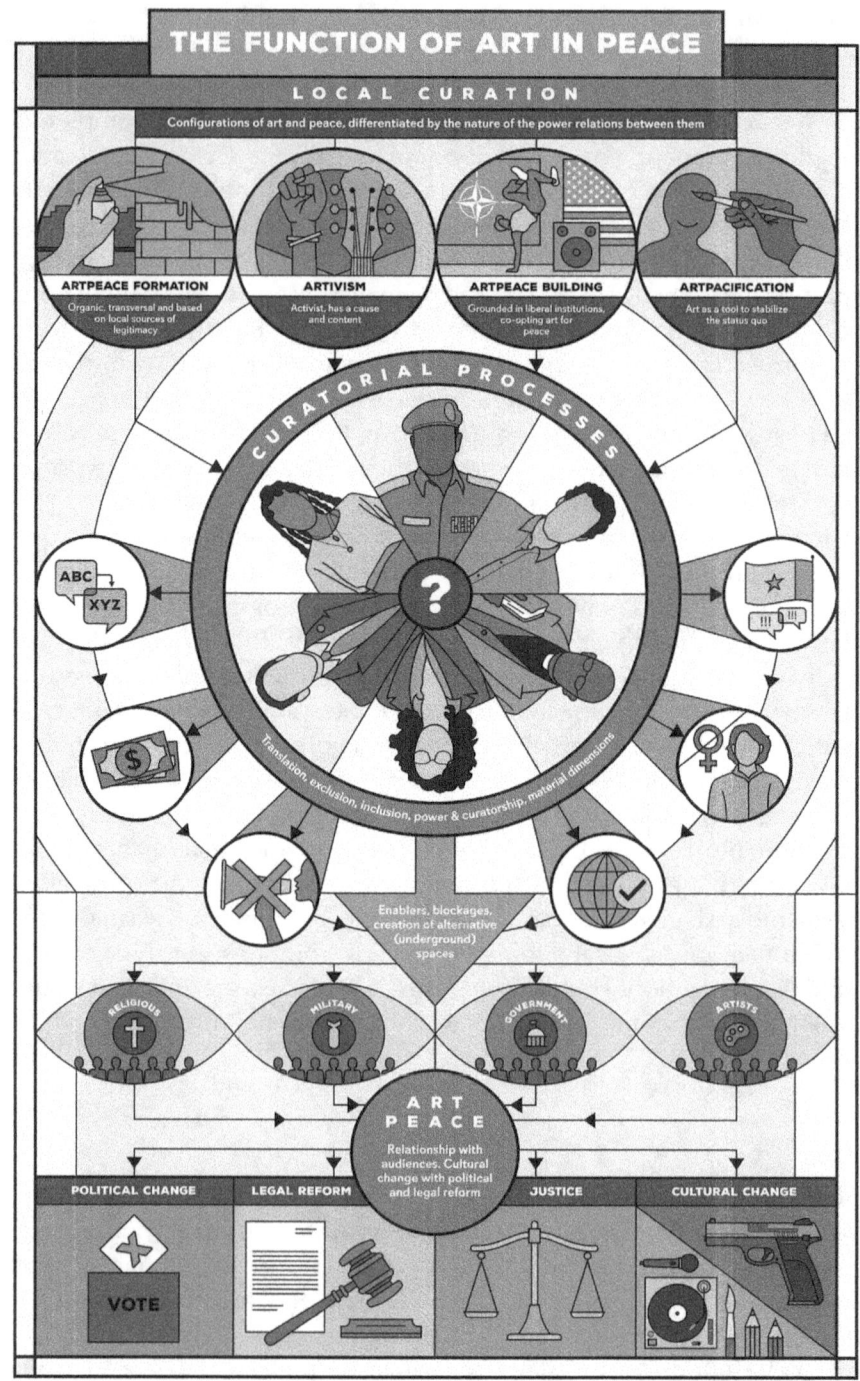

Figure 0.2 Visualisation of the journey from arts to politics, its function and blockages.
Credit: Barney Ibbotson.

power and those who seek to aesthetically resist it. Indeed, there are multiple nodes at which art meets politics in all the chapters. These can be formal and include projects commissioned by the state or big donors, the solicitation of artists in large peacebuilding projects, or campaigns to legitimise political power in a post-conflict environment. They can also be smaller nodes that become only visible in the small cracks of power where they fill power vacuums, build informal new alliances or build the language that is able to challenge the status quo.

Art is thus never free from politics but embedded in a political landscape of legitimising or transformative entanglements, and often both at the same time. Much of the challenging work may require a degree of acceptance of and working with prevailing power relations by the artistic community, so spaces can be carved out through which meaningful change can be instigated. The chapters in this book speak to this complex entanglement between art and politics and ask whether their encounter tends to remain limited to a tokenistic intervention, or is able to eventually lead to tangible political change. The insights from South Sudan, Bosnia-Herzegovina, Colombia, the DRC, Lebanon, South Africa and the Philippines show in fact that the blockages that artists face in an endeavour to create meaningful change can be powerful and sometimes inhibit the kinds of transformation that are articulated in art. The arts, we found however, can play multiple roles in relation to peace: a vehicle for political change, resistance or reconciliation for those actively producing it; a tool for peacebuilding for practitioners and communities; and a site of knowledge about societies and conflicts for scholars.

Returning to our ambition to integrate the arts with scholarship of peace and conflict, and to work with community artists throughout the project, we asked one of the artists on the *Art of Peace* project to visualise the journey from the arts to politics for us from an artistic perspective. The artwork above shows the multiple actors, processes and outcomes that can emerge and that we will theoretically unpack in Chapter 2, after looking first into the historic origins of *artpeace*.

Bibliography

Allport, G. W. 1954. *The nature of prejudice*. Reading, MA: Addison-Wesley.

Arendt, H. 1973. *The origins of totalitarianism* [1951]. New York: Harcourt Brace.

Baker, C. 2021. *Making War on Bodies: Militarisation, aesthetics and embodiment in international politics*. Edinburgh: Edinburgh University Press.

Bergh, A., and Sloboda, J. 2010. Music and art in conflict transformation: A review. *Music and Arts in Action*, 2(2), pp. 1–16.

Boege, V., Brown, A., Clements, K., and Nolan, A. 2008. On hybrid political orders and emerging states: What is failing-states in the global south or research and politics in the west? *Berghof Handbook Dialogue Series*, 8, pp. 15–35.

Björkdahl, A. and Kappler, S. 2017. *Peacebuilding and spatial transformation: Peace, space and place.* London and New York: Routledge.

Bleiker, R. 2017. In search of thinking space: Reflections on the aesthetic turn in International Political Theory. *Millennium,* 45(2), pp. 258–64.

Bleiker, R. 2018. *Visual global politics.* London and New York: Routledge.

Boal, A. 2000. *Theater of the oppressed* [1979]. London: Pluto Press.

Boutros-Ghali, B. 1992. An agenda for peace: Preventive diplomacy, peacemaking and peace-keeping. *International Relations,* 11(3), pp. 201–18.

Chandler, D. 2014. Beyond neoliberalism: Resilience, the new art of governing complexity. *Resilience: International Policies, Practices and Discourses,* 2(1), pp. 47–63.

Chandola, T. 2013. Listening in to water routes: Soundscapes as cultural systems. *International Journal of Cultural Studies,* 16(1), pp. 55–69.

Chouliaraki, L. 2005. Spectacular ethics: On the television footage of the Iraq war. *Journal of Language and Politics,* 4(1), pp. 143–59.

Chouliaraki, L. 2006. *The spectatorship of suffering.* London: Sage.

de Certeau, M. 1985. *The practice of everyday life.* Berkeley and Los Angeles, CA: University of California Press.

Cole, L. C. and Kappler, S. 2022. Soundscapes of Mostar: Space and art beyond the divided city. *Journal of Intervention and Statebuilding,* 16(5), pp. 641–58.

DeGooyer, S., Hunt, S., Maxwell, L. and Moyn, S. (eds). 2018. *The Right to Have Rights.* London: Verso.

Galtung, J. 1969. Violence, Peace and Peace Research. *Journal of Peace Research,* 6 (3), pp. 167–91.

Handler, R. 1986. Authenticity. *Anthropology Today,* 2(1), pp. 2–4.

Kappler, S. 2014. *Local agency and peacebuilding. EU and international engagement in Bosnia-Herzegovina, Cyprus and South Africa.* Basingstoke: Palgrave Macmillan.

Kappler, S. and Lemay-Hébert, N. 2019. From power-blind binaries to the intersectionality of peace: connecting feminism and critical peace and conflict studies. *Peacebuilding,* 7(2), pp. 160–77.

Keane, J. 2005. Eleven theses on markets and civil society. *Journal of Civil Society* 1.1, pp. 25–34.

Lance, K. M. 2012. *Breakin' Beats & Building Peace: Exploring the Effects of Music & Dance in Peacebuilding.* American University ProQuest Dissertations Publishing.

Lederach, J. P. 1995. Conflict transformation in protracted internal conflicts: The case for a comprehensive framework. *Conflict Transformation,* pp. 201–22.

Lisle, D. and Johnson, H. L. 2019 Lost in the aftermath. *Security Dialogue,* 50(1), pp. 20–39.

Mac Ginty, R. and Richmond, O. P. 2013. The local turn in peace building: A critical agenda for peace. *Third World Quarterly,* 34(5), pp. 763–83.

Mitchell, J. P., Vincett, G., and Hawksley, T. (eds). 2020. *Peacebuilding and the Arts.* Cham: Palgrave Macmillan.

Mkwananzi, W. F., Cin, F. M., and Marovah, T. 2021. Participatory art for navigating political capabilities and aspirations among rural youth in Zimbabwe. *Third World Quarterly,* 42(12), pp. 2863–82.

Paffenholz, T. 2015. Unpacking the local turn in peacebuilding: a critical assessment towards an agenda for future research. *Third World Quarterly,* 36(5), pp. 857–74.

Pelto, P. J. and Singh, R. 2010. Community street theatre as a tool for interventions on alcohol use and other behaviors related to HIV risks. *AIDS and Behavior,* 14(1), 147–57.

Pruitt, L. J. 2013. *Youth peacebuilding: Music, gender, and change.* Albany, NY: Suny Press.

Premaratna N. 2021. Dealing with Sri Lanka's demons: Using documentary film for peacebuilding. *Journal of Peacebuilding & Development,* 16(1), pp. 39–54.

Richmond, O. P. 2011. *A post-liberal peace.* London: Routledge.

Richmond, O. P. 2016. *Peace formation and political order in conflict affected societies.* Oxford: Oxford University Press.

Richmond, O. P. 2019. Human rights and the development of a twenty-first century peace architecture: unintended consequences? *Australian Journal of International Affairs*, 73(1), pp. 45–63.

Reimers, B. C. 2016. Peacebuilding in refugee resettlement communities: Using photovoice to find common ground. *Journal of Peacebuilding & Developmen*, 11(3), pp. 108–13.

Ryan, H. E. 2016. *Political street art: Communication, culture and resistance in Latin America.* London: Routledge.

Shank, M., & Schirch, L. 2008. Strategic arts-based peacebuilding. *Peace & Change*, 33(2), 217–42.

Shepherd, L. 2017. Aesthetics, ethics, and visual research in the digital age: 'Undone in the face of the otter.' *Millennium: Journal of International Studies*, 45(2), pp. 214–22.

Spivak, G. C. 1988. Can the subaltern speak? In C. Nelson and L. Grossberg, (eds), *Marxism and the interpretation of culture*. Basingstoke: Macmillan Education, pp. 271–313.

Spivak, G. C. 2000. Translation as culture. *Parallax*, 6(1), pp. 13–24.

Sternberg, P. and Barnett, L. A. 1998. *Theatre for conflict resolution: In the classroom and beyond.* Portsmouth, NH: Heinemann.

Sylvester, C. 2009. *Art/Museums. International relations where we least expect it.* London: Paradigm.

Tan de Bibiana, M. 2017. Changing lenses: Using participatory photography for wide-angle intergroup perspectives on peace and conflict for social change. http://www.diva-portal.org/smash/record.jsf?pid=diva2%3A1128826&dswid=-7769 (accessed 11 November 2022).

Tellidis, I. and Glomm, A. 2018. Street art as everyday counterterrorism? The Norwegian art community's reaction to the 22 July 2011 attacks. *Cooperation and Conflict*, 54(2), pp. 191–210.

Thompson, J. 2007. Performance, globalization and conflict promotion/resolution: Experiences from Sri Lanka. In: Anheier, H. K. and Isar, Y. R. (eds). *Cultures and globalization: conflicts and tensions*. London: Sage, pp. 296–305.

Vogel. B. 2016. Civil society capture: Top-down interventions from below? *Intervention and Statebuilding*, 10(4), pp. 472–89.

Vogel, B., Arthur, C., Lepp, E., O'Driscoll, D., and Haworth, B. 2020. Reading socio-political and spatial dynamics through graffiti in conflict-affected societies. *Third World Quarterly*, 41(12), pp. 2148–68.

ONE

A Critical History of *Artpeace*

Oliver P. Richmond

This critical-historical chapter outlines the early and visible symbiosis of art, power, peace, agency and resistance, mainly examining the Western aesthetic and political tradition. As a background to the later material this book outlines and develops, it outlines how art—in this narrow but hegemonic context—has followed political power for much of history, while erasing representations of social, subaltern and political resistance and experimentation with new approaches to emancipation. This erasure occurred both within the global north, where social, resistance and peace movements were concerned, as well as elsewhere. This chapter helps explains the potential of *'artpeace'* and why it has been so limited and Eurocentric in the past, but also why the symbiosis of aesthetics, resistant and critical agency, reform and political changes lends substantial potential for peacemaking (Kerr 2020).

The growing momentum of critical methodological innovation, uncovering more detailed and complex understandings of emancipation, means that social agency and resistance has become more visible in the connection between art, peace and order in conflict-affected societies. However, it remains marginal, rarely uncovered, preserved and brought to the point of curation or being added to external collections, and still risks being erased by power. As later chapters in this volume indicate, however, the critical convergence that the concept of *artpeace* represents has become more consolidated, and is clearly meaningful to its proponents, even if its impact on peacemaking remains heavily constrained. There has clearly been less erasure of *artpeace* over time, which indicates critical potential for more development.

In the contemporary era, artistic engagements with peacemaking have become more common (Mitchell et al. 2020), and this chapter illustrates the antecedents and growing range of these developments, as they began to debate and contest issues of social agency, ethics and justice (Bloch 1980; Adorno 2020; Rancière 2006). The visual and performative 'spectacle' in peacemaking and political reform (Debord 1967) has shifted from hegemony and the restoration of an unjust status quo (imperialism and authoritarianism, for example) to more substantive, critical and emancipatory contributions (Richmond 2022). Visual, creative and artistic performances, processes, artifacts and dynamics have become associated with social mobilisation and resistance, being open, insightful, wide-ranging and less conditioned by institutions and traditions. This hints at a dialogic engagement with the 'moral imagination' (Lederach 2005) via *artpeace*. It offers the potential to enhance the ethical standing and legitimacy of peacemaking.

This background chapter outlines, with reference to a number of arts-based sources (presented in the reference list via website links),[1] a general evolution and development in the aesthetico-political engagement with, and representation of, peace. It examines the connection of social and ethical claims for peace with artistic representation, and resistance to injustice and hegemony. What emerges from the marriage of arts and peace, represents a radical and emancipatory synthesis that leads to forms of *artpeace*. This chapter firstly outlines some key dynamics in the obscure history of peace art, offering an exploratory conceptual framework for its evolution and symbiotic relationship with critical agency, resistance, and emancipatory thinking (despite its concurrent harnessing by state and elite power). The chapter then outlines the concept of *artpeace* as a basis for critical engagement in contemporary peace and conflict studies and examines its evolution and implications in the following sections.

Dynamics in the Relationship Between Peace, Politics and Art

Battles, Monarchs, Tradition, Victory and Atrocities

Understandings of the development of world history, of politics, society and economy, are all informed by crucial moments in history—often battles or wars won or lost. Violence also dominates media, aesthetics and everyday representations, emphasising the value of sacrifice and the potential of war, as well as its costs, normally from an elite, state or imperial perspective (Bevan 2015). World War I and II memorials are common in city centres, churches, and shrines around the world (King 1998). Most capitals have a 'tomb of the unknown soldier', an eternal flame, and tributes for the heroes who laid down their lives in order to found or save their country, to fight for justice and equality, against (but sometimes supporting) imperialism, fascism, totalitarianism, predation, nationalism and discrimination. Often, in such contexts it is argued that wars were fought for peace. War cemeteries from long forgotten wars and battles are common around the world, even in the most isolated places: they often contain the bodies of people from far away, who often fought in wars that were relatively distant to their own everyday lives and contexts. Rarely are there memorials to those more indirectly caught up in wars and violence, principally women and children, directly or indirectly (though this has become a growing trend more recently). Even less likely are commemorations of peace treaties, processes, peacekeeping or peacebuilding.

Peace in an ethico-political sense has thus been rarely celebrated, noted or described, except in passing, or in juxtaposition with geopolitical, elite or state violence, as a celebration of glory, or as a depiction of the horrors of violence. Depictions of the higher dynamics of peace, in parallel to those of often repeated virtues of war, are rarely referred to. The everyday, state and international dimensions of peace have proven difficult to capture, or artists find them uninteresting, undepictable or even unpopular: more plausibly such representations are easily erased by powerful actors and their narratives. On the one hand it is clear that aesthetic representations of peace, and the support of peace, have been a recurrent interest for some artists, but on the other hand many surviving representations have followed predictable and relatively limited themes which have supported power, militarism, empires and states.

Yet, peace has been documented as a key part of human history, politics and relations from very early on, as the early Kadesh peace treaty illustrates, as an important part of power-relations (Kadesh Treaty, n.d.). Its early stages indicated a limited artistic and creative record and may have reflected a disinterest on the part of elites in general in peace as distinct from war, or the elusive, empathetic qualities of a social peace. They may have also represented an attempt to reduce and censor the wider significance of peace from view to preserve the status quo—and the utility of war—and its associated power relations.

Memorials often underline how violence is always tragic, but more creative, critical and radical representations challenge systems of politics and representation. They tend to intimate that wars can never really be 'won' without immense sacrifice at best, especially in the relational sense of international relations, or in the everyday sense of the local context. Social and cultural reactions to tragedy of World War I are a case in point, even as elite actors battled over achieving victory (Winter 2014). Peace has been elusive and tragic, as Keynes famously warned (Keynes 1919), based upon new waves of domination, boundary setting and establishing new hegemonies, even if it is significant in its everyday senses. An unnuanced 'victor's peace' (Richmond 2005) has all too often been celebrated aesthetically.

Resistance, Rights, Empathy and Subaltern Contributions

From Hiroshima to the Somme, from the Killing Fields of Cambodia to the genocide church in Ntarama, Rwanda, artistic and stylised, visual representations and memorials of war and conflict are increasingly commonplace (Bourke 2017). They have become part of our everyday lived environment. They enable us to navigate around the seminal crises that mark the history of empire, and later, ideology and the state, as well as the development of social agency, resistance, critique and civil society. They have provided a platform, space and creative or critical modes for dealing with issues ranging from marginalisation and injustice to reconciliation, disarmament, identity and commemoration, as well as governance (local and global) regardless of how little formal power participants or its exponents may have. The arts have perhaps been conducive to such critical dynamics because they have connected 'subaltern' resistance and agency (that is critical agency which is generally marginalised by identity, gender, class and nationality) to a wider social and global consciousness (civil or perhaps global civil society, which is mostly anti-war and supports the wide proscription of violence in its multiple forms).

The imprint of *artpeace* on global consciousness has been significant given that the more formal history of the state and international relations is mainly focused on war, conquest, hegemony and governmentality. However, in recent times the association between peace and the arts has returned to more subaltern modes of critique partly because of the rejection of the liberal/neo-liberal peace framework more widely, and partly because of the recent return of multi-polarity at the geopolitical level, as well as the rise of populism and authoritarianism. These new modes are engaging with complex and very entrenched, often hidden power structures in specific localities (such as Colombia, the Balkans, Syria, DRC, or Sri Lanka) and localised issues (AHRC 2018–22). They may point to issues only indirectly associated with violence (e.g., authoritarianism, quasi-liberal states, capitalism, social class and related stratifications) as well as highlighting matters related to identity, environmentalism, historical and distributive justice, such as colonialism, land appropriation and slavery.

Critical currents in the arts tend to be more reflective, creative, emotionally sensitive, culturally and socially attuned and forward looking. In other words, they are able to identify inequality and injustice from below, hidden by the political structures of society, the state and the international system. The arts detect undercurrents and perhaps communicate them, though less tangibly than formal systems of codification: for example, Hans Holbein's painting *The Ambassadors* (1533) clearly depicts the power and mastery of diplomacy. Yet, it also more obliquely suggests its link with death rather than peace through the presence of an anamorphic skull, which can only be seen from an oblique perspective (Holbein 1533; Constantinou 1994). Thus, often the arts in relation to war and peace point to the limitations of political frameworks of agency based on power-relations, which effectively preserve war as a tool of structural violence and inequality. However, artistic endeavour often hints at an alternative, critical vanguard of peace development from a social perspective, even if its engagement is sparse and simplistic in aesthetic terms compared to war. The state or empire has often harnessed the arts for propaganda purposes with respect to the latter (Adorno and Horkheimer 2002; Groys 2008).

The more critical undercurrents in *artpeace* initially foregrounded the beauty, as well as loss, sorrow and horror—the contradictions of peace and war—across multiple dimensions but rarely saw peacemaking as a process that engendered mobilised resistant and critical, marginalised agency. This latter strategy—when it emerged—rather than glorifying power, promised to open up emotional, relational and solidarity elements. It often idealised the endpoint of peace and ignored the processes of peacemaking. However, it may point to cooperation and higher levels of co-existence, and highlights the longer-term political, social and cultural dramas related to war and peace in international relations, rather than merely the brutish immediacy of violence and power (Bleiker 2017).

This is especially so given the role of critique and emancipatory thinking in political and social commentary and in representing and imagining better modes of being for societies in general. The harder aesthetics of war often captured popular imagination, historically at least, and so have seemingly been more successfully translated into power than the aesthetics of peace. The latter often seem ethically correct from a critical perspective that focuses on the positionality of the weak, hidden and marginalised, and the subsequent emancipatory agency, related tactics and strategies of resistance (Scott 1990; Richmond 2011; Vinthagen 2015; Lilja 2022). Consequently, such critical agency (Richmond 2011) is also thoroughly suppressed and marginalised (Sharp 1973) although there has been a strong movement to valorise the 'higher' ethics and aesthetics of war and heroism throughout history, as with just war theory (Walzer 1977). The latter amounts to micro blockages or more substantial strategic blockages to radical imaginaries and their relationship with creative, critical agency, social movements and emancipatory knowledge.

Yet, the critical, radical, undercurrents and imaginaries of peace sometimes present in aesthetic representations now appear to have more social traction in the long term than the oft repeated cul-de-sacs of imperialism, nationalism and fascism (however 'heroic' they may initially appear). The history of art and its relationship with power, peace and emancipation, reflects the age-old struggle between disciplinary power and governmentality, emancipatory agency and resistance, and knowledge (Foucault 1997, 82). The advances that have been made in translating subaltern claims for security, freedom, rights, justice and sustainability, step by step across a range of historical artifacts, into practical political life in the modern world, were thus often imagined first, created, and then reinforced across society (and the global order) through the arts, following undercurrents, resistance and innovation in society (Beales 1931; Spivak 2000). Through various media such aesthetic thinking reached communities widely and deeply, often through undercurrents that may have represented more political legitimacy than more obvious narratives about, and exercises of, unequal power.

There have been chinks or breakthroughs that allowed more critical challenges, revolutionary learning and creative responses to emerge in several stages of the development of a relationship between peace and art (see Table 1.1 below). These often subaltern-style interventions have had world changing impacts over the very long term, perhaps because of the emotive and cultural power and weight they represent, even if they carry little direct, structural or governmental forms of power. Many such breakthroughs emerged from social, creative and radical movements at grassroots levels. They have influenced how the arts reflect and interpret the world, how history is memorialised, how political order is legitimated formally and within society (more to the point within excluded groups) and how peace is maintained, stabilised, rebuilt and developed further.

The Historical Evolution of *Artpeace*

As the following examples endeavour to illustrate, the arts have offered a range of openings for peace within Western traditions, as indicated in the previous section: contesting the consolidation of arbitrary power in mass consciousness and the development of radical, creative and experimental ideas through media designed to resist and bypass the hegemonic. As *artpeace* developed, it offered the possibility of firstly, highlighting violence and injustice; secondly, appealing to human emotions for solidarity, empathy, cooperation and to commemorate; thirdly, advocating and educating different audiences on matters of rights, justice and sustainability across generations and across borders or locations as a precursor to resistance, mobilisation and the construction of wider networks of critical agency; and fourthly, using a common language of aesthetic sensibilities to support reconciliation and pluralism (that is, in later stages).

Thus, the emergent concept of *artpeace* is flexible, wide-ranging, creative and critical, mobile, and often emerges from underground or subaltern groups and their networks, which can build long term community links and consensus. It has historically been networked and has paradoxically been available to powerful actors when they needed symbolic capital for peacemaking or propaganda. *Artpeace* may cut across boundaries via a common language which is non-verbal. It may offer new narratives for mobilisation, calm for reflection, group safety, conflict avoidance and accessibility for the marginal to develop platforms for growth, as well as the potential for elites to understand the experiences of the marginal (depending on the nature of the arts in question). It offers critical social legitimacy through relationality that politics often emulates in its contracts, but often cannot reach because elites are more power-driven than consensus based (Bailey undated).[2]

Yet, underlying this progressive path are the more reductive uses that states, empires and elites have put the arts to in early stages, which have echoed onwards throughout contemporary eras, acting as both a foundation of political order and stability, and obstacles to progress and political change. Indeed, the overwhelming capacity of discursive and state power, when united, can bend critical and challenging representations for peace, justice and emancipation back towards founding narratives associated with nationalism, the state and empire (see Delacroix 1830, as mentioned below).

The Early Stages of Artpeace: The Imperial, Nationalist and Conservative Phase

Building an aesthetics of peace into political and economic systems and settlements has long been an implausible task, given that they have mostly all been founded through clashes of power, war, domination, extraction and hegemony: in its earliest stages, the arts were deployed as validating baubles, if at all. Yet, it was also the first step towards making such systems socially responsive and accountable in their later stages. Historical sources show very small steps towards peace often utilised, or even depended upon, critical and subaltern modes of representation that communicated such needs deeply with their audiences.

For example, the Kadesh Treaty represented a classic stage one type of example of the coming together of arts and politics. It ended the Battle of Kadesh between Ramesses II's Egypt and the Hittites of Muwatalli II in around 1274 BC. This battle is thought to be the largest chariot battle ever fought, involving perhaps 5,000 chariots. The peace was made via a treaty in around 1258 BC. A clay copy of the written treaty—itself now an artifact— survives in the Istanbul Archaeological Museum. A replica is on display at the headquarters of the United Nations, and an Egyptian version survives on papyrus. It has become one of a few global symbols of peace.

Peace, as evidenced by this treaty, was determined by war, power and elite interests, rather than justice or rights at this early stage; it was shaped by violence more than anything else. Yet, it also required documenting and communicating to allcomers, preserved for eternity on stone, to capture the valuable moment that peace was made and to inscribe and guarantee the new political order and its boundaries. Such political orders were generally built on hegemony and coercion, colonialism and imperialism, even if they removed overt violence and communicated from a platform of power and domination to 'lower' social orders. Representing peace in concrete and also emotive ways governed the experience of peace amongst the population, allowing leaders to add to its permanence through forms of communication that worked upon multiple levels, beyond the diplomatic table where powerful and elite signatories of any treaty had once gathered (i.e., drawn on, or written in stone, literally). This elite-dominated, instrumentalised form of the arts, placing it at the service of power, represented perhaps the longest stage in the history of the relationship between peace and the arts, and it continues to form the bedrock of later stages.

The extent of the prevalence of indirect and direct violence in the history of international, domestic, political, social and economic relations and systems was rarely comprehended by its victims until it was too late. It was and often remains widely accepted that peace is 'all other times, except war...' to quote Thomas Hobbes (Hobbes 1642, 1651). The overwhelming dominance of different forms of media, expression and aesthetics by depictions of violence and their aftermath represents a self-fulfilling drama—and a censorship of the possibilities for peace. It might be useful to consider how such a dominant 'print capitalism' (Anderson 1991, 224) associated with violent imperial and state mythologies emerged. The result was the elevation of war and power in thought, politics, society and aesthetics over peace to achieve that which Augustine called the 'tranquillity of order' (Augustine 1993, 690–1). This compromise is reflected in the lack of nuanced politico-aesthetic reflection in the early stages of *artpeace*.

When further evolution emerged, it advanced relatively rapidly, taking in the scope of emancipatory thinking from the classics to contemporary times. This process of development seemed to increasingly hope for the power of the state and international political economy to become more aligned with the anti-war and anti-violence sentiments of more radical peace representations, often drawing on the early classical lineage of Plato, Aristotle, Thucydides, Cicero or Augustine, as with much else in wider remit of the humanities (Boucher and Kelly 2003; Brown, Nardin, and Rengger 2002).

However, representations of a desire for something more than war—or a form of peace—were becoming clearer. Thus, contra Henry Maine, peace was not a 'modern invention' but an evolving concept in the history of world politics, mirroring new ethical and scientific advances (Maine 1888, 8; Kustermans 2018, 57–88). Peace representations received growing attention in a world dominated by imperial and extractive rationalities, and later one dominated by fascism, nationalism and capitalism. Yet, apart from a few pacifist communities (Fabbro 1978, 67–83) or countries with demilitarised constitutional orders (such as modern Germany, Japan or Costa Rica), the rationality of post-war politics was predicated on the controlled use of violence, related to territoriality and sovereignty (and thereby the related search for domination, profit, leadership and heroism), and to reward sacrifice. The tragic, cathartic realist drama of the twentieth century led to peace becoming all the more complex.

Towards a More Enlighted Engagement: Cosmopolitan Discovery and Awakening

The Enlightenment helped develop platforms for the earliest clearly political representations of peace to incorporate both a higher thematic symbolism as well as a more everyday depiction. For example, Lorenzetti, a Renaissance artist, painted a series of frescoes on the walls of the Hall of the Peace (Sala della Pace) in the Palazzo Pubblico of Siena from 1338–40 (Lorenzetti 1338–40). *The Effects of Good Government on Town and Country* represented a rare and early characterisation of what peace may mean beyond non-violence, reiterating the classical lineage of the relationship between certain forms of 'good' government, and peace, order and justice (that is, the good life). His work set the scene for a significant break with the early stages. It proclaimed the importance and benefits of peace by depicting life in a well-ordered and prosperous city, while in a related picture, *Allegory of Bad Government*, the horrors of destruction and disease caused by war were portrayed in the same town by way of comparison. This was not merely an ethical commentary on immediate acts of war, or a representation of a victor's peace, but constituted a substantial politico-ethical reflection upon the relationship between peace and war with the longer-term nature of political order.

A Rubens piece, *Minerva Protects Pax from Mars* (Rubens 1629–30), illustrated a further dimension to this aesthetico-political and diplomatic evolution. This painting illustrated Rubens's hopes for peace between England and Spain even as war loomed, which he, in his role as envoy to Philip IV of Spain, was attempting through negotiation to prevent. The painting depicted the sublime and elevated nature of the gods' relation to peace, as well as symbols of the more mundane everyday aspects of peace. It also became a mechanism for peacemaking itself. Pax (peace) was represented by the goddess of the earth, who was sharing her resources, while Minerva, goddess of wisdom, drove away Mars, the god of war. The picture was presented to Charles I of England as a gift to advocate for peace. It consolidated the idea that leaders had a responsibility to both god and the state not to follow naked self-interest and to deploy the mechanisms of war, but to follow the wisdom of cooperation and trust.

The Lorenzetti and Rubens paintings revolve around the juxtaposition of peace and war, illustrating peace's higher and everyday qualities, with both advocating for peace and warning against war. Both hoped to have a diplomatic and political effect following the interests of elites, nobles and the church, as well as—to an extent more than usual at that time—representing the views of society, intellectuals and artists. They were engaging with the possibility of exercising agency to prevent war, save lives and achieve political change. Both also illustrated the difficulties of depicting peace in the flamboyant or emotive manner that wars are often represented by. Peace tended to be banal, everyday and hard to detect, though its processes were now coming to be seen as depending on elite agency and government, as well as on social activism. Even in these attempts at its depiction, the threat of war or violence becomes their main method through which peace gains its aesthetico-political life, through the mechanism of contrast. Both paintings ultimately provided different avenues (divinity or more earthly politics) towards the social and elite proscription of violence, pointing to the role of social and cultural platforms, new dynamics of agency and mobilisation and new methods of resistance. There was an early sense of the possibility in peacemaking as opposed to the determinism of war.

The repetition of the stereotypes of horror and bravery associated with glory and power versus more marginal possibilities, meant that violence or a victor's peace remained the dominant motif during stage three. It had by now gained a new life that translated into the exceptionalism of empire and the state, summed up in Weber's famous dictum about the state's monopoly over violence (Weber 2015). From this understanding, peace continued to be shorn of its wider, aesthetic, emotional and ethical potential, remaining a narrowly conceived artefact or rarity, an outcome of power-backed war, formed by force relations rather than the emancipatory imagination harnessed to human potential. Art that turned in the direction of power was rapidly discredited, however, for wider society, opening the way for a more radical ethic, which depended on emerging cosmopolitan, social justice-oriented, critical and resistant forms of agency. These were soon to become inherent in *artpeace*.

The efforts of Lorenzetti and Rubens to offer peace as an elite aesthetico-political agenda may have also opened the way for subaltern advocacy and for further explorations of the socio-political potential of peace. This was set against the broader foil of the failings of power. Power had shaped rather than followed society, art and aesthetics, in other words, but there was also growing evidence that power, state and empire were socially constructed, even at the grand scale indicated in such depictions. This realisation gave *artpeace* approaches and social actors substantial agency, and a hitherto little understood capacity to shape politics. The next two centuries were to host an epic aesthetico-political battle over the forces of imperialism, fascism, nationalism and the state (which ultimately was to lead to a nuclear standoff during the Cold War), on view in many state art galleries around the world. In this context, subaltern critical agency began to cohere around the expansion of rights and related issues like disarmament (notably brought together by the Greenham Common campaign of the 1980s) and began to develop new methods of resistance.

Into the Nineteenth and Twentieth Centuries: Revolution, Resistance and Rethinking

Artpeace was often represented by horror and emotion, and an assumption that it was the opposite of what was being depicted: the opposite of death, destruction, injustice and arbitrariness (see for example, *The Apotheosis of War* by Vasily Vereshchagin, also mentioned below [Vereshchagin 1871]). In the high imperial, and the later fascist phases, of the 19th and 20th centuries, the focus tended to be on horror of violence for a radical audience, or the glory and honour that war may represent for a conservative audience who are more taken with motifs of power, nationalism, heroism, stratification, restoration and counter-revolution. *Artpeace* was still generally connected to Augustinian notions of 'just war' as early stages inferred, where war was justified to protect a 'higher' political order (empire, state and elites) and to further its ambitions for itself against others (Guthrie and Quinlan 2007). More sophisticated depictions of peace remained something of a rarity, and the workings of the processes by which peace (even as a limited negative peace inherent in the balance of power) was arrived at were difficult to depict. The ease in depicting war placed its representations in the general terrain of propaganda: to glorify its relationship with individual heroism or to celebrate or disguise imperialism and nationalism. References to peace were often exploited to try to legitimate war in such guises, as with De Neuville's *The Defence of Rorke's Drift*, which heroized the British defence of their colonial garrison against enormous numbers of Zulus, during the Anglo-Zulu War of 1879 (de Neuville 1880).

Countless memorials, sites, museums and galleries around the world continued to depict heroism, battles, war, glory, beauty, sexuality and only very rarely the full horror of war. In these paradigms, war consumed so much political and social-aesthetic energy that the question of what came next was rarely engaged with until social agency began to develop an interest in stopping and preventing war as its scale increased. This represented a turning point where political agency was becoming critical, resistant and democratised; subsequently, *artpeace* expanded its range.

This fork in the road was evident in Delacroix's *Liberty Leading the People*, which celebrated the goals of the French Revolution and its aim of liberty, but also illustrated the sacrifices it entailed (Delacroix 1830). This paint-ing commemorated the July Revolution of 1830, which toppled Charles X. Liberty, represented by a woman holding the *tricolore* flag and a gun and lead-ing the people forward, echoing the French Revolution of 1789 and its goals. Using what has also nationalist iconography, revolutionary violence was offered as a legitimate mechanism to achieve liberty and a resurgent nation. This was to be an area of contestation for peace throughout this period, whether through just war, revolution and resistance to oppression, or later forms of humanitarian intervention. This argument illustrated that peace was subject to power, but that it was also determined by rights claims made by the masses, as well as their experimentations with political agency and goals. It connected peace to a larger project aimed at liberty, equality and justice, though social justice was corralled into a reformed state project: nationalism would become something of a contradiction during the 20th century.

What was significant by this stage in the development of what is now more clearly 'artpeace' was that peace was now something that could be claimed through the exercise of emancipatory agency by subaltern actors, from below. These very actors, previously ignored, were now driving his-tory, preferably non-violently (but often via the mechanism of revolutionary violence), across a range of terrains of human activities: from politics to the arts. Suddenly, the powerless (in Delacroix's context, the Third Estate) had representational, if not practical, leverage in the fundamental terrain of politics and international relations, about the nature of political order. The contested, age-old pairing of peace with war driven by elite power relations and cemented by the state and empire was weakening, and social agency was now being depicted in the context of struggles against the mechanisms of war and power, even if they were again soon deflected into nationalistic or imperial enterprises. This trend also revived the age-old problem of whether violence was justified in the name of peace if there was a just cause (and who determined any such causes). There were increasingly subtle and emo-tive references to explicit justifications for such agency, lying in opposition to violence, war, discrimination, racism and imperialism, and in support of more complex forms of justice. Revolutionary or emancipatory violence lurked in the background of such claims, just as violence lurked in the fore-ground of imperialism, the authoritarian state and other forms of oppressive hegemony.

Vasily Vereshchagin's painting, *The Apotheosis of War*, is thought to be one of the earliest explicitly pacifist paintings (Vereshchagin 1871). It adopted the typical strategy of graphically displaying the horrors of violence pio-neered by the likes of Goya, rather than depicting the pleasures of peace, as with Lorenzetti, or offering liberty as a peace worth fighting for as with Delacroix. This painting was inspired by the horrors associated with the

Russo-Turkish War from 1877–78. In this desolate picture there is no hint of hope or of a cause that justifies the violence portrayed, nor any attempt to produce empathy for its subjects (portrayed merely as objects). Its pacifist message is simply that there cannot be a limited form of peace derived from violence. Peace art had until this point avoided such a stark rejection of violence, but the expanded platform that was now emerging allowed for more radical, non-violent demands to arise. These were being disseminated in an increasingly connected world as fundamental critiques of the way politics had previously been organised.

Artpeace still lacked a constructive vision for the most part, however. When it did endeavour to go beyond war, it often had an unexpectedly large impact as was the case with Goya's *Execution* or later Picasso's *Guernica* (Picasso 1937). Depicting the horror of violence was increasingly being seen as a subversive protest against stratified political power and a foil for subsequent, though still vague calls for peace (as with works by Goya, and later Picasso or Kollwitz [de Goya 1814; Picasso 1937; Kollwitz 1924]). The more graphic the depiction of violence, of futility and loss, the more it pointed to perhaps unspoken alternatives with consequences for the nation, the state and humanity in general. This reflected the growing swell of public opinion and its heightened capacity to influence politics at 'ripe' moments since the start of the 19th century (and to be completely ignored when geopolitics dominated, such as in 1914).

Indeed, *artpeace* still appeared, even in this more sophisticated stage, to depend on the sponsorship of, or influences on the artist: thus, it balanced towards power, glory and honour. However, it was also more clearly beginning to represent and preserve a humanist, critical commentary. As in Goya's piece, *The Third of May 1808*, victimhood, even potential innocence, may be used as a mechanism to underline the injustice of violence and war. So, while the arts may represent and disseminate the architecture of power and the state of exception that allows the monopoly of violence (Agamben 2005), *artpeace* was now directly challenging hegemony as underground movements became aware of a path towards rights and democracy as a standard by which to judge power and violence. The arts were more clearly challenging violence from a subaltern perspective, echoing and amplifying historical undercurrents pertaining to the proscription of violence and the expectation or right for a good life, which required the reimagining of political order. This impulse travelled along the networks that disseminated arts and rights thinking, which were also expanded during industrialisation and the imperial era, from letter writing and small, local meetings, workshops, displays and exhibitions, to large-scale conferences and international campaigning as well as mechanisms of social and political resistance (Randle 1994). These dynamics perhaps were to culminate (at least before the contemporary digital era) with Picasso's *Guernica,* and its 20th century travels and travails (van Hensbergen 2005).

Radical Steps

Increasingly, shocking viewers into confronting the dangers of using violence was problematic if it only supported a political system or form of peace settlement acceptable to power. Until this stage, art had normally been co-opted into imperial or nationalist projects of war, rather than emancipatory collective action: it had constantly flirted with powerful propaganda, or artists had been either dependent on power or unaware of their own underlying assumptions. Representation was dominated by power, with only small corners left available for critical challenges. By this point, however, peace was also slowly mobilised by art at a more residual level, compared to the elite academic texts of the Enlightenment, or the grandiose paintings of Rubens. By the early 20th century, the connections between art, protest against war, the exposure of war's relationship with iniquitous forms of power, and advocacy for peace, as well as intimations of its potential complexity, had been consolidated. A more substantial stage was emerging, which foregrounded subaltern agency in the marriage between art, politics, agency, resistance and peace.

This explosive convergence was present in one of the most famous art movements of the early twentieth century. Dadaism cannot but be seen as a key moment, and emerged at a time of great stress and change in the period during and after World War One (WWI). It began in Zürich—'the peaceful dead centre of the war' as Hans Richter, a leading exponent wrote—at the Cabaret Voltaire and spread to Paris, Berlin and New York. Members of this avowedly anti-war movement were appalled by WWI. Hans Arp, a member of the Zürich Dada movement wrote,

> Revolted by the butchery of the 1914 World War, we in Zürich
> devoted ourselves to the arts. While the guns rumbled in the
> distance, we sang, painted, made collages, and wrote poems with all
> our might. We were seeking an art based on fundamentals to cure
> the madness of the age, and a new order of things that would
> restore the balance between heaven and hell. We had a dim
> premonition that power-mad gangsters would one day use art
> itself as a way of deadening men's minds. (Richter 1965, 7)

Out of this maelstrom of imagination, social and political commentary, resistance, radical rejectionism, and anti-foundationalism, was born an anti-nationalist, internationalist and disruptive movement that hosted some of the great experimental writers, thinkers and artists of the 20th century. Though Dadaism was an internationalist, avant-garde reaction against nationalism, it often adopted a humanist and also universalising tone. It quickly became famous because it was also directly provocative towards its audience. Dadaism was an aesthetic and anarchistic representation of the human and political challenge, not just of rebuilding Europe after WWI, but also of constructing a peace that would be self-sustaining and not reliant on the violence that was materially or aesthetically built into custom, institutions and conservative representations of 'naturalistic' political orders such as monarchy, authoritarianism, militarism or the global political order.

Dadaism's main challenge to war lay in its rejection of the existing order of politics that glorified war, or warned of its excesses, but also saw it as a plausible basis for a victor's peace. It also consolidated the radical, creative energy and insight that the arts offered for a form of peace that was relevant to society, rather than merely celebrating yet another elite victory. For example, Hannah Höch's collage from 1919–20, *Cut with the Kitchen Knife Through the First Epoch of the Weimar Beer-Belly Culture* (Höch 1919–20), portrayed war as self-destructive chaos that would debase humanity, rather than creating peace. However, the methodology of such work suggested an awareness of the potential of transversal networks, relationality and of social power, which connected to peace formation from below as well to social resistance (Richmond 2011, 2016), which were by then growing amongst populations more aware of their status and rights (Cortright 2008, 25–44).

This and similar developments in *artpeace* represented a sharp break with the previous, conservative, and complacent sense that war and the 'higher' representational ethics of arts were comfortably aligned. Art was now challenging power and disseminating scientific thought about progress and the need for radical social and political change. A revolution was required, and it would not be denied. Tentative engagements with the social conditions of peace and justice could no longer be acceptable if the arts were to represent more than a tool of power, push back boundaries and hierarchies, and promote solidarity, empathy and new networks of political creativity.

Artpeace *Radicalism and WWII*

Though emancipatory notions of politics were coming to the fore in *artpeace*, artists still normally eschewed dangerous confrontation for more empathic and subtle modes of engagement that were perhaps less risky during this period of heightened ideology. Those associated with peace movements, or at least with resistance to war, also often portrayed a sensitivity to issues such as identity, discrimination, property and gender inequality as representing negative stratifications (as opposed to historical, conservative arguments which tended to see them as important frameworks for a social Darwinist world). For example, Käthe Kollwitz, a Polish artist who dealt in particular with women as subjects for her art, illustrated the impact of war on women but in particular their agency against war in her image, *Never Again War* (Kollwitz 1924).

Similarly, the level of sectarianism, discrimination and racism often evident in war was represented in the painting by a German Jewish painter in the period leading up to World War Two (WWII). Felix Nussbaum was killed at Auschwitz in 1944, and his painting, *The Pearls* is widely regarded as one of his most important (Nussbaum 1938). It shows a Madonna and child image super-imposed over a battle scene, offering a complex anti-war protest, working on several different levels (especially if the viewer knows anything about the painter's biographical details and context).

Perhaps the seminal example of *artpeace* is Picasso's *Guernica*, which attempted to combine many of the motifs of peace art, including Dadaist confrontation. It was painted for the 1937 Exposition held in Paris, and portrayed the suffering of the small Basque town of Guernica which was attacked by the Luftwaffe in April 1937 (Picasso 1937). Its focus on suffering in an ordinary, everyday context, caused by a cynical, surprise air attack against innocent civilians, was underpinned by allusions to long standing Spanish myths of survival and power. It brought together radical epistemic-aesthetic innovations in modernity: artistic experimentalism with radical political challenges to fascism and the violence it valorised, as well as emotional, social appeals for solidarity and empathy. It deployed the tactic of relying on empathy to expose war and its connection with underlying, elemental and structural forces of nationalism, evil and violence, while also appealing to a certain national character of resilience and eternality.

It became a powerful symbol of the international and transnational peace movement during and after WWII, becoming associated with a number of different anti-war campaigns, including against the Vietnam War. The remarkable transversality of these movements—ordinary, powerless, global networks of people opposing total war as a political tool, along with all the power it engendered, and proposing various alternatives—were to become perhaps defining features of the post-war world. This was the basis for another stage in the *artpeace* evolution. *Guernica* spent most of its life at the Museum of Modern Art in New York before it was returned to a newly democratic Spain in the 1980s, in accordance with the wishes expressed by Picasso in his will. Basques have been calling for its relocation from Madrid to Bilbao ever since, as a symbol of the suffering the Basque country has endured and the peace it now hopes for.

Picasso also produced the most well-known emblem for contemporary peace movements, drawing on a common historical metaphor. His *Dove* from 1949 is now widely recognised in many different guises (Picasso 1949). It made no reference to violence but offered a globally resonant symbol through an allusion to a more environmental, 'commons' perspective of peace at a time in the Cold War when social movements were beginning to mobilise in the East and the West (Goedde 2019, 43–4). He also composed several other peace images that focused on symbolising peace independently (Picasso n.d.).

Also, around this time, his creation *War and Peace* was painted onto the walls of a chapel in Vallauris in France during a period sometimes referred to as 'the summer of War and Peace.' It depicted 'war' as a tank, a figure with a bloody sword, a basket of bacteria and a sack of skulls. These were opposed by a 'peace fighter' carrying a shield with a dove on it and a child ploughing the sea, drawn by a winged horse. This was the last major political composition produced by Picasso and made explicit a more complex motif: the balance between war and peace (Picasso 1952). This perhaps prefigured peacebuilding practices later in the century, which attempted to maintain and improve peace through a variety of different military, economic, political, social and cultural tools. His support and recognition of peace movements both endorsed and heightened the transnational and transversal 'rights' revolution that emerged after WWII, which challenged war and uncovered structural forms of violence (Moyn 2018).

New Possibilities

The evolving depiction of *artpeace* and its relationship variously with power, hegemony, domination, imperialism, totalitarianism, authoritarianism, territory, heroism, tragedy and inequality, as well as with balance, justice and sustainability, was now gathering pace in a variety of different media. Late in the century the sophistication of the message was perhaps eclipsed by the possibilities inherent in global mobilisation and advocacy, especially when subaltern *artpeace* connected with like-minded international or transnational actors and formed cross-cutting alliances (assuming these were not formed for superficial purposes on either side). The arts provided a common grammar that was now becoming more widespread.

Soon after WWI, and after it had destroyed the fabric constructed over previous generations, there emerged the phenomena of 'peace museums'. There are now many of these around the world. Probably the most famous is the Hiroshima Peace Memorial Museum. This museum is sited on the original 'ground zero', where the US atomic weapon, absurdly named 'Little Boy', was detonated. This location is marked by the remains of a building in Hiroshima Peace Park called 'Genbacku'. It is the sole architectural reminder of the damage and death caused at 8.15 in the morning of August 6, 1945.

About 70,000 individuals were killed instantly, and many more in the period afterwards. The city of Hiroshima is now closely associated with civil resistance to nuclear weapons (Hiroshima Peace Memorial Museum, n.d.).

The use of the A-bomb was commonly justified by western scholars and policymakers on the grounds that the 140,000 deaths it caused were significantly less than the many possible deaths a land invasion of Japan would have caused, given the complete militarisation of Japanese society at the time. A politico-aesthetic, humanities-influenced approach would underline this philosophical ethical dilemma, probably making it extremely difficult to justify the level of violence applied. Such issues are not referred to in the rather anodyne museum. Instead, it focuses on cataloguing the events of the day and the suffering the bombing caused in an understated manner, perhaps because of acute political sensitivities over the admittance of Japanese or western guilt. However, the museum's presence speaks for itself: a terrible catalogue and a warning, as well as place of memorialisation, tranquillity and reflection about how to avoid such catastrophes in the future. Its reflectiveness points the observer to sophisticated concerns about radical alternatives from the subaltern perspective.

The preservation of widespread war damage and its use in public monuments or symbols became common after WWII. This practice reconnected the post-war epoch with the pre-war period, travelling over the rupture that war represented. This was the case with Marienkirche in Lübeck in Germany. This church, dating from 1250, was badly damaged in Allied bombing of civilian areas during World War II. Its church bells, in what is now a UNESCO listed church, fell from their tower in the Allied bombing, and have since been left as a reminder on the floor of the rebuilt tower (for a photograph, see Arnoldius 2006). This dramatic, thought-provoking scene operates on several different levels, again pointing towards complex concerns.

Cartoons in newspapers have also been widely used to critique the incompetence and hypocrisy of war leaders, war and inconsistent peace settlement processes. For example, J. N. Ding Darling drew a series of cartoons opposing war during WWI, WWII and after. These relied on the shock factor of futility, atrocity or tragedy, and represented peace as a necessary alternative. Others incorporated an element of satire, humour and irony (in Koss 2004).[3] Cartoons continue to be used to critical effect in contemporary media to highlight a popular desire for peace and a resistance to war, particularly during the Iraq War (2003–11), for example in the work of Steve Bell (Bell n.d.).[4]

As noted above, peace art has become a part of public architecture (though mainly decorative rather than structural),[5] whether through the concurrent glorification of war and a victor's peace, through the vilification of war and its mechanisms, the celebration of peacemaking, peacekeeping, peace treaties, the UN, peacemakers, civil society actors or, more marginally, the attempted depiction of peace as a form in itself. For example, representing the common peace, disarmament and development theme of the early post-war era, of converting the implements of war into those of peace, one public sculpture at the UN headquarters in New York depicts a figure holding a hammer aloft in one hand, and a sword in the other, which he is making into a ploughshare (Buchetich 1959).

Also at the UN Secretariat building in New York is Marc Chagall's stained-glass window in the Public Lobby. It was a gift from United Nations staff and Chagall in memory of Dag Hammarskjöld, the second Secretary-General of the UN. He and fifteen other people died with him in a plane crash while on a peace mission in the Democratic Republic of Congo in 1961. The window contains several well-known symbols of peace (Chagall 1964). Indeed, the United Nations' family of organisations has been active in documenting peace within its own institutional terms, in the context of its work in the areas of international security, refugees, development and health, via an extensive archive of historical photographs and posters. Many of them highlight the cooperative, legal and institutional, as well as the human stories of peace and war, though many also point to the fact that states remain the pre-eminent actors in international relations (Marks 2000).[6] Again, these images span the later, more sophisticated stages of *artpeace* development but do so via a rather traditional aesthetic form. Another well-known piece at the UN Headquarters in New York is *Non-Violence*, by Carl Fredrik Reuterswärd (1988). This portrays a giant revolver with its barrel twisted into a knot, making the gun useless (ironically, this sculpture became less public after the security perimeter of the building was expanded after 9/11).

Ambivalent references to peace through violence, threat or force remain common. The ambiguity of war and peace art remained visible in post-Good Friday Agreement (1998) murals on house walls in Belfast long after the agreement was struck. These murals became a tourist attraction and though some are still expressions of militantism, many have been repainted with less ambiguous messages about the benefits of the peace process. Walls, with their fluid aesthetic, that once glorified violence, now reflect more optimistic messages illustrating how representation itself is renewed after war (even if aimed at tourists) (Hocking 2012). Murals tend to be repainted repeatedly, representing the changing environment and shifting politico-aesthetic responses to the dynamics of the post-Good Friday Agreement (1998) period. They were originally quite traditional representations of *artpeace*, but increasingly have shifted towards more critical, radical and resistance-oriented forms.

Overall, during recent times, the artistic representations of peace have diversified substantially, as seen with arts deployed in the Campaign for

Nuclear Disarmament (CND) resistance movement around Greenham Common since 1981 (Artworks n.d.), or as mentioned above in Northern Ireland. One of the most poignant tragedies of the early post-Cold War era, until the massive civilian losses that occurred in the Iraq war or the Rwandan Genocide in 1994, was the siege of Sarajevo during the breakup of Yugoslavia during the early 1990s. This drawn-out conflict was the scene of many poignant reminders of the hubris of the claims that peace had arrived after the Cold War, when set into relief by the political claims for justice, economic assistance, restitution, reparations and a sustainable political order that conflict-affected populations were now raising. Many Sarajevans remember the U2 rock concert of 1997 as a realisation that the war was over, and the constant bombing and sniping that the city had endured for around 1,000 days from 1992–95 would not return. The strange process behind the realisation of this unlikely concert reflected indigenous *artpeace* movements that had arisen underground particularly in Sarajevo during the siege, and was related in a quirky book, which may also be said to offer a more literary dimension to *artpeace* (Carter 2005). Of course, this book stands in a long but relatively recent line of examples in the literary peace genre, spanning Leo Tolstoy in the 19th century to Ernest Hemmingway, George Orwell and beyond (Tolstoy 2007; Hemmingway 1940; Orwell 1949).

Another creative example could once be found in the divided capital of Cyprus, Nicosia, Lefkosia or Lefkosha. From the late 1950s until 2003 an impassable so-called 'green line' divided the city's Greek and Turkish Cypriot inhabitants. One General Young marked the line on a Nicosia map to establish a buffer zone between the two communities. This was a strategy of divide and rule or divide and pacify, particularly after the city became the scene of intercommunal riots in December 1963. After a war in 1974 the green line became part of an island-wide buffer zone, patrolled by a UN peacekeeping force. In 2005, a painted pink line also appeared in the city, which was supposed to transgress the green line's patriarchal demarcations, categorisations and divisions (Kamerić 2005). In a sophisticated challenge to the related dynamics of war, division, nationalism and patriarchy, the pink line implied that war and division in Cyprus could be blamed on such traditional categories. There is some truth to this.

More radical and satirical stances on the inadequacies of mainstream politics—as well as the exploration of completely new directions—were developing at pace, and, on the way, they scarred the social landscape with violence. They were also more visible to various global audiences than ever before because of new communication technologies. They partly converged in the work of Banksy, a self-described 'guerrilla graffiti artist' known for his resistance to war and violence in his public, hit and run style art, which has a habit of randomly appearing all around the world. He is associated with anti-capitalist and anti-Establishment pieces of work, as well as opposing various wars and oppressive political systems, including in the Middle East, the Iraq War, and War on Terror after 9/11, using the popular appeal of his work to discredit established modes of order and to raise the issue of what should come next (Banksy 2006; BBC News 2007). His painted window view through to a seeming paradise beyond the Israel/Palestine buffer wall (2005) pointed to radical possibilities of peace despite conflict and division (Banksy Explained 2021). His interpretation of the peace dove for Christmas in Bethlehem, in the West Bank in 2007, was also far more complex than Picasso's earlier drawings mentioned above (Daily Sabah 2021). Yet, even during *artpeace*'s recent development, it is still common that exhibitions purporting to be about peace generally fall back on campaigning against war (a trend reflected in an exhibition in the Tate Britain in London in 2007, which touched on the Iraq War).[7]

The Evolution of the Relationship Between the Arts and Peace

The diagram below (Table 1) outlines a tentative historical typology of six stages for this relationship. This chronology is not concrete, as these stages

Table 1.1 The Evolution of the Relationship Between the Arts and Peace

Imperial, Nationalist and Conservative Phase

Stage 1: In ancient times, art was used to delineate territory, to embed centralised authority and to spread hegemony or law, through or after war. It was used to legitimate and expand authority.

Stage 2: It was used to memorialise and heroize, through a linkage between art and war, especially as empires grew and were replaced by nationalism and sovereignty, buttressed by conservative thinking on the role of war in the state and empire.

Cosmopolitan Discovery and Awakening

Stage 3: With the emergence of rights struggles during the last millennia a more critical, subaltern (often underground) wing of the arts became more prominent. It was used to highlight victimhood, arbitrary power and to evoke an emotional response to injustice within a more cosmopolitan domestic and international framework.

Mainstream arts also continued to valorise empires, the state, battles and heroism, and diplomacy.

Stage 4: After the Enlightenment the subaltern arts were used to promote tolerance, independence and self-determination, and to campaign against violence as a political tool, creating a more heterogeneous understanding of cosmopolitanism. Disarmament and pacifism became common motifs, as well as labour rights, equality, resistance and explicit social and transnational empathy.

Mainstream sources continued to valorise empires, the state, battles and heroism, and diplomacy in the context of various ideologies.

Table 1.1 (continued)

Revolution, Resistance and Rethinking

Stage 5: By the 19th century new wings of the arts, more plausibly able to represent more marginal views and groups from below, because of new formats, were being used as a revolutionary force to mobilise groups and networks across a wide range of rights claims. They targeted power structures deemed to be unjust, to help advocate, mobilise, codify and to incentivise campaigns of resistance, such as those against slavery, imperialism, war, armaments, discrimination, racism and poverty within both a state-centric and international framework. Disarmament and pacifism remained common motifs, as well as labour rights, equality and an explicit social and transnational empathy. Along with a new experimentalism in media this allowed for more subaltern expressions (as opposed to the 'high arts' epistemology that often valorised war and power).

Mainstream approaches were also being deployed to support war recruitment, intelligence gathering, nationalism and self-determination struggles simultaneously, along with their traditional pursuits of enabling empires, the state, battles and heroism, and diplomacy. States and empires adopted (or co-opted) such representations and discourses over time because they carried such wide global legitimacy by the 20th century.

Stage 6: The concept of *artpeace* is consolidated. More recently it has shifted to a subaltern, bottom-up, grassroots mode and turned against the state, empire (formal and informal), capitalism and extraction, and began to align itself with global justice debates (distributive, historical and environmental). Artists have used increasingly experimental modes of engagement, mobilisation, networking and resistance across a broadening range of the arts. These modes have been used to satirise power and its corruption, often through intense experimentalism in content and format, as well as to promote and disseminate subaltern and creative thinking about the evolving conditions of peace across multiple dimensions. In particular, they unpick the intellectual and practical limitations of centralised power, sovereignty, capitalism, injustice and related and arbitrary reductionism during the Anthropocene, demanding global and environmental justice.

In parallel, it has become increasing implausible to legitimately disseminate the values of old-fashioned empires, the state, valorise battles and heroism and maintain elitist approaches to diplomacy (unless via propaganda, authoritarianism and coercion). Indeed, high-level representations as in earlier stages are now seen often to represent hypocrisy or to be anachronistic.

overlap and often run forwards to the present, forming a sort of sediment for each other (connecting them to the evolution of the International Peace Architecture that I have outlined in other work [Richmond 2022]). Many of the artworks alluded to in this chapter to are not explicitly about peace, but their relevance to peace (and its related elements) as one of the eternal issues in the evolution of political philosophy, political theory and history, is clear.

Implications of Stages 1–6

In the selections above of a range of aesthetic representations of war and peace, familiar and simple dynamics are illustrated associated with stages one and two, in which war and violence are glorified and power is delineated in the service of empire, state or powerful elites. By stages three and four *artpeace* is being used as a subaltern form of resistance and for advocacy against war. Peace art was openly starting to represent critical resistance to war, often by appealing to emotion, religion, solidarity and community, or focusing on its tragedy. However, *artpeace* also openly operates within the parameters of the state or empire, just as much as it may challenge iniquitous and unjust exercises of power. That both dynamics are represented indicates its power as a tool.

Peace innovation has thus mainly been dominated, often in reductive ways, by formal political and policy actors and powerful propaganda, at least until recently. This deficit illustrates an ambivalent attitude towards war but often also supports its metastructures via bureaucratic, technocratic, management and stabilisation techniques aimed mainly at propping up an imperfect, negative form of peace and a relatively crude international order. This parallels the paucity of ideas beyond the ideological and mainstream theoretical debates on peace of modern times. Peace and conflict studies debates have recently focused on descriptive and methodological approaches (such as issues of locality and positionality), partly perhaps because of the regressive dynamics emerging that are pushing back scientific and ethical progress. Yet, the more marginal, critical edge of peace art has continued to develop, pointing peace more broadly to issues of agency, resistance and global justice (historical, distributive and environmental) (Reid and Taylor 2010; Nussbaum 2015, 68–79; Pogge 2001, 6–24; Kohn 2013, 187–200; Gonzalez 2017; Della Porta et al. 2007).

This has produced an elusive commentary. It guides peacemaking towards primary emotional and empathetic responses, considerations of subaltern voices, resistance, agency and representation. The latter implies peacemaking probably becomes much less Burkean and more focused on reform, experimentation, much improved systems of law and government and improved institutions, as well as equality, rights, justice and sustainability as responses. The performances of the arts, their ability to transcend convention, boundaries and systemic enclosures juxtaposes with the brutal oversimplifications of war and violence as power has been historically transmitted through empires, states, militaries, alliances, international political economy and classes to the modern era of rights expansion (Moyn 2019). From stages four to six *artpeace* thus invites a broad social and subaltern consideration of the philosophical, ethical considerations of war as a political tool or historical event.

While earlier stages left open the question of what must be done for there to be a good peace for the long term, later stages have clarified the imaginary of a peace with global justice (UN 2018). As media and platforms for networked production and representation proliferate, the subaltern perspective is for the first time also much more accessible across, rather than enclosed by, international boundaries of empire, state, region, gender, race and class.

However, while more accessible it also still represents a substantial lacuna when compared with mainstream representations of victor's peace or peace that follows power. It reiterates the question of why technical and aesthetic representations of peace remain so limited, widely scattered and occur in such a low volume (despite some acceleration over time). Censorship and the erasure of emancipatory political arguments have been historically common in imperial and state history, as well as in ideological terms, and the same appears to be true for *artpeace*, even in a digital age (where disinformation and propaganda can muddy the waters so easily) (Zuboff 2019). There can be little other explanation for the paucity of historical exemplars, which mainly exist today in state-backed art collections, or the fact that ethnographic methodologies are required to recover deeper historical and contemporary evidence for *artpeace*. Aesthetico-political projects also mirror power-relations in their survival and influence. Ultimately, much artistic peace work challenges war through broad brush emotions, or associates peace with elite and northern power or ideas, challenging, perhaps, the direct use of violence but less frequently the political systems that mobilise it.

Conclusion

Translating all of the above into a valuable contribution for peace and conflict studies, which provides indicators for future emancipatory paths, offers an overall conceptual framework for *artpeace*. This represents a confluence and a synthesis of historical political and creative forces to make peace, one often overlooked or blocked for disciplinary reasons or by power. The grammars of humanities, social sciences and the arts merge in this conceptual framing, often despite powerful interests and opposition. The arts have historically offered a platform of creativity for political innovation and alternative perspectives on violence not easily identifiable from a Eurocentric rationality, as well as creating alternative frameworks for a peaceful solution. They suggested them centuries before they became social, state and international practice in many cases, rehearsing the emancipatory and non-violent potential of social imaginaries when fed into reformed political systems.

This suggests that in a contemporary setting, *artpeace*—as a platform for imagining emancipatory improvements to political systems that rest on violence and war—could offer new methods that would help solve power deadlocks, build legitimacy, reconciliation and justice, and contribute to peace formation processes. It would reimagine the nature of the state, good life and international political order (by promoting positive forms of peace, highlighting unseen violence and supporting the proscription of violence across the different scales of analysis from local to global). Its synthesis would be a source of practical reform in the longer term. It offers a grounded, resonant, alternative grammar of representation, that utilises transnational and transversal networks for peace-oriented communication, advocacy, reciliation, justice, reform and non-violence.

Artpeace thus represents an overall conceptual framing of the synergy between arts and peace, as well as a methodological strategy for addressing conflict through the arts. In turn, '*artpeace*building' represents an amalgamation of medium-term, peacebuilding strategies often dominated by top-down, external factors. Even so it provides useful platforms for further creative, subaltern networks and synergies to be rediscovered or to emerge. '*Artpeace* formation', connected to social movements, resistance and civil society engagements, represents long term, social, cultural and bottom-up engagements with peace, including dynamics related to cultural shifts, emotions, representation, memorialisation and reconciliation.

Notes

1. I have used this method, rather than direct illustrations in the text, because copyright costs for most are prohibitive.
2. See various outcomes of the *Art of Peace*, AHRC research project at the University of Manchester (2018–22) amongst others.
3. See for example, "We Have Gained 200 Yards of the Enemy Trenches—Dispatch from the Front—1916", "Sign Him Up Before He Gets Over His Headache", "Waiting for the Sword to Fall", and "Eventually, Why Not Now?" in Koss (2004).
4. See for example the many cartoons of Steve Bell in *The Guardian* on President G. W. Bush's conduct during the Iraq War (Bell n.d.).
5. Thanks to Stefanie Kappler for this important point.
6. See the wide variety of UN posters spanning the end of WW2 to the contemporary era (Marks 2000).
7. See the recreation of peace campaigner Brian Haw's Parliament Square protest (Wallinger 2007).

References

Adorno, T. W. and Horkheimer, M. 2002. The culture industry: enlightenment as mass deception. In *Dialectic of enlightenment: Philosophical fragments*. Stanford, CA: University of Stanford Press, pp. 94–136.

Adorno, T. W., Benjamin, W., Bloch, E., Brecht, B., and Lukacs, G. 2020. *Aesthetics and politics*. London: Verso.

Agamben, G. 2005. *State of exception*. Chicago: University of Chicago Press.

AHRC. 2018–22. *The Art of Peace*, University of Manchester https://sites.manchester.ac.uk/the-art-of-peace/home/about/research/ (accessed 17 August, 2023).

Anderson, B. 1991. *Imagined communities: Reflections on the origin and spread of nationalism*, London: Verso.

Arnoldius. 2006. Germany Luebeck St Mary melted bells. Available at: https://commons.wiki media.org/wiki/File:Germany_Luebeck_St_Mary_melted_bells.jpg (accessed 17 August, 2023).

Artworks. n.d. Our Greenham. https://www.theartworks.org.uk/our-greenham (accessed 17 August, 2023).

Augustine. 1993. *The city of God*. New York: Random House.

Bailey, A. n.d. *The art of peace*. British Council.

Banksy. 2003. *Bomb Middle England*.

Banksy Explained. 2021. The Segregation Wall, Palestine, 2005. https://banksyexplained.com/the-segregation-wall-palestine-2005/ (accessed 17 August, 2023).

BBC News. 2007. Record price for Banksy bomb art. *BBC News*, 8 February. http://news.bbc.co.uk/1/hi/entertainment/6340109.stm (accessed 17 August, 2023).

Beales, A. C. F. 1931. *The history of peace: A short account of the organized movements for international peace*. New York: The Dial Press.

Behr, H. and Shani, G. 2021. Rethinking emancipation in a critical IR: Normativity, cosmology, and pluriversal dialogue. *Millennium*, 49(2), pp. 368–91.

Bell, S. n.d. Cartoons in *The Guardian* on President GW Bush's conduct during the Iraq War. https://www.theguardian.com/Iraq/cartoons/0,,912730,00.html (accessed 16 August, 2023).

Bevan, S. 2015. *Art from contemporary conflict*, London: Imperial War Museum.

Bleiker, R. 2017. In search of thinking space: Reflections on the aesthetic turn in international political theory. *Millennium*, 45(2), pp. 258–64.

Bloch, E. 1980. *Aesthetics and politics*. London: Verso.

Boucher, D. and Kelly, P. (eds). 2003. *Political thinkers from Socrates to the present*, Oxford: Oxford University Press.

Bourke, J. (ed.). 2017. *War and art: A visual history of modern conflict*. London: Reaktion Books.

Boutros-Ghali, B. 1992. Report of the Secretary-General 1992. An agenda for peace, preventive diplomacy, peacemaking and peace-keeping, *A/47/277 - S/24111*, 17 June, paras 3 & 5.

Brown, C., Nardin, T. and Rengger, N. (eds). 2002. *International relations in political thought*. Cambridge: Cambridge University Press.

Buchetich, E. 1959. *Let us beat our swords into ploughshares* (A Gift to the UN from the Soviet Union). United Nations Art Collections, New York.

Carter, B. 2005. *Fools rush in*. New York: Wenner Books.

Chagall, M. 1964. *The Window of Peace and Human Happiness*. UN Headquarters, New York.

Constantinou, C. 1994. Diplomatic representations...or who framed the ambassadors? *Millennium*, 23(1), pp. 1–23.

Cortright, D. 2008. *Peace: A history of movements and ideas*. Cambridge: Cambridge University Press.

Daily Sabah. 2021. Political street art: Best of Banksy. *Daily Sabah*, 5 March. https://www.dailysabah.com/gallery/political-street-art-best-of-banksy/images?gallery_image=39191 (accessed 17 August, 2023).

Debord, G. 1994/1967. *The society of the spectacle*, translation by Donald Nicholson-Smith. New York: Zone Books.

Delacroix, E. 1830. *Liberty leading the people*. Louvre, Paris.

Della Porta, D., and Andretta, M., Calle A., Combes, H., Eggert, N., Giugni, M. G., Hadden J., Jimenez, M. and Marchetti R. 2007. *Global justice movements: Cross-national and transnational perspectives*. London: Routledge.

Fabbro, D. 1978. Peaceful societies: An introduction. *Journal of Peace Research*, 15(1), pp. 67–83.

Foucault, M., 1997. *Society must be defended: Lectures at the Collège de France, 1975–1976*. London: Penguin.

Goedde, P. 2019. *The Politics of Peace*. Oxford: Oxford University Press.

Gonzalez, C. G. 2017. Global justice in the Anthropocene. In Kotze, L. (ed). *Environmental Law. and Governance for the Anthropocene*. New York: Hart Publishing Seattle. University School of Law Research Paper No. 17–06. https://ssrn.com/abstract=2929042 (accessed August 17, 2023).

de Goya, F. 1814. *The third of May, 1808: The execution of the defenders of Madrid*, Museo del Prado, Madrid, Spain.

Groys, B. 2008. *Art power*. Cambridge, MA: MIT Press.

Guthrie, C. and Quinlan, M. 2007. The structure of the tradition. *Just war: The just war tradition: Ethics in modern warfare*. London: Bloomsbury.

Hemmingway, E. 1940. *For whom the bell tolls*. New York: Scribner.

Hiroshima Peace Memorial Museum. n.d. http://hpmmuseum.jp/?lang=eng (accessed August 17, 2023).

Hobbes, T. 2013/1642. *De Cive*. Scotts Valley, CA: CreateSpace Independent Publishing Platform.

Hobbes, T. 1996/1651. *Leviathan*. Cambridge texts in the history of political thought. Cambridge: Cambridge University Press.

Höch, H. 1919–20. *Cut with the Kitchen Knife Dada Through the Last Weimar Beer-Belly Cultural Epoch of Germany*. Nationalgalerie, Staatliche Museen, Berlin. Available at: https://www. khanacademy.org/humanities/art-1010/dada-and-surrealism/dada2/a/hannah-hoch-cut-with-the-kitchen-knife-dada-through-the-last-weimar-beer-belly-cultural-epoch-of-ger many (accessed August 17, 2023).

Hocking, B. T. 2012. Beautiful barriers: Art and identity along a Belfast 'peace' wall. *Anthropology Matters Journal*, 14(1), pp. 1–12.

Holbein, H. 1533. *The Ambassadors*. National Gallery, London.

Kadesh Treaty. n. d. Istanbul Archaeological Museum, Turkey.

Kamerić, Š. 2005. *Pink line vs green line*. Public project; Nicosia, Cyprus. https://sejlakameric. com/works/pink-line-vs-green-line/ (accessed August 17, 2023).

Kerr, R. 2020. Art, aesthetics, justice, and reconciliation: What can art do? *AJIL Unbound*, 114, pp. 123–7.

Keynes, J. M. 1919. *The economic consequences of the peace*. London: Macmillan.

King, A. 1998. *Memorials of the great war in Britain: The symbolism and politics of remembrance*. Oxford: Berg Publishers.

Kohn, M. 2013. Postcolonialism and global justice. *Journal of Global Ethics*, 9(2), pp. 187–200.

Kollwitz, K. 1924. *Never again war*. Käthe Kollwitz Museum, Köln. Available at: https://www. kollwitz.de/en/never-again-war-kn-205 (accessed August 17, 2023).

Koss, C. D. (ed.) 2004. *A Ding Darling Sampler: The Editorial Cartoons of Jay N. Darling*. New: York: Maecenas Press.

Kustermans, J. 2018. Henry Maine and the modern invention of peace. *Journal of the History of International Law / Revue d'histoire du droit international*, 20(1), pp. 57–88.

Lederach, J. P. 2005. *The Moral imagination: The art and soul of building peace*. Oxford: Oxford University Press.

Lilja, M. 2022. The definition of resistance. *Journal of Political Power*, 15(2), pp. 202–20.

Lorenzetti. 1338–40. *Allegory of good government: Effects of good government in the city*. Frescos. Palazzo Publico, Siena, Italy.

Maine, H. S. 1888. *International law: A series of lectures delivered before the University of Cambridge*. London: John Murray Press.

Marks, E. B. 2000. *For a better world: Posters from the United Nations*, Maldon: Pomegranate Europe.

Mitchell, J., Vincett, G., Hawksley, H. and Culbertson, H. 2020, *Peacebuilding and the arts*. London: Palgrave Macmillan.

Moyn, S. 2018. *Not enough: Human rights in an unequal world*. Cambridge, Massachusetts: Harvard University Press.

Ndlovu-Gatsheni, S. 2018. A world without others? Spectre of difference and toxic identitarian politics. *International Journal of Critical Diversity Studies*, 1(1), pp. 80–96.

de Neuville, A. A. 1880. *The Defence of Rorke's Drift*. New South Wales Art Gallery.

Nussbaum, F. 1938. *The pearls*. http://www.painting-analysis.com/pearls.htm (accessed August 17, 2023).

Nussbaum, M. C. 2015. Political liberalism and global justice. *Journal of Global Ethics* 11(1), pp. 68–79.

Orwell, G. 1949. *1984*. London: Secker & Warburg.

Picasso, P. 1949. *Dove*. 9 January. https://www.tate.org.uk/art/artworks/picasso-dove-p11366 (accessed August 17, 2023).

Picasso, P. 1937. *Guernica*. Museo Reina Sofía, Madrid.

Picasso, P. 1952. *War and peace*. https://www.tate.org.uk/whats-on/tate-liverpool/exhibition/picasso-peace-and-freedom/picasso-peace-and-freedom-explore- (accessed August 17, 2023).

Picasso, P. n.d. *The Face of Peace, The Dove of Peace*. Poster for the Congress of the National Movement for Peace, Picasso, May 1962.

Pogge, T. 2001. Priorities of global justice. *Metaphilosophy*, 32(1/2), pp. 6–24.

Querejazu, A. 2022. Cosmopraxis: Relational methods for a pluriversal IR. *Review of International Studies*, 48(5), pp. 875–90.

Rancière, J. 2006. The ethical turn of aesthetics and politics. *Critical Horizons*, 7(1), pp. 1–20.

Randle, M. 1994. *Civil resistance*. Boulder, CO: Paladin Press.

Reid, H. and Taylor, B. 2010. *Recovering the commons: Democracy, place, and global justice*. Chicago, IL: University of Illinois Press.

Reuterswärd, C. F. 1988. *Non-violence*. New York: UN.

Richmond, O. P. 2011. *A post-liberal peace*. London: Routledge.

Richmond, O. P. 2016. *Peace formation and political order*. Oxford: Oxford University Press.

Richmond, O. P. 2020. *Peace in IR*. London: Routledge.

Richmond, O. P. 2022. *The grand design*. Oxford: Oxford University Press.

Richmond, O. P. 2010. Resistance and the post-liberal peace. *Millennium*, 38(3), pp. 665–92.

Richmond, O. P. 2011. Critical agency, resistance and a post-colonial civil society. *Cooperation and Conflict*, 46(4), pp. 419–40.

Richmond, O. P. 2005. *The transformation of peace*. London: Routledge.

Richter, H. 1965. *Dada: Art and Anti-Art*. London: Thames and Hudson.

Rubens, P. P. 1629–30. *Minerva protects Pax from Mars* ('Peace and War'). National Gallery, London.

Scott, J. C. 1990. *Domination and the arts of resistance: Hidden transcripts*. New Haven, CT: Yale University Press.

Sharp, G. 1973. *The politics of nonviolent action*. Boston, MA: Porter Sargent Publishers.

Spivak, G. C. 2000. Translation as culture. *Parallax*, 6(1), pp. 13–24.

Tolstoy, L. 2007/1867. *War and peace*. London: Penguin.

UN General Assembly and Security Council. 2018. Peacebuilding and sustaining peace. *Report of the UN Secretary General*, A/72/707-S/2018/43, 18th January.

UN General Assembly. 1966. *International Covenant on Economic, Social and Cultural Rights* (ECOSOC), United Nations General Assembly Resolution 2200A (XXI), 16th December.

UN General Assembly. 1984. Right of peoples to peace. *UN General Assembly Resolution 39/11*.

van Hensbergen, G. 2005. *Guernica: The biography of a twentieth-century icon*. London: Bloomsbury.

Vereshchagin, V. 1871. *The apotheosis of war*. State Tretyakov Gallery, Moscow.

Vinthagen, S. 2015. *A theory of nonviolent action: How civil resistance works*. London: ZED Books.

Wallinger, M. B. 2007. *State Britain*. Tate Modern, London.

Walzer, M. 1977. *Just and unjust wars: A moral argument with historical illustrations*. New York: Basic Books.

Weber, M. 2015. *Weber's rationalism and modern society*, trans. and edited by Tony Waters and Dagmar Waters. New York: Palgrave Books.

Winter, J. 2014. *Sites of memory, sites of mourning: The great war in European cultural history*. Cambridge: Cambridge University Press.

Zuboff, S. 2019. *The age of surveillance capitalism*. London: Profile Books.

TWO

Theorising Peace Formation and the Arts

Stefanie Kappler, Oliver P. Richmond and Birte Vogel

Arts projects are being developed in conflict and post-conflict contexts all over the world (Mitchell et al. 2020). They often connect aesthetics, emotions, performance and the dissemination of creative commentary or ideas with political, social, economic and cultural conflict and ways beyond it. They may appear to merely engage with everyday dynamics of conflict, violence, war and peace, but they may also address structural and persistent problems, with critical commentary, and perhaps even creative propositions. There is a long back-history to the evolution of the relationship between peace, politics and emancipatory thinking on the one hand, and the arts on the other hand, as we discussed in the introduction and Chapter 1. Across the artistic range, from visual arts to music, film and exhibitions, as well ritual and performativity, this relationship often provides a platform to debate and contest issues of social agency, ethics and justice (Bloch 1980; Adorno et al. 2020; Rancière 2006).

As pointed out in the previous chapter, the debate also raises the questions of what the role of the visual and performative 'spectacle' is in peacemaking and political reform (Debord 1967), how the latter are associated with hegemony and the restoration of an unjust status quo, and how to understand more substantive, critical and emancipatory contributions (Richmond 2022), critiques associated with visual, creative and artistic performances, processes, artefacts and dynamics. These are questions long associated with social mobilisation, resistance and political conflict (Kerr 2020, 123). Such engagement is open, insightful, wide-ranging, less conditioned by institutional and traditional order and offers a dialogic engagement with the 'moral imagination' (Lederach 2005) necessary for peacemaking to move beyond negative forms of peace. For example, approaches such as photovoice, community theatre or dance therapy are commonly used by non-governmental organisations in refugee camps or trauma workshops as ways of engaging local communities and addressing (psychological) needs emerging during and in the aftermath of violent conflict.

Such approaches may be in support of hegemony by communicating creative yet censored perspectives. In some instances, they resist, contest, engage and network, rearticulating and reimaging the nature of a peaceful political order. There are indeed a wide spectrum, range, mode and type of dynamics to and productions to consider here (Kerr 2020, 125).[1] Investigating these dynamics also means uncovering hidden, submerged and blocked perspectives that offer potential innovations which enhance the ethical standing and legitimacy of peacemaking. Yet to what extent is the effect of such practices more than therapeutic, ephemeral and short-lived (Pupavac 2005), developing responses to structural issues related to political economy, social and global justice, reconciliation, and sustainability (UN 2018)? Do we see wide-ranging political and social change as a result of the energy and resources now devoted to art-based projects? Peace processes, after all, have to contend with regional geopolitics and elite power competition as well as coordinate local representation, rights and restitution. Power relations are inevitably balanced towards the former. Is it plausible to expect civil society and arts-based agency, activism or productions to make a political impact (as so many policy and advocacy papers recently published argue [e.g., Woods, 2015]) and if so, in what ways?

To understand the potential political ramifications of art-based peace work, this chapter develops a framework that enables us to capture the impact of the arts beyond the linear narratives of transformation dominant in the recent literature. Instead, it provides a more complex understanding of the factors that could drive radical or hybrid potential in the arts—or prevents these from developing. It investigates the complex factors that drive or block radical or hybrid, social agency-derived potential in the arts and identifies the various manifestations that the intersection between aesthetics and politics can produce (Bleiker 2009).

This chapter first investigates the relationship between art, power and politics (domestic, international and global). It shows that the arts are not immune from the power relations from which they emerged in the first place, but that there are significant attempts by artists to challenge the status quo in aesthetic terms (Premaratna and Bleiker 2010; Mitchell et al. 2020). It is at these points where art meets politics, ranging from possibilities of effecting radical change to stabilising the status quo, with different forms of experimentation and hybridisation possible in between those two ends of the spectrum (Richmond 2007).

On this basis, we map our analytical framework through a typology of *art-peace* based on these parameters (Richmond, 2022), which we capture in the concept along with supporting research conducted by the multiple authors in this book, in order to assess the possible impacts the arts can have on political change and conflict dynamics. This is carried out within the critical framework of peace formation (Richmond 2016) that we discussed in the Introduction. We outline *artpeace* as an umbrella term to capture the various possibilities of interaction between art and the politics of peace processes, where art can have productive, community-centred effects on politics on the one hand, or sit in spheres completely isolated from the politics of peace on the other (Richmond 2016, 180).

Overall, we suggest that, while there is a plethora of positive effects in community-based, therapeutic and individual benefits of their work, artists tend to find it difficult to make a larger difference to the material and formal underpinnings of peace processes at state or international level. This exposes them to elite power clashes, regional geopolitics and the limitations of the liberal international peace frameworks (Paris 2004; Pugh 2005; Chandler 2010; Richmond 2005, 2022). Blockages at play include funding and political constraints, different ideological agendas and attempts to co-opt art by political elites for their own ends, such as through propaganda (see Pogodda, Richmond and Visoka 2023). Blockages operate at the local, tactical level, as well as at the state and international strategic level. At all scales, blockages are deployed to support elite justifications of inequality and domination across different forms of media against subaltern claims, minority rights and local networks, as well as to block their connection with wider regional and global emancipatory movements. More subtly, elites are often in the position to curate art in ways in which some of the radical potential that shapes much of the inspiration of art dissipates and is depoliticised. Our framework therefore casts light on the various blockages at play in making art a radical component of peace and seeks case studies in which these blockages are articulated in different ways.

Peace, Art and Power

The arts can be seen as embedded in, and constitutive of, socio-political processes. There is also a strong sense in the literature on the arts that they are prescient, hinting at undercurrents of praxis not readily accessible within the public rationalities of everyday or political life (liberal, neoliberal, bureaucratic and so on). What interests us specifically in this project are the ways in which art allows for the translation of messages between different types of audiences. How does politics travel from one space to another, and what is the role that art can play in this process, particularly with respect to developing experimental, radical and more deeply legitimate ways of enabling human security, justice, rights and representation beyond the limited rationalities of the state and the liberal international? These social and global justice aspects that emerge from the rationality of peace formation certainly cannot be viewed in isolation from questions of power and agency in that they drive

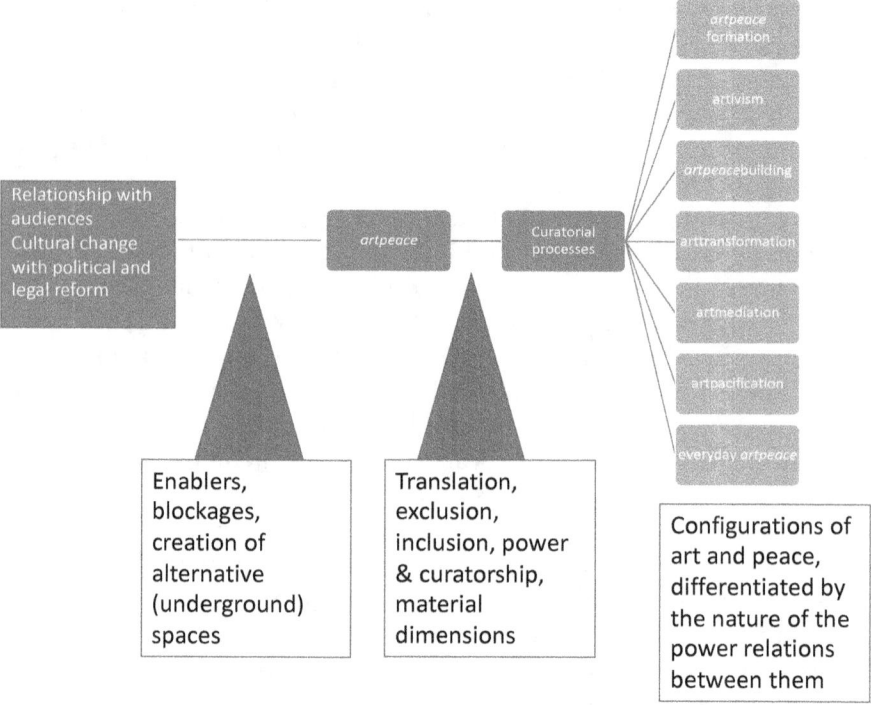

Figure 2.1 Mapping *artpeace*.

the ways the connections between art and politics interact. Figure 2.1 lays out these dynamics of *artpeace*.

Importantly, as much as artwork can be directed and guided by powerful top-down actors, such as elite-level curators and museums (Sylvester 2009), it can also be a tool of expression for those most oppressed by hegemonic power structures (Boal 2006). Community-based forms of curation also exist, sometimes supporting top-down curatorial practices, other times challenging them from their points of view. However, there is much room within that binary, and it is rarely clear-cut as to whether artistic messages are *either* hegemonic (often the most dominant and long-lasting post-war aesthetic form) *or* expressions of resistance to oppression (rarely dominant and easily erased). Instead, the relevant points lie in the subtle nuances and variations of power and agency as they can be expressed through artistic engagement and consumption alike. Gell's book on the relationship between art and agency accounts for exactly this, namely the ways in which artwork mediates social agency (Gell 1998, 7). In Gell's view, the agency of the artist, viewer, artwork and 'prototype' (artistic reference points) are inextricably linked (Gell 1998). In that sense, we could argue that art does not necessarily address, but is able to highlight multiple lines of inequality in society, both as they relate to the production and the consumption of artworks. Who has the means to produce art and what narratives are they choosing or having to follow? Who is able and willing to contemplate the artwork and how do they use it to build their own political messages on this consumption process? To take this further, how does this possibly indicate a process of 'ethical witnessing' (Little 2017) in which an audience is encouraged to move into an active, transformative role? In this process, the boundaries between creator and spectator are somewhat merged, and the translation process between agents and audiences becomes one loaded with political ideas and networks of agency. Certainly, expressions of agency by audiences are not limited to constructive participation, but equally take the form of vandalism and the destruction or removal of artwork that is perceived as offensive, or transgresses hegemonic rationalities (cf. Kappler 2017).

Further questions raised in this context are questions of access as well as in- and exclusion in view of power relations at the state and elite levels as well as international liberal peace rationalities—again, both in relation to the producers and consumers of artworks as well as their interaction with each other and with hegemonic forces. In peace formation contexts specifically, inequalities between a variety of actors (not just local and international actors, but also in relation to gender, class, race and so forth) often are materialised via artistic expressions. The latter can be used as ways of reading marginalised, complex, intersectional inequalities (cf. Kappler and Lemay-Hébert 2019). In (post-)conflict contexts, such inequalities can be the essence of contestation and agonism, transported, amongst others, through artistic engagement. The narrow framing and partial marginalisation of cultural and artistic agency from liberal peacebuilding contexts is therefore an important indicator of a particular power constellation which deems art as unsuitable for, or marginal to, peace-related engagement (cf. Kappler 2014). Such processes of marginalisation lead to an increasing bifurcation of social ideas and norms and prevent agonistic discussions, as they are often transported through art, from feeding into institutional policies. However, we suggest that a focus on the arts as mediators of power and agency can be helpful not only in understanding power differentials within societies, but also the ways in which the latter are stabilised, shattered and transformed over time. For the eventual reconstruction of legitimate authority that peace requires, this is more significant than is generally understood, introducing social and cultural dimensions of mediated political agreements and peacemaking where normally, power-based, diplomatic, securitised, military approaches have the monopoly. The following section will look at this in more detail.

Translating and Mediating Power: From Peace Aesthetics to Peace Politics

Translation, communication and discourse are important parts of any peace process, establishing the basis for political negotiation, reform, agreement and reconciliation. Traditionally this occurred at an elite and state level in formal diplomacy, but increasingly, with the advent of civil and global civil society, local actors, social movements and local to global shifts, informal networks have become involved in peace formation. This process has created a parallel and concurrent shift in how we understand violence, and how peace is constituted, also requiring a broadening of its conceptual framework (from power, politics or law) to more elemental features of human politics and communication, where political claims can be made from outside of accepted norms of hegemony. However, what is less clear is the role that aesthetics can play, not only in communicating politics, but also in translating their messages into formal political processes.

In this context, post-colonial scholarship has contributed to our understanding of *translation* as a social, political and normative practice. According to Spivak (2000, 14), translation is more than moving between two languages; instead, it is about 'the production of the ethical subject'. Pointing to the interplay between the creators and recipient of translations, she claims that '[n]o speech is speech if it is not heard. It is this act of hearing-to-respond that may be called the imperative to translate' (Spivak 2000, 14). The translation of discourses between different communities thus takes on a highly politicised nature, implicating either side in the constitution of a political community. Bhabha's reading of translation as a non-binary, but nonetheless subversive political act is well in tune with this approach (Bhabha 1994, 38).

Specifically, in relation to art and their capacities to translate, we can take a closer look at the processes of heritage authorisation and legitimation vis-à-vis conflict-affected communities. Just as heritage is discursively legitimised and authorised (Smith 2006), so is art. Douglas (2017, 4) indeed reminds us how museums (both of art and heritage more generally) are constitutive of political communities through their curatorial powers, arguing that '[m]useums, like constitutions, function as authorisers of the world, its history, its reality, and its possibilities'. Of course, this often relates to nationalist arts, which confirm the longevity of a nation's claims, presence on a particular territory, or authenticity, and confirms its current political organisation. In this sense, art can be counter-revolutionary, block peacemaking, undermine progressive movements and confirm the authenticity of unjust power structures, just as it can hint at expanded rights and revolutionary change. Douglas (2017, 14ff) points to the 'counter monumental' abilities of the museum in that it can shape political processes not only in terms of legitimising, but also in terms of challenging them. The unsettling of norms is thus part and parcel of curatorial processes, which may transcend the abilities of the respective artist. Yet, most formal art tends not to do that, but instead operates within accepted parameters. It is more often new, radical art forms and spaces that challenge norms, offering a connection with peace formation, which is ultimately about changing state formation from a process favouring power-structures, war and violence as formative of the state (Tilly 1985), to a state based upon the political process that arise from subaltern claims for emancipation. The power inherent in the ability to choose, translate, juxtapose and present artwork can be seen as instrumental to post-conflict processes, which are often left with the legacies of 'difficult histories' (Lehrer and Milton 2011). Unsettling engrained narratives about the past can thus be a key challenge, not only for artists but also for curators in such spaces. Whether they perpetuate engrained narratives of divisions or contrast them with alternative interpretations of history and visions of the future, they remain an integral part of the scripting of narratives and the processes of translation between past and present, as well as between the different constituencies that are embedded in divided political settings.

Within the constraints of the political field, artists can, in theory, choose their political alliances. Yet, their choice is usually limited to existing political parties and other power holders or complete isolation; this can be progressive in contexts where there are such power holders in the public sphere, as well as amenable to engaging with subaltern actors, networks and dynamics from below. It is restrictive in contexts in which the political situation is static, narrow or inflexible, conditioned by nationalism, elite power and a defence of sovereignty. In conflict-affected societies, such alliances often fall victim to pressure from powerful actors (such as war profiteers), and artists may feel that working underground is more beneficial to their agenda than to collaborate with a narrow set of elites that was institutionalised by violence to begin with. Artists' agency can thus not only consist of forging new alliances but also of refusing cooperation in other cases. Thus, the political landscape prepares certain options for the arts and excludes others, more so as elite, state and colonial power dominate social actors and networks. What remains to be seen is if art agency means choosing alliances in this landscape to shift the 'field of gravity' within that landscape away from the rent-seeking and power-seeking violence that often dominates stratified societies and geopolitical balances. Are art-based actors making particular pathways of peace or conflict more politically/socially acceptable? There certainly is a synergy between politics and the arts where the arts provide symbolism and legitimation of political projects, for example where art-based projects promote messages of reconciliation to broader audiences, as seen with community theatre projects in Sri Lanka (e.g., Premaratna 2018) or South Sudan (e.g., Verjee, this book). This can obviously also be used for the opposite end, and the connection between arts and nationalism is well documented too. One only has to think of the militarised murals in Northern Ireland. Likewise, power holders, such as political actors, can provide funding and exert their influence to support arts-projects and their political messages if they feel this is in their interests (or at least does not contradict them). They can also erase arts-projects which undermine their interests very easily, given the flimsy nature of art-based agency, especially when connected with peace as a critical response to hegemony, nationalism and domination. The changing mural landscape in Kabul is another case in point: pro-democracy and human rights murals were systematically erased after the Taliban came to power in 2021 and sometimes replaced with conservative Islamic messaging (*The Guardian* 2021).

In understanding the ways in which art meets formal politics, we can also look at art as a space in which ideas can meet and be negotiated publicly or semi-publicly. This refers to both discursive and material spaces: some ideas generate a discursive space of agency (Kappler 2014), others need to be given a physical presence in order to circulate effectively (Björkdahl and Kappler 2017). Such physical places can present themselves in the form of micro-spaces, such as museums or galleries (cf. Sylvester 2009), or alternatively in macro-spaces, including particular urban or rural zones of peace formation (Vogel 2016, 2018). They can act as microcosms of peace formation in that they may facilitate discussions about the nature of peace and political order as well as the various debates that surround its conceptualisation. They can foster or inhibit particular forms of social mobility, encourage or discourage movement in particular ways. Artworks can make certain urban zones more inviting and accessible to outsiders, whilst closing others off, symbolically and materially (cf. Forde 2019). In that process, liminal spaces can emerge, but they can also be turned into more popular and widely accessible spaces. This particular technique has often been used in projects of urban regeneration (Cape Town, Medellín or Belfast are notable examples here), where artists were invited to turn seemingly desolate and violent areas into lively places through artistic means. Street art, graffiti or art festivals are particularly popular tools in this context. For instance, one of the most deprived and violent neighbourhoods in Medellín, Colombia, now successfully hosts graffiti tours and has thus become a tourism hotspot, generating new economic possibilities within the neighbourhood (Vogel et al. 2020; Ó Brádaigh Bean, this book). Nevertheless, the spatial presence of art can be highly controversial, particularly in contexts where a particular type of artwork gives space to perpetrators of violence and thus increases their everyday visibility in public space. This is not least the reason for which the murals employed on Belfast's peace walls have long been subject to debate and keep being replaced by seemingly less militant ones (cf. Kappler and McKane 2019).

Having said that, peace formation can take place in the most acutely experienced spaces where violence occurs and is experienced 'intersectionally' (Crenshaw 1991), and indeed elements of existing peacebuilding practice may reinforce the structures behind violence rather than peace formation itself. Likewise, violence, human rights violations and oppressive systems also might drive some of radical arts activities into less visible and underground spaces. This shift offers the chance of survival for some projects and ideas, but also bears the risk of projects being easily erased. It makes the idea of the arts (just as with scholarship) as a platform for emancipatory, transversal, trans-national networks—rather than physical spaces—particularly important. What is striking is that these networks often find their alliances horizontally rather than vertically, again pointing to the already discussed disconnect between the different levels within arts-based peace formation processes. Horizontal networks can indeed be an important part of this process, especially in restrictive political environments. While controversial or system-critical individual arts projects are more likely to be targeted (at both participants and viewers), transversal cooperation between a number of artists and curators is more likely to be able to challenge national and regional political processes and contribute to peace formation. Thus, while individual projects may seem less influential and threatening to power, their collective presence might be more of a target for power and a risk for participants.

From Arts for Peace to *Artpeace*

In this edited volume, we propose to map and chart the journey 'from art to politics', which is not always a directly identifiable and traceable journey, but one that meanders through various communities, obstacles and channels in order to convey messages aimed to bring about societal transformation. We term this entanglement *artpeace* to highlight the ways in which art and peace are often inseparable, but in a potentially frictional relationship (cf. Björkdahl et al. 2016), and one which certainly transgresses the concepts, theory and pathways of formal politics and liberal or authoritarian forms of peacebuilding (Paris 2004). The overarching concept of *artpeace* points to a mixed aesthetic and political praxis of emancipatory peace (Richmond 2022) in its contemporary format, hints of which can be gleaned from its historical development as a primary power-based nexus. This includes a broad understanding of the role that art can play in relation to peace processes, ranging from more traditional practices of reconciliation to revolutionary, frictional politics subverting the status quo (Mitchell et al. 2020). We therefore posit the following potential outcomes of mapping the journey between arts-based interventions and politics with three theoretical outcomes. These involve the challenge of uncovering or discovering marginalised examples, and then producing, mediating, curating and even 'resolving' *artpeace* for: a) radical change, b) mediation and hybridisation, or c) the status quo. In any of these cases, new voices and positions would emerge, which are necessary for local legitimacy in peace and reform processes (Richmond and Mac Ginty 2020).

Radical Change

This scenario reflects an understanding of the arts as essential generators of politics by themselves, as posited by Bleiker (2017), as well as responding to ethical deficits sensed in politics, discovering, uncovering, enabling, mobilising and bringing them to public attention and even suggesting possible ways forward. This means they offer more than critique, but mainly in the context of micro social networks—which may also be more widely connected beyond the state. It points to a practical and ethics-based vision of expanding rights, reform and change uniquely tailored to the context and situation the artist is representing. We can witness some of these articulations in the work with Syrian and South Sudanese artists (see Sobout's and Verjee's chapters) as well as, in less visible ways, in the ways in which ballads in the Philippines point to very specific local grievances vis-à-vis the peace process (see Ragandang's chapter). This is based on an understanding of art as inherently radical and political, with the ability to bring about political and aesthetic transformation in its own creative ways. It includes processes of creatively uncovering injustices, attracting attention, producing embryonic cultural networks of legitimacy that are transnational, transversal and informal. It may also span different agendas, may attack and shift power structures from outside and inside and might undermine the legitimacy of existing institutions. Such transformation is necessary for a viable peace process if it is to respond to subaltern claims. At the same time, the existing literature remains vague on how such processes of change translate into tangible benefits for those affected by violence and engaged in peace formation ('the peace dividend'). Sobout's and Schouten's chapters in this volume speak to these questions, investigating whether the arts can create some form of social movement that challenges and transforms the status quo, not as a result of one specific project or actor, but as a collective undertaking in a particular community.

Mediation and Hybridisation

In this case, through a less reductionist view of agency, the arts act as mediators in the Latourian sense (Latour 1996, 378). As a result, the arts are somewhat transformative and thus have an impact on politics and vice versa, but only to a limited extent. Initially, they allow the expression of marginal and creative voices, with the possibility of recording the political claims that are made in influential ways that reach certain key audiences. There is a connection between arts, marginal quarters of society, and politics, yet connections are not always clear and less traceable, while their political impacts are limited to the micro-level rather than transforming the structural politics surrounding and conditioning them. However, subaltern political claims and alterity (Spivak 1988), when set against liberal and authoritarian political orders, tend to lead to heightened agency, resistance, and thus mediated, hybrid forms of peace and order emerging (Boege et al. 2009; Richmond 2011). These are aimed at maintaining both local, state level and international legitimacy. There are fields of dialogue between politics and art, but other fields of silence, where the confrontation of the two spheres becomes too controversial. This process continues to favour the powerful, who are able to instrumentalise processes of mediation and hybridisation in their favour, as Verjee's chapter shows. Similarly, Cole and Ó Brádaigh Bean reflect on the ways in which urban politics can be inspired by creative powers on the one hand, but be constrained by powerful administrative and infrastructural constraints that continuously seek to contain transformation through mechanisms of urban governance.

Status Quo

In this scenario, the arts act as intermediaries in the Latourian sense (Latour 1996, 373). We assume a blocked connection between arts, society and political systems, which is also connected to the historical tendency for subaltern voices and political claims to be erased or silenced (Spivak 1988, 2000), or at best to be allowed if they contribute to propaganda discourses framed by elite power and sovereignty (Tilly 1985). The arts do not bring in political energy themselves, but instead represent a 'black box' disconnected within a political environment, unable to generate politics but indicative of new, creative thinking with political implications, and potential ethical and methodological innovations related to issues of justice and legitimacy (Kerr 2020). The blockages that prevent the arts from effectively engaging with society and politics can be manifold and may either be structural, or deliberately placed by different powers that resist the changed envisioned by arts-based activism. They can even serve as a propaganda or power tool to support dominant narratives. This assumption echoes Spivak's cautions about the agency of the subaltern (Spivak 1988).

A postcolonial reading of the arts can be helpful in this context in that it touches on foundational norms and values reflected in aesthetics, questions of translation, radical change, subalternity and resistance (cf. Bhabha 1994).

Such approaches, however, have been largely neglected in the design and implementation of peace agreements and processes around the world, despite their potential to raise questions of injustice and marginalisation, as the chapters by Nkosinkulu and Ragandang demonstrate. This has often been for reasons of practical parsimony, but this realism has also often limited the local legitimacy of peace processes. It is a double-edged sword though: while the exclusion of arts-based agency indeed limits the connectivity of the peace process to grievances that may be articulated through the arts, their inclusion might in turn risk their critical capacity and coopt them into a system they may be wary of. Mindful of this tension, Nkosinkulu's and Ragandang's chapters discuss the ways in which progressive developments inherent in aesthetic practices are, at least partially, governed and silenced to render the translation of their claims into political actions difficult.

Certainly, what remains difficult to see is how such outcomes of artistic interventions in the political sphere can be measured and assessed although there is a common agenda often to be found centred on questions of local, social and global justice. Often, such change remains deliberately subtle and hidden in order to be sustainable over a longer period of time. Other changes may be more directly visible in the longer term, for instance, through changing goals of the UN Sustaining Peace Agenda (UN 2018) or changes of political practice on the ground—although such changes may often not be directly attributable and traceable to artistic interventions. Certainly, whilst peace formation theory proposes the possibility of emancipatory outcomes, such outcomes are often only achieved when different societal and political sectors work together (including the arts), but they are rarely traceable to one social sector alone. Legitimacy for peacemaking, in other words, is complex and multidimensional, whereas the practice of peacemaking tends to focus on security and political interests, and associated elites, which ultimately restore the status quo. The collection of case studies in the following chapters, indeed, illustrates that the arts record, reflect, generate and mobilise diverse understandings of justice and legitimacy through creative methods, but often struggle to translate these into major political change, particularly as its challenge becomes more radical.

In this vein, there are a variety of ways in which art-based approaches and the politics of peace can intersect, ranging from scenarios where art is subdued into pacification politics and reduced to a quasi-propagandistic tool of legitimising the status quo, to scenarios where peace is negotiated through creative practices and art serves as a mobilising tool through which new networks of peace politics can emerge. We therefore propose a typology of ideal types that describe the different possibilities of *artpeace*, depending on who holds the defining power, where and how the *artpeace* intersection is negotiated, what norms they promote and under what structural conditions they operate

Table 2.1 The Relationship between Artistic Agency, Peace and Political Reform

	Radical change	Mediation and hybridisation	Status quo
artpeace formation	x		
Artivism	x		
*Artpeace*building		x	
Arttransformation		x	
Artmediation		x	
artpacification			x
everyday *artpeace*			x

(see Figure 2.1). These complex pathways result in different *artpeace* config-urations, which we conceptualise as: 1) *artpeace* formation, 2) artivism, 3) *artpeace*building, 4) arttransformation, 5) artmediation, 6) artpacification and 7) everyday *artpeace*. We now turn to each of those concepts individually.

1)   *Artpeace* formation
Artpeace formation is the expression of *artpeace* that places most agency in the hands of the communities peace is to serve. Drawing on different local forms of legitimacy, in this constellation, art grows into the peace process quite organically, is transformative and shapes politics but also cultural and social practice—at least in certain spaces and at community level. *Artpeace* forma-tion suggests a sort of organic connection between art and politics, where one grows out of the other and art-based processes impact political processes nat-urally. *Artpeace* formation is driven by bottom-up local agency, and utilises arts-oriented agency in order to represent subaltern voices and influence both state reform and the nature of any peace settlement, whilst also influencing international attempts at enabling peace and engaging with transnational and transversal non-governmental networks (Richmond 2011). This points towards hybrid peace outcomes (Richmond and Franks 2008; Mac Ginty and Richmond 2015) which seek to transcend the negative political versions that emerged in the 2000s (Richmond 2015) by combining different forms of political, social and cultural organisation. It suggests the necessity of moving beyond territorial sovereignty in order to achieve reconciliation, justice and sustainability, and according cultural registers political significance even if they appear to represent only marginal agency and have little in the way of structural power.

This type of dynamic can arise at micro- or macro-levels of politics, depending on which community the peace that is being formed responds to. This scenario assumes that there are long-standing networks between artists, communities and community representatives, and political conver-sations about rights, grievances, needs and visions of peace are discussed in such networks. Often, artists and curators will work together to articulate those and will manage to channel these into informal and formal political networks. In that sense, *artpeace* formation acts transversally across a set of actors, with art embedded as a legitimate form of public engagement in communities. Findings from our chapters on South African graffiti (Nkosinkulu), Colombian youth activism (Ó Brádaigh Bean) and the ballads in the Philippines (Ragandang) point to such possibilities of political art, embedded in community structures and channelling grievances and visions into political processes, even attaining global influence. At the same time, we also observe the various blockages that such endeavours face when meeting formal politics: they are often pushed back, minimised or localised in a broader (sometimes) national peace process. Political power-holders find it easy to erase the artefacts and performances *artpeace* produces, and to reduce such processes—especially where they take place in local communities—to notions of marginality or specificity, thus undermining their ability to enter a wider conversation beyond their immediate circle of activity.

2) Artivism

Artivism is a term already well established in contemporary scholarship, often describing the fusion of artistic production and political activism, and pointing to its organic symbiosis. This notion is specifically evoked in Sobout's and Schouten's chapters, exploring the common interlacing of artists and activists. The former may have a dedicated political cause at the heart of their activities, or the latter may mobilise art-based forms of mobilisation to articulate specific political goals. Artivism uses art as a particular kind of mobilisation that connects to certain issues and agencies in society and is usually process-oriented, collaborative, antihierarchical and self-organising (Danko 2018). It relies on the notion that art can not only critique and portray what is there (and therefore mobilise) but is also able to imagine (and advocate for) alternative futures. One could argue that artivism highlights the agenda-setting role of arts in politics and is often used, as our chapters show, by actors marginalised by contemporary politics. Both the process of creating and curating art can act as activist practices and deliberately challenge the political status quo. Such political engagement tends to run counter the political status quo and, for this very reason, faces strong opposition by incumbent political powerholders. Despite—or because of—that, artivism can be a potentially powerful tool for those excluded from politics to make their voices heard, yet with different outcomes depending on what kinds of alliances they can build, nationally or globally.

Derived from the notion of 'celebrity activism', which denotes the involvement of high-profile individuals in political campaigns (Huliaras and Tzifakis 2010), some of this can turn into 'celebrity artivism' during the course of which celebrities (such as Banksy, Pussy Riot or Ai Weiwei) mobilise their artwork to capture attention to specific political issues. There are also many examples of larger national and transnational social movements connecting to artistic performances to draw international attention to their causes. Here, examples such as the use of graffiti during the Arab Spring, the Occupy Movements in the US or the national efforts of a number of prominent South Sudanese organisations that Verjee describes in his chapter come to mind. On a smaller scale, Sobout's chapter on art forms emerging in the Syrian refugee community in Lebanon illustrates the ways in which artivism can also play out on a locally-based, yet no less important, level. These are examples of powerful ways of using art-based engagement for larger political goals, some more connected to grassroots concerns, others more connected to individualised agendas. It may not always be clearly discernible whether the role of art in these processes is primarily for the sake of art or for the sake of politics. What is more, the effects of artivist practices are at risk of being ephemeral when not fed and sustained by continuous political resources at all levels of society, when not engaging with questions of political reform at the state level, or when not connecting with global networks. Such contingencies explain why some projects have followed political trends and been vulnerable to resource depletion, while others have thrived over a longer period of time.

3) *Artpeace*building

Connected to the liberal peace tradition, *artpeace*building essentially follows the liberal political theory of using the arts as a peacebuilding tool to support democratisation, human rights, economic liberalism and a vibrant role of civil society (Paris 2004; Richmond 2005). It foregrounds the civil and the social within these liberal parameters (Lederach 1997). It relates and supports a substantial and multidimensional intervention into the social fabric of society, one that challenges the autonomy and independence of civil society and social movements, whilst also aiming to support its struggle with predatory elites or the authoritarian state. This paradox rests on the claim of basic universal values, which also often figure in artistic engagements with peace across the world. It offers local-to-global, comprehensive dynamics of peacemaking, indicating that social and cultural, small-scale dynamics are essential to the wider legitimacy of comprehensive peacebuilding approaches.

In this scenario, art is used to transport pre-defined values by donors, as shown in the discussion on the current literature on arts and peace in the introduction. International non-governmental organisations and foreign governments thus achieve a buy-in of a (post-)conflict society into the traditional civil society peacebuilding discourse, whilst restraining the exercise of unaccountable power by elites. As such, *artpeace*building is intricately connected to top-down structures and forms of external interventionalism but has also captured the imagination and support of local, community actors in the short term at least. Longer term, they expect a peace dividend as well as acceptance into a broader, global community. Art is therefore not immune to the power politics at play in peacebuilding politics at large, but represents a dynamic yet weaker part of the equation: co-opted into the politics of peace, it serves the agendas set by powerful elites, who are often from outside the realm of those most harshly affected by conflict.

*Artpeace*building can manifest itself locally, for instance in cases where artists are commissioned by well-funded NGOs to undertake particular projects, or on a bigger scale where organisations involved in post-conflict institution-building use artwork as a way of consolidating their agendas. Here, the political curation of artwork is not necessarily undertaken by professional curators in the narrow sense, but instead by proxy organisations, such as NGOs or international organisations. In other cases, artwork can be 'discovered' by peacebuilders and subsequently used as part of their wider political ambitions of intervention. Aspects of this approach can be seen in both Sobout's and Schouten's chapters, which outline the ways in which some art projects in Lebanon and the DRC have undergone a process of 'NGOisation' and thus been curated by actors with a clear stake in the wider peacebuilding mission. In this context, curation becomes an effort to embed art in liberal institution-building policies, with the latter setting the agenda over the former. This is not to say that art necessarily becomes a mere platform on which power politics are transported—although this can be the result—but it points to the often-uneven resource distribution between art and politics, where artists tend to be in a particularly vulnerable situation in terms of precarious labour and employment.

4) Arttransformation

Arttransformation refers to the integration of art with the conflict transformation toolkit which ultimately aims to achieve a social transformation in post-conflict societies by turning destructive and oppositional dynamics into positive change (Curle 1990). It is ontologically based on the assumption that political and civil conflict can be transformed into positive social processes, which can help mitigate and transform wider conflicts—an assumption that is shared by some artists. Thus, it mainly focuses on social dynamics, thought it expects small scale processes to trickle up towards elite, state and even international actors (Garson 2020).

As Cole's chapter on the divided city of Mostar illustrates, there is a transformative element in Mostar's Street Art Festival, as it hopes to positively impact on the urban fabric of an infrastructurally divided city. Such an approach draws on a notion inherent in conflict transformation work, namely that conflict can be a positive, creative micro-force leading to social change, while, perhaps more tenuously, art can help replace a violent conflict through social and ultimately political reform (Dukes 1999) and thus have a longer-term impact on a divided society. Here, art tends to be used instrumentally, as a functional tool to channel social change, but also as a black box without a politics of its own. Curatorial work then mainly consists of exploiting the transformative elements of artwork for social transformation, which, if not enjoying the buy-in of the respective artists themselves, can lead to a problematic decontextualisation on the aesthetics inherent in artwork. This is especially difficult in cases where the intended aesthetico-political ambitions of artwork may conflict with the political transformational goals of those using the work for conflict transformation. In cases where the goals align, social transformation may be driven by the joined-up forces of art and politics. Yet, as the example of Mostar aptly illustrates, where such arttransformation work is confronted with a paralysed (here also ethnicised) political landscape, it is blocked from having an effect that reaches beyond the immediate local, urban or rural community in which it is placed.

5) Artmediation

Artwork has also been deployed as a supporting tool in negotiations and diplomatic efforts, which we identify as artmediation. This represents a narrow, quasi-diplomatic function relating aesthetics to mediation (Constantinou 1996). This is primarily for its capacity to represent multiple meanings and positions, and to explore their contradictions, which points to a second, less obvious function: mediating meaning, claims and difference within the parameters of political conflict. A study commissioned by the British Council, for instance, identifies art as a form of soft power (British Council 2017b), while another of the institution's commissioned reports outlines the importance of arts (understood here primarily as cultural relations) and specifically details the strategic role of the arts in international negotiation processes (British Council 2017a). Very clearly referencing peace work, the Swiss Embassy in the UK researched the ways in which art could serve 'as an additional tool to assist and possibly unblock mediation and peace processes' (FDFA n.d.). In other ways, the Constitutional Court in Johannesburg, South Africa, includes an art exhibition at its buildings, setting the tone to visitors and employees of the court of the nature of the state.

These examples reflect the increasing extent to which art is being used by governments in their strategic political goals, both internationally and domestically. It is no longer unthinkable to include an arts-element in high-profile negotiations. Instead, artmediation views art as a way of softening attitudes in protracted peace negotiations, exploring contradictions, raising otherwise hidden or obscured issues and questions, and highlighting features of shared humanity. These capacities may help ease negotiations at the official level as well as in social contexts by fleshing out ambiguous issues, highlighting subjectivities and reconfiguring how peace is understood in specific contexts.

Curation in this context consists primarily of the effort to link influential artists with political power holders who have a say in the selection of art and artwork in the setup of negotiations, as well as navigating their presentation to the public. The content of the artwork is preselected in a sense that only the artwork that seems to conform with political goals is likely to be chosen, funded and featured. This also means that artmediation is somewhat limited in its transformative potential, feeding into the strategic positions of those in negotiating positions, unless mediation is sponsored by external actors and their normative and legal agendas and standards (such as the United Nations or European Union). While such approaches may soften attitudes and make conversations more likely, it remains questionable as to what effect of this is due to the (possibly restricted) autonomy of the artist and to what extent it presupposes a political openness of the negotiating parties to begin with. Again, long-standing relationships and networks between artists and diplomats seem to be key to understanding the extent to which an artist may enjoy freedom of expression beyond confined political boundaries.

6)   Artpacification

Artpacification describes a situation in which particular groups are allowed (very confined) spaces in which they can 'be radical', while ensuring that what happens in those spaces remains confined within them. They attempt to display diverse opinions whilst making sure they are not mainstreamed. Such approaches might also be associated with counter-insurgency practices, internment camps, rump states and secessionism, as well different forms of socio-economic and identity hierarchies with a state, where the dominant actor seeks to maintain hegemony and reduce opposition, without undermining majority consent. Discontent and non-consent may be expressed within those spaces but not beyond, where they become merely a spectacle of subversion and impractical idealism. In mediated forms this is a way of making sure that the political status quo is not challenged even if there are marginal areas of rejection in a political order. Art, in this scenario, is primarily used to stabilise the status quo as it serves as a tool through which grievances are channelled into managed and mediated spaces, where they can potentially be depoliticised or separated from the wider society (Adorno and Horkheimer 2002, 94–136; Groys 2008). As some of the art and peace work developed in the buffer zone in Cyprus's capital Nicosia has suggested, its impact may be somewhat restricted to the very buffer zone, struggling to make a difference beyond its confines (cf. Kappler 2014).

One could argue that expressions of social justice are possible in this scenario (within the spaces that are allocated), and may yet seep out or upwards into the wider political milieu. However, they are also moderated and targeted to contain and manage grievances that might otherwise have translated into political—violent or non-violent—energies. People and artists inhabiting those managed spaces may well feel that they are able to express their political messages, yet are blocked when attempting to voice those concerns beyond those spaces. The blockages they face are substantial, including those deployed by state elites, state institutions, the military and security services, the market environment, tradition and conservative elements of wider society (Pogodda, Richmond, and Visoka 2023). This is an issue that has been identified in some peace work as creating a significant degree of withdrawal and the alienation of socially engaged artists into underground spaces (Debord 1967), as we have seen in the political landscape of Bosnia-Herzegovina where the formal political landscape has long been largely hostile to arts-based change (Kappler 2013) and, furthermore, the arts have long been used to amplify marginal and often futile resistance to war and domination (Zelizer 2003; Balkan Diskurs 2015).

Curation by formal political actors, in such contexts, involves the funding of artwork that supports the de-politicisation of peace agendas and instead engages in processes of therapy, deradicalisation, categorisation and confinement of political activities into closed spaces. Indeed, some elements of Ó Brádaigh Bean's chapter on Medellín illustrate the difficulties when political activities are vibrantly used among particular parts of society and subcultures but are prevented from having an impact at a level beyond their confinement.

7) Everyday *artpeace*

By everyday *artpeace* we refer to a scenario in which art remains largely isolated from specific policy areas and issues though it may engage with politics (de Certeau 1984, xi), such as with parallel and isolated versions of peace formation (Richmond 2016) and everyday approaches to peace (Mac Ginty 2014, 2022; Richmond 2009). Hard security policy has, for instance, long shied away from an engagement with the arts and even today actors such as the North Atlantic Treaty Organisation (NATO) may not see it as particularly relevant for their policies to include arts-based approaches in their work. Some changes have emerged in the last few years: while the EU would have found it unusual to connect artwork to its activities in Bosnia and Herzegovina (BiH) ten years ago, today there is a wider range of art-based activities, which obtain EU funding and are used for peace-related purposes in some shape or form. This indicates that isolated arts activities may well move into a relationship with formal peace processes and actors at some point. At the same time, there are still areas and activities that artists cannot reach or engage—at times because they are deliberately excluded, or at times because they may not feel welcome in those spaces. This may be linked to elitist discursive frameworks of politics, which maintain rigid power relations that impinge on particular political or artistic spaces, or due to a lack of funding to enable artists to work hand-in-hand with political actors.

The formal domestic political arena in BiH is still largely immune from art-based engagement, so much of the creative energies from the cultural sector has previously been channelled into parallel political processes, as the set-up of citizens' plenums, sometimes termed the 'Bosnian spring' has shown (cf. Belloni et al. 2016). Cole's chapter reflects similar processes in which arts-based change in Mostar takes place in isolation from a city administration that has been dysfunctional for years. This scenario is not too disimiliar to the situation in Cyprus where some artists have decided to stay away from bi-communal organisations, primarily NGO-based peace work, as they feel the rigid framing of bi-communalism may inhibit their space for creative intervention. This could be because they may be embedded in one community specifically (through which they may obtain funding, political standing or legitimacy), or because they remain suspicious of the NGO-isation and, at least partially internationally directed, nature of the peace process.

Conclusion

We have seen numerous attempts around the world of where art initiatives and artists engage with local communities and individuals, and this book provides a range of case studies to demonstrate exactly that. Art-based projects seem to be widespread and influential at this level (as therapeutic tools, as local networking platforms, as ways of expressing activism about rights, justice and reconciliation). They attempt to challenge deeply held preconceptions about the nature, processes and goals of peacemaking, perhaps less overtly than direct political dialogue. They attempt to bring in a wider range of experiences and senses in a longer temporal span than traditional formal politics or peacemaking can address, and seek to function across networks of creative, critical, resistant agency (as with peace formation, thus producing a hybrid of agencies and approaches). *Artpeace* attempts to transcend the constraints of formal, track 2, and state-oriented approaches to peacemaking, and shift beyond even the informal networks of conflict transformation or resolution thinking. Yet we also observe a substantial disconnect between such transversal and local effects where art meets community and their political claims for representation and justice. *Artpeace* indicates the production of communicational forms that transcend traditional power-relations inherent in peacebuilding, peacekeeping or mediation, and the more formal macro-politics of peace, aiming to achieve more creative forms of reconciliation between the social and the constitutional. Economic reform is also often highlighted, along with the proscription of violence as a political tool, and wider forms of justice. Art-based initiatives imply a distant challenge for international reform and the geo-politics of peace.

We propose that *artpeace* represents critical and emancipatory claims, with the capacity for dissemination within and beyond society on a significant scale through their concurrent network formation capacities. At both levels of analysis, we see a range of tactical and strategic blockages designed to limit the capacity of *artpeace* agency and the networks around which they travel. These blockages mirror the ways in which state sovereignty and elite power maintain control and legitimacy, but also the nature of embryonic, radical challenges that might eventually be scaled up. Based on the notion of *artpeace* and its different manifestations in terms of the intersection between art and politics, the chapters in this book explore the following questions: what happens to the radical potential of the arts when it meets politics under conditions of unresolved violence? Does *artpeace* agency evaporate, become tamed, censored or co-opted, withdraw or comply? Who curates the remaining, unerased art in a way that supports social reconciliation and justice in a peacemaking framework?

Note

1. With respect to transitional justice, Kerr lists: films, posters, graphic novels, exhibitions, fine art, photography, film-making, theatre, dance, creative writing, photographs, drawings and sketches. In addition, she notes that there is a wide spectrum of creative activity driven by community workers, NGOs, heritage institutions, arts organizations and artists.

References

Adorno, T. W. and Horkheimer, M. 2002. The culture industry: Enlightenment as mass deception. In *Dialectic of enlightenment: Philosophical fragments*. Stanford, CA: University of Stanford Press, pp. 94–136.

Adorno, T., Benjamin, W., Bloch, E., Brecht, B., and Lukacs, G. (2020) *Aesthetics and politics*. London: Verso.

Balkan Diskurs. 2015. The art of peace: Bosnia and Herzegovina. *Peace in Sight*, 31 March, https://www.peaceinsight.org/en/articles/art-peace-bosnia-herzegovina/?location=west ern-balkans&theme=culture-media-advocacy (accessed 18 August, 2023).

Belloni, R., Kappler, S. and Ramovic, J. 2016. Bosnia-Herzegovina: Domestic agency and the inadequacy of the liberal peace. In Richmond, O. P. and Pogodda, S. (eds), *Post-liberal peace transitions: between peace formation and state formation*. Edinburgh: Edinburgh University Press, pp. 47–64.

Bhabha, H. 1994. *The location of culture*. London: Routledge.

Björkdahl, A. and Kappler, S. 2017. *Peacebuilding and spatial transformation: Peace, space and place*. London and New York: Routledge.

Björkdahl, A., Höglund, K., Millar, G., van der Lijn, J., Verkoren, W. (eds). 2016. *Peacebuilding and friction: Global and local encounters in post conflict-societies*. London: Routledge.

Bleiker, R. 2009. *Aesthetics and world politics*. London: Palgrave Macmillan.

Bleiker, R. 2017. In search of thinking space: Reflections on the aesthetic turn in international political theory. *Millennium*, 45(2), pp. 258–64.

Bloch, E. 1980. *Aesthetics and politics*. London: Verso.

Boal, A. 2006. *The aesthetics of the oppressed*. London and New York: Routledge.

Boege, V., Brown, A. and Clements, K. P. 2009. Hybrid political orders, not fragile states. *Peace Review*, 21(1), pp. 13–21.

British Council. 2017a. Arts, Cultural Relations and Soft Power: Developing an Evidence Base. https://www.britishcouncil.org/sites/default/files/arts_cultural_relations_final_report_for_british_council.pdf (accessed 18 August, 2023).

British Council. 2017b. Soft Power Today: Measuring the Influences and Effects. https://www.britishcouncil.org/sites/default/files/3418_bc_edinburgh_university_soft_power_report_03b.pdf (accessed 18 August, 2023).

Chandler, D., 2010. *International statebuilding: The rise of post-liberal governance*. London: Routledge.

Constantinou, C. 1996. *On the way to diplomacy*. Minneapolis, MN: University of Minnesota Press.

Crenshaw, K. 1991. Mapping the margins: Intersectionality, identity politics, and violence against women of color. *Stanford Law Review*, 43(6), pp. 1241–99.

Curle, A. 1990. *Tools for transformation*. Stroud: Hawthorn Press.

Danko, D. 2018. Artivism and the spirit of avant-garde art. In Alexander, V. D., Hägg, S., Häyrynen, S., and Sevänen E. *Art and the Challenge of Markets Volume 2*. Cham: Palgrave Macmillan, pp. 235–61.

de Certeau, M. 1984. *The practice of everyday life*. Berkeley, CA: University of California Press.

Debord, G. 1994/1967. *The society of the spectacle* (translated by Donald Nicholson-Smith). New York: Zone Books.

Douglas, S. 2017 *Curating community. Museums, constitutionalism, and the taming of the political*. Ann Arbor, MI: University of Michigan Press.

Dukes, E. F. 1999. Why conflict transformation matters: Three cases. *Peace and Conflict Studies*, 6(2), November, pp. 47–66.

FDFA. n.d. https://www.eda.admin.ch/countries/united-kingdom/en/home/representations/embassy-in-london/embassy-tasks/culture/art-in-mediation.html (accessed 18 August, 2023).

Forde, S. 2019. *Movement as conflict transformation, rescripting Mostar, Bosnia-Herzegovina*. Basingstoke: Palgrave Macmillan.

Garson, M. 2020. Defying gravity: Evaluating the trickle-up effects of reconciliation programmes. *Ethnopolitics*, 19(2), pp. 188–208.

Gell, A. 1998. *Art and agency: An anthropological theory*. Oxford: Clarendon Press.

Groys, B. 2008. *Art power*. Cambridge, MA: MIT Press.

Huliaras, A. and Tzifakis, N. 2010. Celebrity activism in international relations: In search of a framework for analysis. *Global Society*, 24(2), pp. 255–74.

Kappler, S. 2013. Everyday legitimacy in post-conflict spaces: The creation of social legitimacy in Bosnia-Herzegovina's cultural arenas. *Journal of Intervention and Statebuilding*. 7(1), pp. 11–28.

Kappler, S. 2014. *Local agency and peacebuilding: EU and international engagement in Bosnia-Herzegovina, Cyprus and South Africa*. Basingstoke: Palgrave Macmillan.

Kappler, S. 2017. Sarajevo's ambivalent memoryscape: Spatial stories of peace and conflict. *Memory Studies* 10(2), pp. 130–43.

Kappler, S. and Lemay-Hébert, N. 2019. From power-blind binaries to the intersectionality of peace: Connecting feminism and critical peace and conflict studies. *Peacebuilding*, 7(2), pp. 160–77.

Kappler, S. and McKane, A. 2019. 'Post-conflict curating' the arts and politics of Belfast's peace walls. *De Arte*, 54(2), pp. 4–21.

Kerr, R. 2020. Art, aesthetics, justice, and reconciliation: What can art do? *AJIL Unbound*, 114, pp. 123–7.

Latour, B. 1996. On actor-network theory: A few clarifications. *Soziale Welt*, 4: 369–81.

Lederach, J. P. 1997. *Building peace: Sustainable reconciliation in divided societies*. Washington DC: US Institute of Peace Press.

Lederach, J. P. 2005. *The moral imagination: The art and soul of building peace*. Oxford: Oxford University Press.

Lehrer, E. and Milton, C. E. 2011. Introduction: Witnesses to witnessing. In Erica, T. L., Milton, C. E. and Patterson, M. (eds), *Curating difficult knowledge: Violent pasts in public places*. Basingstoke; New York, NY: Palgrave Macmillan, pp. 1–19.

Lewis, D., Heathershaw, J. and Megoran, N. 2018. Illiberal peace? Authoritarian modes of conflict management. *Conflict and Cooperation*, 53(4), pp. 486–506.

Little, S. 2017. The witness turn in the performance of violence, trauma, and the real. In O'Toole, E., Kristić, A. P. and Young, S. (eds), *Ethical exchanges in translation, adaptation and dramaturgy*. Leiden: Brill, pp. 43–62.

Mac Ginty, R. 2014. Everyday peace: Bottom-up and local agency in conflict-affected societies. *Security Dialogue*, 45(6), pp. 548–64.

Makoi, Akhtar Mohammad. 2021. 'The soul of Kabul': Taliban paint over murals with victory slogans. *The Guardian*, September 7. https://www.theguardian.com/world/2021/sep/07/the-soul-of-kabul-taliban-paint-over-murals-with-victory-slogans (accessed 3 October, 2022).

Mitchell, J., Vincett, G., Hawksley, T. and Culbertson, H. 2020. *Peacebuilding and the arts*. London: Palgrave Macmillan.

Paris, Roland. 2004. *At war's end*. Cambridge: Cambridge University Press.

Pogodda, S., Richmond, O. P. and Visoka, G. 2023. Counter-peace: From isolated blockages in peace processes to systemic patterns. *Review of International Studies*, 49 (3), pp. 491–512.

Premaratna, N. 2018. Theatre for peacebuilding. In *Theatre for peacebuilding*. London: Palgrave Macmillan, pp. 65–103.

Premaratna, N. and Bleiker, R. 2010. Art and peacebuilding: How theatre transforms conflict in Sri Lanka. In Richmond, O. P. (ed.), *Palgrave advances in peacebuilding: Critical developments and approaches*. London: Palgrave Macmillan, pp. 376–91.

Pugh, M. 2005. The political economy of peacebuilding: a critical theory perspective. *International journal of peace studies*, 10(2), pp. 23–42.

Pupavac, V. 2005 Human security and the rise of global therapeutic governance. *Conflict, Security and Development*, 5(2), pp. 161–81.

Rancière, J. 2006. The ethical turn of aesthetics and politics. *Critical Horizons*, 7(1), pp. 1–20.

Richmond, O. P. 2022. Artpeace: Validating Power, Mobilising Resistance, and Imagining Emancipation. *Journal of Resistance Studies*, 8 (2), pp. 74–110.

Richmond, O. P. 2016 *Peace formation and political order in conflict affected societies*. Oxford: Oxford University Press.

Richmond, O. P. 2011. *A post-liberal peace*. London: Routledge.

Richmond, O. P. 2022. What is an emancipatory peace? *Journal of International Political Theory*, 18(2), pp. 124–47.

Richmond, O. P. and Franks, J. 2008. *Liberal peace transitions*. Edinburgh: Edinburgh University Press.

Richmond, O. P. and Mac Ginty, R. 2020. *Local legitimacy and international peacebuilding*. Edinburgh: Edinburgh University Press.

Richmond, O. P. 2015. The dilemmas of a hybrid peace: Negative or positive? *Cooperation and Conflict*, 50(1), pp. 50–68.

Richmond, O. P. 2005. *The transformation of peace*. London: Palgrave.

Richmond, O. P. 2007. Dadaism and the peace differend. *Alternatives: Global, Local, Political.* 32(4), pp. 445–72.

Richmond, O. P. 2009. A post-liberal peace: Eirenism and the everyday. *Review of International Studies* 35(3), pp. 557–80.

Mac Ginty, R. and Richmond, O. P. 2015. The fallacy of constructing hybrid political orders: A reappraisal of the hybrid turn in peacebuilding. *International Peacekeeping,* 23(2), pp. 219–39.

Smith, L. 2006. *The uses of heritage*. Abingdon: Routledge.

Spivak, G. C. 1988. Can the subaltern speak? In Nelson, C. and Grossberg, L. (eds), *Marxism and the interpretation of culture*. Basingstoke: Macmillan Education, pp. 271–313.

Spivak, G. C. 2000. Translation as culture. *Parallax,* 6(1), pp. 13–24.

Sylvester, C. 2009. *Art/museums: International relations where we least expect it*. London: Paradigm.

Tilly, C. 1985. War making and state making as organized crime. In Evans, P. Rueschemeyer, D. and Skocpol, T. (eds), *Bringing the state back in*. Cambridge: Cambridge: University Press.

UN Secretary-General. 2018. Report of the secretary general, peacebuilding and sustaining peace (A/72/707–S/2018/43). New York: United Nations.

Vogel, B. 2018. Understanding the impact of geographies and space on the possibilities of peace activism. *Cooperation and Conflict,* 53(4), pp. 431–48.

Vogel, B. 2016. Civil society capture: Top-down interventions from below? *Journal of Intervention and Statebuilding,* 10(4), pp. 472–89.

Vogel, B., Arthur, C., Lepp, E., O'Driscoll, D. and Haworth, B. T. 2020. Reading socio-political and spatial dynamics through graffiti in conflict-affected societies, *Third World Quarterly.* 41(12), pp. 2148–68.

Woods, K. 2015. *The arts and peacebuilding: An emerging approach*. Washington DC: USIP.

Zelizer, C. 2003. The role of artistic processes in peace-building in Bosnia-Herzegovina. *Peace and Conflict Studies.* 10(2), pp. 62–76.

THREE

Peace through Performative Art, Theatre and Wrestling? The Intersubjective Co-constitution of Art by 'High' and 'Low' Peace Processes in South Sudan

Aly Verjee

South Sudan's few years as an independent country have been troubled. Although widely celebrated by the South Sudanese, independence in 2011 occurred in the context of continuing, long-running subnational violence in large parts of the country. In December 2013, a new civil war began, was momentarily interrupted by a 2015 peace agreement, resumed and expanded with that agreement's collapse, and was again put in abeyance by a revamped agreement in 2018. As of mid-2022, the 2018 agreement holds, but implementation of most of its provisions has not occurred or lags well behind schedule, scepticism in its durability is widespread and there are significant holdout groups who reject the agreement (John 2022).

Subnational violence remains commonplace in South Sudan and is motivated by multiple factors. While local, subnational, national, transnational and international developments in war and peace in South Sudan are often described separately, there are many intersections between these levels and forms of conflict. However, for the most part, international interventions to address South Sudan's 'national' conflict have not considered subnational dynamics, nor had the ambition to resolve these issues in the context of the mediation of elite disputes (Verjee 2020). Meanwhile, domestic efforts to resolve everyday local conflicts are numerous. Conflict resolution efforts in South Sudan are thus often conceptually bifurcated between 'high-level', elite-focused negotiations held outside the country, while 'low-level' or 'local' disputes are mediated within South Sudan, often by respected individuals, traditional authorities or faith-based institutions, with comparatively little foreign involvement or support, invoking the idea of peace formation outlined in this book's Introduction. The manifestations of peace and conflict in South Sudan are a complex interplay between these levels; a hard, binary distinction between conflict types may sacrifice complexity for (often international) comprehensibility (Craze 2020). Further, because there is not one single conflict in South Sudan, but a web of overlapping conflicts, the country qualifies as in-conflict, post-conflict and (likely) pre-conflict, depending on one's lived experience, geographic location or place of origin and point of view, which makes both the cause and effect of peace interventions on conflict even more difficult to disentangle.

Public opinion surveys show that most South Sudanese want peace, although views vary as to what accounts for the absence of peace and how peace should be achieved (Deng 2018). Demands for peace are often situated both in relation to South Sudan's relative youth as a country, and the many decades of past conflict when the country was still part of Sudan. Consequently, almost all endeavour in South Sudan—whether state or private-led, individual or collective, formal or informal—is discussed, narrated and measured in terms of its real or perceived contribution to and possible effects on peace and conflict on multiple levels. Artistic and cultural expression, including sports, are not exempt from this omnipresent national accounting. In a context of persistent insecurity and considerable uncertainty, artists and cultural creators are subsumed in these liberal narratives of *artpeace*building, and further submerged by the discourse of headline writers. Children 'dance for peace' (EU 2014); visual artists are 'painting for peace' (BBC News 2016b); musicians are 'singing for equality' (Louro 2021) and 'sing for peace' (BBC News 2016a); wrestlers 'fight for peace' (Vice News 2016; AFP 2016); and dramatists and actors stage 'theatre for peace' (Namubiru 2018). There is no shortage of hyperbole, either: wrestlers keep 'the country's return to peace alive' (Africanews 2016), while others ask whether music can 'save South Sudan' (ABC News 2016).

In this chapter, I consider three leading artistic and cultural endeavours in South Sudan: an artists' collective which initially focused on visual and performance art, a theatre group and organised wrestling competitions. Each endeavour became prominent post-independence, with most growing after the 2013 war began or recurred in 2016. These cases show how peace and art in South Sudan intersect and evolved in the last decade along three main, but not mutually exclusive, pathways: an evolution to activism (the artists' collective); broad continuity (the theatre); and major interruption (wrestling), followed by imitation by successors. The first case, of artists' collective Ana Taban, shows a movement evolving from art to activism. Ana Taban's initial impetus for formation was the national crisis of the collapse of the 2015 peace agreement, and the resulting deterioration of peace. Though its early focus was largely local, it subsequently became more active at the national-international level, including at high-level peace talks. The second case, that of the internationally famous South Sudan Theatre Organisation (SSTO), is one of significant continuity, despite the context of war and peace—it is

COVID-19 that has arguably had more of an impact on the organisation's recent work. While SSTO was founded with the explicitly outward orientation of putting on a production of a Shakespeare play outside of South Sudan (Walkling 2012), it subsequently became anchored in local community and forum theatre, where the themes of politics, peace and peace agreements frequently recur. The third case, of South Sudan Wrestling Entertainment (SSWE), is an example of cultural expression interrupted by war and peace. SSWE was the first to commercialise wrestling in the country, and thus provide an incentive to change the orientation of young men who might otherwise consider engaging in forms of intercommunal violence. Beyond its impact on its contestants, SSWE used the occasion of convening tournaments to organise peace meetings on the margins of its events, paralleling more formal peace initiatives. Its initial focus was local peace, but the goals of Peter Biar Ajak, its founder, and his own trajectory as a political activist re-orientated the organisation towards broader national questions of peace and governance; ultimately, its efforts interrupted when Biar was imprisoned. SSWE was a secondary victim in Biar's misfortune; it has not organised another inter-state tournament since January 2018. Others have borrowed elements of the SSWE model, however, and continue to organise matches (albeit again constrained by the COVID-19 pandemic), still explicitly framing their efforts in terms of contributions to peace, while more explicitly seeking to make money (Biar 2021; Garang 2021).

I argue that all three of these cases adopted, with varying degrees of introspection, classical liberal discourses of peace and conflict—the concept this book names as *artpeace*building. All have been shaped by their founders' own personal as well as wider popular demands for everyday and elite peace, by the presence of conflict and awareness of peace processes, and by a desire to influence—whether directly at the negotiating table or indirectly through mockery and social critique—South Sudan's various engagements with peace. At the same time, it is these attempts at peace that have also played a role in constructing art, both in its organisational and aesthetic dimensions. Were it not for the collapse of a peace agreement, Ana Taban might not have emerged in the same form and at the moment it did (Bul 2021; Chol 2021). For its part, SSTO leveraged its newfound international credibility, and an appealing narrative of overcoming the odds (Milner 2016) to initiate more participatory, domestically focused theatre, albeit one that built on past dramatic foundations. Finally, SSWE's case illustrates that the rise and fall of a single individual, in line with the country's own tribulations of war and peace, can impinge on an otherwise successful effort that is tangibly contributing to one form of peace, even if the desired wider impact on national peace was much less certain. Before turning to the case studies, I briefly discuss the relationship between peace, violence and art in South Sudan as well as the constraints and blockages faced by the sector in influencing peace beyond the local level.

The Relationship between Peace, Violence and Art in South Sudan

As creators themselves assert, many artistic and cultural movements have been founded in direct response to the country's conflicts. Many of these artistic initiatives, from the moment of their formation, explicitly articulate a connection between their art and peace, broadly defined, albeit heavily influenced by liberal discourses and aspirations of ideas of peace and conflict resolution. Much like conflicts in South Sudan, artistic endeavours thus operate in interlinked dimensions and seek to influence peace and peace formation at multiple levels: the local 'low' level, aiming to address everyday forms of grievance and improve intercommunal tolerance and co-existence; and the national-transnational-international 'high' level, where artists seek to influence externally-led peacemaking efforts (artmediation).

While much of the discourse of cultural creators in South Sudan, their patrons, and the media coverage and analysis focuses on the extent to which art can promote peace, I argue that the relationship between art and peace is intersubjective and co-constitutive, rather than unidirectional. As Potgieter (2016, 9) observes, 'much contemporary artmaking is no longer predicated on subjective, disinterested aesthetic contemplation, but rather on intersubjective, relational artistic practices typified by social communion, anonymity, collaboration, interaction, participation, sharing, forming connections, art co-ops, happenings, interactive internet art, [and] 'solution-orientated'… art' instead. This intersubjectivity, in the South Sudan context, invokes the idea that art is, in its methods, an object of inquiry, pursued and conceptualised between and among its participants (Efland 2004; Young 1996). The relationship is also co-constitutive: while many artists have explicitly aimed to influence the country's peace processes, artistic development is affected, too, and is not a one-way process driven exclusively by the artists. Artistic expression and organisation may not only be a demonstration of agency in response to the shifting context of peace and conflict in South Sudan, but is, in part constructed by ongoing interactions with both high- and low-level processes of peace and conflict. Some South Sudanese artists thus function as local and national 'peace entrepreneurs', while also being constrained, and sometimes blocked, by the paradigmatic limits of liberal forms of peace and conflict resolution. Some may also risk co-optation by donor-driven peacemaking agendas.

These constraints can take several forms. First, there are practical, financial realities. Making a living from art is particularly difficult in South Sudan. This incentivises artist groups to frame what they do in terms of peace, as this is more likely to attract and interest international funders already predisposed to a pro-peace agenda than would funding art for art's sake (or for other forms of instrumentalisation) alone. At the same time, most of the initiatives profiled in this chapter are conscious of the tension this brings. Some are savvy enough to instrumentalise donor agendas, rather than only be instrumentalised by them. As one interviewee noted, whether it was taking funding by using the rhetoric of peace or for performing art as part of the public health campaign against COVID-19, it did not matter, as long as it could sustain the artistic endeavour. In terms of fundraising, 'corona is the new peace', he said (Interview, identity withheld, April 2021). At the same time, others see donor priorities as complementary to their own understandings and desires for peace and are therefore not resistant to tailoring their activities and outputs to the funder's requirements. As another South Sudanese interviewee noted, 'it is difficult to delink our lives [as proponents or practitioners of the arts] from the political' (Bosco 2021), whether that be in relation to the agendas of donors, war and peacemakers, or politicians (or all three).

A second form of constraint are the inherent structures of peace efforts in South Sudan. While there are numerous critiques of the multiple liberal-international peace processes in South Sudan (e.g. Rolandsen 2011; Srinivasan 2021; Young 2019), and detailed insider accounts of the design and process deficiencies of South Sudan's recent peace mediations led by the regional organisation the Intergovernmental Authority on Development (IGAD), comprising the countries of northeast Africa (Verjee 2021; Verjee and Vertin 2021; Vertin 2018), the liberal peace remains the dominant peacemaking paradigm, and IGAD remains the lead mediator. Although these high-level peace efforts have also been criticised by some artists and cultural creators, artists are not necessarily able to escape the confines of the liberal *artpeace*building, either; in their own discourse and activities, they may even inadvertently reinforce such a paradigm. For example, some dramatists see it as their role to inform and educate the public about the content of the IGAD-mediated peace agreements. As one actor and dramatist explained, 'people don't understand what is written in that [2018] agreement. They can't read, write, don't have access to TV...we have access to this information [about the agreement], so we can include the peace agreement in the play, and translate it in terms that people can understand' (Gorgory 2021). Others see the role of artists as 'pointing the direction [towards a peace process]...putting the signposts towards mediation [of whatever form], and also the signposts towards the resolution of the conflict' (Bosco 2021). For some, this has meant attempting to become involved or directly influencing these high-level peace processes, which apart from taking considerable time and energy, risks trapping artists in the same framework they may otherwise claim to resist.

A third constraint of the liberal paradigm of peace for South Sudanese artists is to conceive of peace in limited, rather than transformative, terms, and often tie this to a wider liberal state-building agenda. For many, conceptions of negative peace—seeking to achieve the absence of violence—remain common aspirations. While some have alternative views of peace that could be classified as positive forms of peace, edging towards the *artivism* concept— for example, to promote peace among communities, or to work for reconciliation and justice—these too are often liberally-oriented endeavours. Although some see art as a way to 'speak truth to power' (Bosco 2021), others assert that they are doing work that the state would or should do if it was functioning appropriately. Given that most of the artists interviewed for this research, like most South Sudanese, remain ardently in favour of South Sudan's independence, criticism of the state quickly brushes up against strong feelings of nationalism and patriotism, and with it the risks of conflating criticism of the state with that of the government or individual politicians.

Ana Taban: From Art to Activism

Ana Taban, which in Arabic means 'I am tired', is perhaps South Sudan's most prominent artists' group (Zaremba 2018). This collective of young visual artists, musicians, actors, poets and fashion designers has painted murals, organised music and poetry festivals, produced music videos and a comic book, and has been at the forefront of an advocacy campaign explicitly targeting the IGAD peace process. Ana Taban has therefore been involved in both 'high' and 'low' forms of peace formation in South Sudan. The group was initially established as an 'art-driven peace campaign' (Bekenova 2019, 49) in the aftermath of the collapse of the 2015 peace agreement in July 2016. For some of those behind Ana Taban, the 2016 collapse was pivotal in developing the group's cohesion and identity. As one founder, Ayak Chol Deng, asserted:

> if not for 2016, Ana Taban would have been different. [The start of the war in] 2013 was considered a mistake, something that was fixable, [the collapse in] 2016 made me/us realise it is bigger than what we thought. It cast gloom over the independence. It made me/us as citizens feel utterly helpless and easily manipulated and it made me/us realise that this is a system versus her people. (Chol 2021)

For another founding member, Jacob Bul Bior, 'we felt crushed because the 2015 agreement failed. When [Opposition leader] Riek Machar was coming to Juba…there was euphoria in the air…then such disappointment [when the agreement collapsed]' (Bul 2021). Despite being founded by artists, the group's name was deliberately chosen for its political implications.

As another founder, Manasseh Mathiang, explains: 'the war has basically snatched our joy as a people, we also see the [name] as an action point to do something about it, by taking ownership of our country knowing that we as a youth have a great role in solving our own problems' (Bekenova 2019, 45–6). However, while Bul felt that the events of 2016 were a 'trigger' for Ana Taban, if it had not been that collapse, 'there might have been something else' to coalesce the group. Since the government had 'succeeded in silencing different voices' even before the conflict, he said, '…we wanted to do something' (Bul 2021).

Having come together, Ana Taban's founding members explicitly sought to draw on art for its potential positive influence on war and peace, having perceived that politicians were dominating the public discourse with their version of events. For Bul, previously 'civil society groups neglected art… [despite] art being political…[and] a way to entice the public' (Bul 2021). And, as Chol explains:

> In all our local cultures, art, particularly music and poetry, has been used to mobilise for war and peace. The power of these artistic forms in particular to speak to a broader audience beyond politics, age and in some instances tribes/communities, prompted politicians and community leaders to include them as part of their mobilisation strategy [for war or peace]… In every community there is a song for a coward who won't fight, but likewise there is a song that praises the peacemaker. (Chol 2021)

The connections between music, particularly song, and politics are well established in South Sudan (Impey 2013; Vambe 2014). The logic behind Ana Taban was to use the same methods for its own aims. In 2016, Bul explained that 'our idea was to host arts-based community events—including performances and street art—to spread messages of peace and reconciliation. No one refuses to be entertained so, if you put message in [the event], people will listen' (Daldorph 2016).

From initial activities such as painting murals and organising events like the Hagana (Arabic for 'ours') Festival (Maluak 2017) and catering to local dimensions of peace, Ana Taban has developed significantly beyond its initial artistic endeavours and ventured into elite peace processes. The High-Level Revitalisation Forum (HLRF) peace talks were held by IGAD in 2017 in an attempt 'to revive the stalled 2015 peace agreement' (Verjee 2017, 1). The HLRF continued into 2018, during which Ana Taban joined other civil society groups to conduct the #SouthSudanIsWatching social media campaign specifically to target the HLRF negotiations (Nyaga 2019). This direct advocacy aimed to affect and pressure negotiators and mediators, as well as their international backers, while promoting the normative agenda of inclusive peace processes. Bul asserts that traditional civil society meetings had limited public engagement, and that this campaign broadened engagement beyond the usual elites:

the message [of the #SouthSudanIsWatching campaign] reached the representatives of the warring factions and made an impact on the negotiations. Previous talks fell apart because citizens were not involved, so we mobilised citizens online and on the ground so politicians would know that people were watching. (Nyaga 2019)

At the same time, Bul acknowledges that the influence of Ana Taban on the peace talks as a single organisation was limited, 'but as part of a broader civil society [coalition], our participation would have more of an impact' (Bul 2021). Ana Taban representatives also travelled to the peace talks to target negotiators in person. They distributed some printed materials with key messages to the delegates to the talks, which prompted some strong reactions: 'there were some spices about that' Bul noted (Bul 2021).

While the empirical evidence for the impact of such actions remains contested and difficult to measure (Price and Orrnert 2017, 5, 31), such activities would for some clearly fit more in the realm of activism than artistry, even accepting that an arbitrary distinction between the two is over-simplistic and risks overlooking any act's multiple motivations and purposes. Still, the attempt to influence the HLRF was a change in Ana Taban's focus and significantly affected the group's thinking and future work. For Bul, being on the sidelines of the negotiations 'did change how we thought about the talks…[at] first, we wouldn't understand ourselves what the peace deal was… we were complaining about the process. Now we were part of it. It brought in the eye of monitoring [as something we needed to think about in future]' (Bul 2021). For him, the experience after the 2015 agreement was instructive:

We know what happened in 2015. Civil society was part of the peace deal. They came back to sit in Juba and the only thing they would do is disseminate over the radio. How many people have access to this? We added some thinking to the whole process [about how to do things differently]. (Bul 2021)

There were also important reputational and organisational consequences for Ana Taban following its involvement in the HLRF peace talks. For Chol, that experience 'has given us more confidence, and more recognition by our peers as a family they would definitely want to identify with…There is recognition in the power of the arts [by youth and political leaders] and also a newfound respect for artists' (Chol 2021). It also served as a mobilising tool for the organisation. As Chol asserted, the respectability provided to Ana Taban by the peace process meant that 'more and more parents are encouraging their children to join Ana Taban…You see most parents wouldn't normally encourage their children to join art, music etc., because it is considered a world with drugs and dropping out of school' (Chol 2021).

While Bul and Chol differed about the possible aesthetic impact the experience of the peace process had had on Ana Taban, Chol noted 'alleviating panic' and 'curbing online misinformation' as two areas of work that had resulted from their engagement in the peace process. Still, in relation to the group's message, it was the same in principle but tailored to the audience' (Chol 2021).

The shift towards the explicitly political continues outside of the elite peace process. In April 2021, in response to the death of the singer, Trisha C, who died after Juba Hospital was unable to provide blood for an emergency transfusion, Ana Taban painted two authorised murals on the wall of the national blood transfusion service in honour of the singer, while also aiming to mobilise blood donors (Ana Taban 2021). The mural was vandalised by unknown perpetrators shortly after it was completed, provoking outrage from Ana Taban (Ana Taban 2021).

As a result of these engagements, for some observers, Ana Taban was now less about art, and more about activism and lobbying. One observer of South Sudan's art scene said, 'we have not heard much from them [artistically] for a while'. She continued that it was often now 'difficult to distinguish what is done by Ana Taban', versus that of other groups, such as Defy Hate Now (Interview, identity withheld, April 2021). For Ana Taban, however, the resulting attempts by government authorities to limit its activities was a sign it was making an impact. Incidents of harassment at airports, the need to obtain clearance from the authorities for events, other organisations being told to desist from inviting Ana Taban members to their events, smear campaigns trying to link the group to a prominent opposition politician, a fake Facebook page set up to discredit the group and its murals being defaced were all signs Ana Taban was seen as a meaningful nuisance by the government and its allies. At the same time, Ana Taban's popularity makes it desirable for other civil society groups and international donors to associate with the group's positive brand, sometimes as part of their own state-building agenda. Ana Taban is certainly aware of others' possible ulterior motives, even if it sees, in principle, no problem in working with others: 'We take it issue by issue', asserts Bul, 'in seeing what to join and what not to join...If you are giving resources, we make the visibility of Ana Taban [in the funded programme] a condition of accepting the funding' (Bul 2021).

In summary, Ana Taban's formation was the direct consequence of (negative) developments in a high-level peace process. While, at the outset, the group sought to focus on local peace concerns, it ended up changed by its initially unforeseen involvement in the elite peace process, which became pivotal in the organisation's evolution. While members insist that its original artistic identity remains, the case of Ana Taban shows the limits of the indirect influence on peacebuilding through the arts. Although originally situated in the more ambiguous realm of peace formation, and while the group's members continue as practising artists, it is the legacy of its engagement in the HLRF and subsequent implementation processes of the 2018 peace agreement that now risks constraining Ana Taban in its more everyday and local artistic and peace ventures. Having now become 'political', Ana Taban's activities are closely scrutinised by the authorities, easily disrupted and vulnerable to being smeared.

The Continuity of Drama: The South Sudan Theatre Organisation

On the basis of two performances of one of Shakespeare's lesser-known plays, *Cymbeline*, at the Globe Theatre in London in 2012, the South Sudan Theatre Organisation (SSTO), formerly known as the South Sudan Theatre Company (SSTC), became perhaps South Sudan's most famous cultural export since independence in 2011 (Bloomekatz 2012; Oakley 2012; Trueman 2012; Wynne-Jones 2012; York 2014). Established in 2012 by veteran South Sudanese dramatists long active in drama scenes in Sudan and elsewhere in East Africa to specifically adapt and perform *Cymbeline*, this production of SSTO is the subject of considerable scholarship, with no less than three book chapters written about it (Elfman 2017; Matzke 2013; Solga 2013), in addition to other academic scrutiny (e.g., Mancewicz 2018).

Matzke, who conducted contemporaneous interviews with the play's co-director, SSTO founder Joseph Abuk, notes the most pertinent contextual allusions in *Cymbeline*'s adaptation 'related to the experience of war' (2013, 74). She cites Abuk as comparing the signing of the Sudan Comprehensive Peace Agreement of 2005 with the truce between Britain and Rome depicted in the play. By her own admission provocative, Solga (2013, 101) instead argues that SSTO's production functioned primarily 'as a neo-liberal social good', with the implication that 'the (quite radical) differences between "Global North" and "Global South" [could be assuaged] merely by coming together to see the SSTC's show', while Elfman (2017, 509) argues that the production 'contributed to a more complex perception of South Sudanese people as agents capable of self-determination rather than passive subjects awaiting external help'. As Abuk himself notes, missing from these scholarly analyses was much if any mention of a subsequent performance of *Cymbeline* by the SSTO in Bangalore as part of an international Shakespeare festival in India, where the reaction to the performance was much less enthusiastic (Datta 2012; Abuk 2021), not to mention the performances in South Sudan itself.

Building narratives about South Sudan's emergence from war based on this single production of the SSTO, which although symbolically impor- tant, was little known among the wider South Sudanese public living in South Sudan, misses both the story of the long history of theatre among South Sudanese (Campbell 2006; Dixon 2006; Lorins 2007; Milner 2016), what one supporter calls its 'strong tradition of resistance,' (Milner 2021) and, more immediately, where the SSTO invests most of its time and focus (Gorgory 2021; Abuk 2021). The bulk of SSTO's work inside South Sudan has consisted not of Shakespeare, but of interschool theatre competitions and forum theatre modelled on Boal's Theatre of the Oppressed, rebranded as citizens' theatre (Boal 2006; Milner 2021; Abuk 2021). In adopting the method of citizens' theatre, SSTO sought to promote change, local peace and reconciliation (Murray 2018). While SSTO is not alone in using citizens' theatre, SSTO's efforts have been sustained the longest and have perhaps the widest reach across the country.[1]

Although multiple experiences of war were personally and profession- ally formative for individual dramatists and organisationally developed the SSTO, the 2013 war, somewhat paradoxically, provided an opportunity. While some characterise theatre in South Sudan as being disrupted by the 2013 war (York 2014), Milner, who worked closely with the SSTO in this period, argues that 'to some extent [the war] had positive aspects for the SSTO. Spaces emerged for voices to talk about reconciliation. Because the international community was somewhat lost about what to do, and there was growing awareness of the [importance] of the local', it was possible to find donor support for forum theatre initiatives (Milner 2021). This view was echoed by donor representatives (Oyediran 2021). While there was cer- tainly an impact from the conflict, SSTO kept going. As SSTO actor Dominic Gorgory recalls, 'we were really interrupted in 2013...now it [was] difficult to be critical'; Abuk concurs, arguing, '2013 was more catastrophic [than earlier conflicts] by being self-inflicted, [although it was]...not only the war of 2013 that has inflicted deformity on theatre' (Gorgory 2021; Abuk 2021). However, the conflict offered some means to make the theatre financially sustainable; Gorgory points out that 'we [still] need to feed ourselves in that environment', regardless of the violence (Gorgory 2021). For Abuk, it was 'the coming of the corona that was a bigger war' (Abuk 2021). SSTO's work to organise theatre in schools drew on earlier traditions of theatre work in secondary schools in Sudan in the 1980s, as well as independent efforts to work with students in parts of southern Sudan in the late 1990s (Bosco 2021). As Abuk observes, drama work with schools had been a form of resistance to the Khartoum government of Omar al-Bashir, which prevented literature from being taught in secondary schools. Although 'we did not call it forum theatre then' Abuk said, we saw 'drama as a way for advocating issues' (Abuk 2021). After 2013, forum theatre became more explicitly the method, in what its supporters freely acknowledge was a way for SSTO to, as Milner states, 'instrumentalise peace...SSTO offers a tool [for] citizens' theatre for dialogue...which was flexible...whether about conflicts over water, resource conflicts, and so on...it was instrumentalising the narratives of a political project, of donors' (Milner 2021). For Abuk, the enduring purpose of drama as a political endeavour remained, regardless of the specific historical circumstances:

> The writer of a play has an objective. It is not purely for entertainment. Even a comedy has other observations. A playwright will have a message intended to influence to the particular context of what has gone on...the architect of conflict in that country [Sudan] was the political system. This is the same thing here [in South Sudan]. (Abuk 2021)

SSTO organised school drama clubs and interschool competitions in various parts of the country, as well as theatre festivals, where political themes were common. There were many comedy conflicts over chairs, and 'a rich vein of peace satire', remembers Milner (Milner 2021). While this clearly provided an outlet for both performers and the public to air their grievances, as well as to inform the public of developments in the high-level peace processes, to, as Gorgory put it, 'share the peace of the politicians with the public' (Gorgory 2021), the more systematic impact of citizens' theatre on peace, as conducted by SSTO, is more uncertain. As an evaluation of SSTO's programming found, there was:

> a lack of communication between SSTO, and actors and audiences, about what was expected of the two in terms of engagement. Almost as if there was no clear understanding of the objectives of [citizens' theatre] on the part of SSTO staff and young actors—other than to entertain—or of the pathways to meet the programme's overarching aims. ... SSTO purposely avoided turning [citizens' theatre] into just 'another NGO activity', thereby allowing open and creative debate...[But] for participatory theatre to work, audiences must be fully aware of their right (and need) to engage at any point during a given performance—this does not require them being informed that they are a 'beneficiary' of a project. Second, young actors need to be fully aware of their roles as performers in [citizens' theatre]: promoting the fullest participation from audiences; and to spark debate, promote awareness and encouraging behavioural change. (Murray 2018)

Such critiques of forum theatre and questions of effectiveness are not unique to South Sudan (e.g., Aguiar 2020; Baú 2018; Burns et al. 2015; Obasi et al. 2021; Stephenson and Zanotti 2017). Perhaps more particular to the case of South Sudan is Milner's observation about the effect, or lack thereof, of national-international political developments on SSTO's activities. For Milner, South Sudan's dramatists 'were so far away from these [peace] processes...the theatre remained incessantly satirical. Whether you had any moment of optimism [in the peace process], I never saw any large change in response to these moments' (Milner 2021). He continued: 'What was happening on high...for the artistic community, naturally anti-authority, scepticism [at those developments] was reflecting a broader [public] mood.' Instead, the national peace process was of immediate concern for how it affected the broader political space for groups like SSTO. For Abuk, the primary impact was practical:

> To apply for a space [to perform], you had to get permission from NSS [the National Security Service, South Sudan's intelligence agency]. After 2013, [there were] real difficulties in getting permission...Our methods were to go to the markets and invite the audience to the stage to talk, in all the suburbs of Juba...[there were] certain security [officials watching], very close to the shadows of the president...There were difficulties in reaching other parts of South Sudan, insecurity risks, and not easy to travel... even now [in 2021] we have not gone to many places with significant displacement and destruction. (Abuk 2021)

Overall, however, SSTO's means and methods have not changed dramatically despite South Sudan's recent conflicts, even as there are practical, logistical and political limits to its work. War constructed and provided new opportunity for SSTO and other drama groups to organise and take their participatory methods to non-elite, ordinary citizens (the so-called communities). Still, although impacts on peace are evidenced largely by anecdote, participants in SSTO's citizens' theatre commonly cited direct positive impacts on their own lives, including safer neighbourhoods, improved social networks and that the theatre had served as an informal forum for psychosocial counselling (Murray 2018). By design, citizens' theatre work did not seek to directly interact with the high-level peace process, which was both distant and mistrusted. Rather, SSTO's international reputation gave it the credibility to pursue its own aims, as well as inspired other drama groups to become active, knowing that there was precedent for (international) success. Regardless of the critics, in this respect, the domestic consequences of SSTO's *Cymbeline* endure: as one observer noted, the production was an 'embodiment through culture of what South Sudan could be' (Oyediran 2021). Even though the impetus of SSTO initially was not about promoting peace, it deftly used demands to support and promote peace to expand participatory and inclusive drama in South Sudan, even if any resulting causal influences on peace itself are hard to conclusively determine.

The Rise and Fall of South Sudan Wrestling Entertainment

The wrestler Magot Khot may not be a household name to most South Sudanese, but for Abit Mayen, operations manager of South Sudan Wrestling Entertainment (SSWE), Khot shows how wrestling can practically develop mutual respect among communities that have a reputation for feuding. As Mayen observed, in general, 'it is difficult to bring [South Sudanese] people together, even to eat together, let alone [to consider] how to live together in peace...so it is positive that Mundari people now have [composed] songs praising Magot Khot' in recognition of his success as a competitor (Mayen 2021). The Mundari often consider themselves and are usually perceived as rivals of the Dinka Twich and Dinka Bor communities from which Khot hails, and which neighbour Mundari lands to the south of Bor. Khot came to prominence in part because of his participation in wrestling competitions, including a 2016 inter-state competition organised by SSWE, which he won (Radio Tamazuj 2016).

The sport of wrestling was not recently introduced to South Sudan. As a cultural practice in Sudan and South Sudan, it may well date to antiquity (Carroll 1998). However, despite this long history and some perceptions the sport is ubiquitous (Africanews 2016), wrestling is not historically practised by all Sudanese and South Sudanese communities. War, displacement and changing socio-economic contexts have also affected the practice of the sport, although they have also led to its reproduction in diaspora South Sudanese populations (Ajang and Ngong 2013). Historically, the Nuba of Sudan (Bromber, Krawietz and Petrov 2014), and the Dinka, Mundari, and Lotuka of South Sudan (Hungerford 1953; Carroll 1998) are the communities most closely associated with wrestling, but even among the Dinka, South Sudan's largest ethnic group, there is significant variation; not all Dinka sections and sub-sections have wrestling as a common traditional practice. As SSWE's founder, Peter Biar Ajak explained, in addition to the Lotuka of Eastern Equatoria, the Mundari of Central Equatoria, and a few sections of the Dinka, the Atuot of Yirol in Lakes State and the closely related Dinka Twich and Dinka Bor of Jonglei State, are most known for their participation in wrestling (Biar 2021). However, seeing the potential to widen participation beyond these few communities, Biar, a former World Bank economist and wrestling enthusiast, led outreach to the Dinka Agar in Lakes State and the Dinka Malual of Northern Bahr el Ghazal, as well as the Lou Nuer in Jonglei State, to encourage individuals in those communities to take up the sport more systematically and send representatives to the competitions SSWE would go on to organise.

Biar founded the SSWE in 2010, and initially asserted that wrestling could 'promote peace among the tribes of South Sudan' (AFLI 2016; Leposo 2011).

As Biar notes, at that time, Jonglei State was embroiled in conflict, and many, himself included, were worried that the upcoming South Sudan independence referendum scheduled for January 2011 would be put at risk by the ongoing turmoil in the state (Thomas 2015; Verjee 2010). As he describes, 'there were a lot of peace initiatives at that time [in Jonglei], but little that was unique'. In remarks that could have described events in South Sudan in any subsequent year, he continued: 'there were local disputes, cattle raids, abductions, intercommunal violence. We asked ourselves, how do we build peaceful co-existence over time? We felt that this [wrestling] was something that could be used [for this purpose]' (Biar 2021).

Thus, from its inception, SSWE had an explicitly normative peace formation aim: to promote peace between communities that engaged in wrestling, most of whom are cattle-keeping agro-pastoralists. Biar's reasoning was that by commercialising wrestling and offering cash and other prizes (for example, livestock) to the top fighters, communities and the wrestlers themselves, they would have an incentive to fight for money, rather than, say, fight each other with arms or raid each other's cattle. As Biar explains, with a prize pot of US$400–500 a match, a wrestler could make more in a single bout than in any other economic pursuit likely open to them. The narrow aim of the wrestling tournament was therefore to prevent conflict by creating a purposeful alternative activity. As Mayen asserts, 'Champion wrestlers are leaders of their communities…If they are without activities, they would be cattle rustlers. If they stay idle, they would be the ones [stealing cattle from other communities]…If we engage them, cattle rustling will not happen' (Mayen 2021).

Yet, acknowledging that even if this was true, it had a fairly narrow impact, Biar asserts that organising wrestling allowed peace to be pursued beyond the competition itself, in parallel to other, more conventional attempts to attain local peace. For Biar, wrestling was 'a vehicle to do other things'. It allowed us 'to organise peace meetings on the sidelines of the competition, since [the wrestlers] were there in Juba for a fairly long time, 3–4 weeks…This was a long time for them to get to know each other…' Further, he continues, 'wrestling allowed us to bring [to Juba] others who matter[ed] [in their communities]…to talk about the issues they faced' (Biar 2021). Both Biar and Mayen assert that this familiarity helped advance intercommunal peace, and a better understanding between individual cattle-keepers and their respective communities. Mayen recounts several agreements, in 2013 and 2016, that allowed people coming from Twich and Bor to pass in safety on the Nile, through Terekeka (in Mundari territory) to come to Juba, on the basis of their affiliation with competitive wrestlers. As he explains:

Wrestlers intervened in Terekeka to allow free transport. There were no formal talks with the government about this, the wrestlers arranged it themselves. From a water point from Twich, they pass[ed] along the Nile, using a small boat from Twich to Bor, then Mundari land to Juba...[The Mundari community said], we won't attack them [because the wrestlers asked us not to].

Although SSWE's initial aim was to promote local peace 'between tribes', the popularity of the tournaments with the wider public as well as political elites provided SSWE's organisers with new opportunities to seek to influence peace at the elite level. By Biar's own admission, 'we hadn't intended this [elite influence] when we started up'. But having found that politicians and elites were interested in the sport and SSWE's tournaments, and were impressed by the thousands of spectators who attended, Biar saw matches as an opportunity to speak freely to disseminate a broader, more political message to both ordinary citizens and politicians, about a lack of development, the absence of services like hospitals and clean water, and the failures of leaders to govern well. Explaining that there were always seats set aside for 'VIPs', Biar recalls that those encounters gave politicians some exposure to how normal people were thinking, and that there was at least some, albeit very temporary, impact on politicians, sardonically observing: 'they [politicians] feel good for that one hour or two and then they go back and cause a crisis' (Biar 2021).

SSWE organised tournaments in 2013 (the tournament's final match was cancelled by the outbreak of the civil war), 2015, 2016, 2017 and 2018. The January 2018 tournament faced a lot of difficulties, with the NSS significantly curtailing what the organisers could do. Meanwhile, SSWE was far from Biar's only engagement, and by the time of the 2016 conflict, Biar was increasingly critical of the government. After calling for the leading political figures of South Sudan to step down, Biar was soon detained and ultimately imprisoned for his views, before being pardoned and freed eighteen months later (Akram 2018; BBC News 2020). 2018 was the last tournament SSWE organised in Juba; SSWE has no plans to organise another. As Mayen (2021) laments, there is

no problem with wrestling itself. The problem is with the organisers. The politicians don't look at the wrestlers, they look at who is behind it. It was not easy when Peter [Biar] tried to give his own opinions about how the government is operating. It did not make it easy for us to continue.

However, SSWE's abeyance has left space for others to enter the proverbial arena, including a SSWE knock-off (SSWE-Jonglei) that Mayen half-jokingly threatened to sue for brand infringement, the South Sudan Wrestling Championship (SSWC), established in 2019, and a wrestling betting operation, South Sudan Wrestling Bet (SSWB), begun in August 2020. Ajang Chol Biar, the founder of the SSWC, was careful to commend the SSWE for commercialising the sport and paving the way for others, while noting that wrestling could also damage peace. 'When somebody loses a match, people get angry', Ajang said (Ajang 2021). Wrestling organised 'community by community—sometimes it brings conflict....While wrestling brings people together to support their sons, the bitterness in their hearts is still not eased' (Ajang 2021). Instead, Ajang said, he wanted to organise the SSWC on the basis of individual merit, rather than on the basis of teams from individual communities or states. If a 'wrestler could become a star on his own', Ajang remarked, it might help avoid intercommunal rivalries (Ajang 2021). For Michael Achiek Garang of SSWB, wrestling too could lead to problems. There was 'a lot of argument about who should compete [in wrestling]...SSWE was good, but since others are continuing to wrestle, we need to find a way to avoid [today's] problems' (Garang 2021). In Garang's view, the way to address this is to get people to put 'money where their mouth is' and avoid disparaging other communities. For Garang, betting was a way to replace physical and verbal arguments and avoid unnecessary provocations. Aware of the cautionary story of Biar and the SSWE, neither Ajang nor Garang saw it as their responsibility to make wrestling influence the thinking of elite politicians, while both argue there is a real connection between the sport and a possible contribution to local peace. Perhaps, for them, more modest ambitions were less risky, and a more certain approach to ensure operations could continue, even while elements of imitation and emulation are quietly borrowed from the example of SSWE.

For SSWE itself, there are clear, concrete examples of how its activities contributed to local peace, as the examples of improved relations between some cattle-keeping communities attest, as well as ongoing links between past and present wrestlers from different communities. SSWE eventually sought to influence the high-level, national dimension of peace and evolved in response to these external dynamics. Ultimately, the organisation's destiny was inextricably intertwined with its founder and most prominent organiser. Once the government's suspicion and mistrust became disturbingly heightened, SSWE's efforts were, as a consequence, interrupted. The SSWE, so closely affiliated with its founder, was not able to replicate its past successes. Neither its former participants nor other organisers were able to sustain what had been previously achieved. Yet, to an extent, the imitations of others are recognition that at least part of the local model of peace promotion that SSWE pioneered is worthy of emulation.

Conclusion

The three cases considered in this chapter on South Sudan focus on very different artistic and cultural endeavours. What unites them across varied spaces, beyond becoming active in the same period, is the importance of peace—in its contrasting dimensions and arenas—to their organisational purposes. To varying extents, all three endeavours sought to influence peace by 'subaltern' agency, while working along a local-national-international spectrum. This was usually in the liberal tradition of *artpeace*building, and sometimes aspiring to *artivism*. Initially, SSWE focused more locally, attempting to use alternative methods to foster local peace, situating agency among the wrestlers and their communities. However, in time it became more nationally and internationally focused and connected with the formal political process because of its founder. Ana Taban was driven by national events, although initially expressed itself locally in micro arts-based approaches, only later becoming involved in an international peace process. After an international debut, SSTO remained locally focused, but adjusted its discourse of peace as it saw necessary to ensure its activities could continue. Moving along this spectrum of peace is driven by both circumstance and opportunity at home and in the wider framework of peace and conflict in the country. While concerns that artistic and cultural movements are vulnerable to external instrumentalisation are valid, artists are savvy too. Peace entrepreneurism and material survival have also led artists and cultural creators to, in the name of peace, promote, sustain and expand their arts. At the same time, these efforts are still often localised in Potgieter's (2016) collaborative, intersubjective, 'solution-orientated' forms of expression.

Based on the evidence of these cases, artistic and cultural projects can play a role in peace formation in South Sudan, but this is sometimes modest (e.g., safe passage for some people on the Nile) or anecdotal (e.g., safer neighbourhoods in Juba), sometimes temporary and often in need of careful nurturing and maintenance to endure (e.g., Ana Taban's monitoring of peace agreement implementation). This may suggest that arts-based initiatives have greater agency and relative influence in local peace processes, compared to those at the national and international level where there is both a multiplicity of actors and more exogenous factors. Further, in most of the cases featured, it is easier for creators to recognise the impact they sought to achieve, or did achieve, on conflict, peace and peace processes, rather than to recognise the impact that conflict, peace and peace processes may have had on them. While they may not describe their personal and organisational evolutions in such terms, it seems apparent that the development of these artistic organisations has been intersubjective, relational and co-constitutive: not entirely determined by the creators themselves. Rather than having a solely unidirectional effect, artistic expression and organisation in South Sudan has in part been co-constructed by its ongoing interactions with processes of peace and conflict, and particularly so when organisations interact with high level processes, as the Ana Taban and SSWE cases show. Although the direct aesthetic impacts may be more variable, these are present too, in both the subjects and themes of art, as with Ana Taban, and in the activities pursued, as with SSTO. At the same time, the magnitude of impact also varies clearly: while Ana Taban has evolved considerably, and SSWE is now largely dormant, SSTO has maintained a degree of continuity, albeit one subject to the vagaries of donors' funding and the unforeseen COVID-19 pandemic.

Even in a comparable context over a comparable period of time, therefore, the conditions under which arts and culture can promote locally directed peace efforts thus vary. One limitation may be the pursuit of an elusive liberal peace in a resource-poor environment without disinterested patrons, who want quick and measurable results. By such measures, disappointment is likely. More broadly, while a degree of latitude to critique and criticise is provided for by visual art or theatre, or even wrestling, and the prestige of international recognition and big crowds provides cultural creators with some protection, the directness with which dissent and resistance is pursued in South Sudan is, for now, a key determiner of whether it will be tolerated. Collectively, all three of these case studies have not succeeded in making their wider aspirations of peace into realities. In part, this is only conceding that aspirations are, by definition, aspirational, and that peace is a process, and not only a destination. It is also tacit acknowledgment that while crossing the Rubicon of 'art' into 'politics' or 'activism' may be possible (it may also be crushed), such a transition is alone insufficient to produce the change these artists may seek. There are other blockages, too. Financial limitations are a preoccupation; while framing art as a peace intervention may attract sponsorship or patronage and the ability to continue activities, this also establishes boundaries between art as an ideal or radical practice and art as a bounded 'project'. Further, peace-orientated artists and cultural creators are contextually limited, both by the available political space, by their own paradigmatic understandings of liberal and negative peace in general and *artpeace*building in particular, as well as by their own conception of function to sometimes replace or substitute the state. In an already polarised national political environment, the critical role of art and cultural expression is very quickly interpreted as being part of an anti-government agenda, whether or not this is explicitly present. Repression of art is an all too common response. Producing that robust, repressive response signals, perhaps, that artistic and cultural critique does matter to seemingly uncaring, self-interested and hardened politico-military elites. While individual organisations may thus wax and wane for many reasons, the broader method of influence endures; in this era of persistent conflict in South Sudan, it may thus be more important to entrench artistic methods, rather than (organisational) mechanisms, in the promotion of and search for peace.

Note

1. The *Likikiri* (the Bari word for 'stories'), a collective theatre group, established in 2015, uses similar methods and states its aims are 'to create a national network of theatre practitioners working for reconciliation and social justice' (Likikiri 2021).

References

ABC News. 2016. Can music save South Sudan? 2 August. [Video]. https://www.youtube.com/watch?v=ZnzAZ3A_A1A (accessed 30 April 2021).

AFLI (Africa Leadership Institute). 2016. Tutu fellows: Peter Biar Ajak PhD. https://alinstitute.org/tutu-fellows/about-fellows/287-peter-biar-ajak (accessed 30 April 2021).

Africanews. 2016. South Sudan: Wrestling for peace. https://www.youtube.com/watch?v=jqkvEWUpsEM (accessed 30 April 2021).

Aguiar, J. 2020. Applied theatre in peacebuilding and development. *Journal of Peacebuilding and Development*, 15(1), pp. 45–60.

Ajang, G. P. and Ngong, A. A. 2013. East Coast beats Midwest in Dinka Bor inter-regional U.S. wrestling competition. *New Sudan Vision*, 30 May. https://www.newsudanvision.com/781-2/ (accessed 30 April 2021).

Akram, S. 2018. Amid peace efforts, South Sudan arrests activist Peter Biar Ajak. *Al Jazeera*, 15 August. https://www.aljazeera.com/features/2018/8/15/amid-peace-efforts-south-sudan-arrests-activist-peter-biar-ajak (accessed 30 April 2021).

Ana Taban. 2018. [Twitter], 17 March. https://twitter.com/AnaTabanSS/status/975135416105005057 (accessed 30 April 2021).

Ana Taban. 2019. Our story. https://www.facebook.com/AnatabanSouthSudan/about/ (accessed 1 April 2021).

Ana Taban. 2021. Clarity on the vandalized Trisha C Mural. 17 April. https://www.facebook.com/AnatabanSouthSudan/posts/2896325387255925 (accessed 30 April 2021).

Baú, V. 2018. Participatory communication, theatre and peace: Performance as a tool for change at the end of conflict. *Communicatio*, 44(1), pp. 34–54.

BBC News. 2016a. South Sudan conflict: Artists sing for peace. 25 July. https://www.bbc.com/news/world-africa-36883957 (accessed 30 April 2021).

BBC News. 2016b. South Sudan artists paint for peace in Juba. 25 October. Available at: https://www.bbc.com/news/world-africa-37754047 (accessed 1 April 2021).

BBC News. 2020. Peter Biar Ajak: Imprisoned Cambridge student released, lawyer says. 5 January. https://www.bbc.com/news/uk-england-cambridgeshire-50998906 (accessed 30 April 2021).

Beck, L. 2015. Wrestling for peace. UNHCR. 15 January. https://www.unhcr.org/news/stories/2015/1/56ec1e7d1b/wrestling-for-peace.html (accessed 30 April 2021).

Bekenova, K. 2019. *In their own voices: Conversations with African emerging leaders*. Stuttgart: Ibidem Press.

Bloomekatz, A. 2012. South Sudan troupe sees new country's struggle in Shakespeare. *Los Angeles Times*, 16 May, https://www.latimes.com/entertainment/arts/la-xpm-2012-may-16-la-et-globe-to-globe-shakespeare-20120512-story.html (accessed 30 April 2021).

Boal, A. 2006. *The aesthetics of the oppressed*. London: Routledge.

Bromber, Krawietz, K. B. and Petrov, P. 2014. Wrestling in multifarious modernity. *The International Journal of the History of Sport* 31(4), pp. 391–404.

Burns, M. A., Beti, B. N., Okuto, M. E., Muwanguzi, D. and Sanyu, L. 2015. Forum theatre for conflict transformation in East Africa: The domain of the possible. *African Conflict and Peacebuilding Review*, 5(1), pp. 136–51.

Campbell, A., with J. Plastow. 2006. Promenade theatre in a Sudanese reformatory. In Etherton, M., ed., *African Theatre: Youth*. Oxford: James Currey, pp. 61–77.

Carroll, S. T. 1988. Wrestling in ancient Nubia. *Journal of Sport History*, 15(2), pp. 121–37.

Craig, J. 2016. South Sudanese artists call for peace in song. *Voice of America*, 9 August. https://www.voanews.com/arts-culture/south-sudanese-artists-call-peace-song (accessed 30 April 2021).

Craze, J. 2020. *The politics of numbers: On security sector reform in South Sudan, 2005–2020*. London: London School of Economics, Centre for Public Authority and International Development.

Dahir, A. L. 2016. 'I am tired': Young South Sudanese are using art to protest the endless cycle of violence and death. *Quartz*, 21 September.https://qz.com/africa/786411/south-sudans-ana-taban-campaign-calls-for-change-as-the-country-is-marred-in-civil-war/ (accessed 30 April 2021).

Daldorph, B. 2016. 'Tired' of war, young South Sudanese artists form 'Ana Taban' movement. *France24*, 28 October. https://observers.france24.com/en/20161028-south-sudan-art-ana-taban-youth-music-peace-war (accessed 30 April 2021).

Datta, S. 2012. The Bard in new lands. *The Hindu*, 14 November. https://www.thehindu.com/features/friday-review/theatre/the-bard-in-new-lands/article4094981.ece (accessed 30 April 2021).

Deng, D. 2018. *Revitalizing peace in South Sudan: Citizen perceptions of the peace process*. Juba: South Sudan Civil Society Forum (SSCSF).

Dixon, L. 2006. Youth theatre in the displaced people's camps of Khartoum: Kwoto. In Etherton, M., ed., *African theatre: Youth*. Oxford: James Currey, pp. 78–85.

Efland, A. D. 2004. Emerging visions of art education. In Eisner, E. W. and Day, M. D. eds, *Handbook of research and policy in art education*. Mahwah, NJ: Lawrence Erlbaum Associates, pp. 691–700.

Elfman, R. 2017. Slapstick against stereotypes in South Sudan's *Cymbeline*. In Bulman, J. C., ed., *The Oxford handbook of Shakespeare and performance*. Oxford: Oxford University Press, pp. 495–511.

European Union Civil Protection and Humanitarian Aid. 2014. EU Children of peace 2014: South Sudan dances for peace. 26 September. https://www.youtube.com/watch?v=O-Yte huqLNA (accessed 30 April 2021).

Gordon, C. Sharing history: South Sudan Theatre Company's *Cymbeline* at the Globe. *Blogging Shakespeare*. https://bloggingshakespeare.com/reviewing-shakespeare/year-of-shakespeare-sharing-history-south-sudan-theatre-companys-cymbeline-at-the-globe/ (accessed 30 April 2021).

Harragin, S. 2011. *South Sudan: Waiting for peace to come*. Copenhagen: Local to Global Protection.

Hungerford, G. 1953. The northern Nilo-Hamites: East Central Africa part VI. In Forde, D., ed., *Ethnographic survey of Africa*. London: International African Institute.

Impey, A. 2013. The poetics of transitional justice in Dinka songs in South Sudan. *UNISCI Discussion Papers* 33, pp. 57–77.

John, M. 2022. Peace partners in South Sudan agree to unify security command structures. Conflict and Resilience Monitor. *ACCORD*. https://www.accord.org.za/analysis/peace-part ners-in-south-sudan-agree-to-unify-security-command-structures/ (accessed 15 September 2022).

John, M., Wilmot, P. and Zaremba, N. 2018. Resisting violence: Growing a culture of nonviolent action in South Sudan. United States Institute of Peace Special Report 435.

Johnson, V., Lewin, T. and Cannon, M. 2020. *Learning from a living archive: Rejuvenating child and youth rights and participation*. REJUVENATE Working Paper 1, Brighton: Institute of Development Studies.

Leposo, L. 2011. Wrestlers fight to unite world's newest nation. *CNN*. http://edition.cnn.com/2011/WORLD/africa/08/16/south.sudan.wrestling.ajak/ (accessed 30 April 2021).

Likikiri Collective. 2021. About. http://www.likikiri.org/about/ (accessed 1 April 2021).

Lorins, R. 2007. Inheritance: Kinship and the performance of Sudanese identities. PhD dissertation, Austin: University of Texas at Austin.

Louro, D. 2021. Singing for equality: Joy Mbraza. UN Mission in South Sudan, 8 March. https://unmiss.unmissions.org/singing-equality-joy-mbraza (accessed 30 April 2021).

Malish, D. B. 2015. There are many connectors for South Sudanese. *Transformedia*, 19 September. http://www.transformedia.org.uk/connectors-for-south-sudanese/ (accessed 30 April 2021).

Maluak, A. 2017. The Hagana festival. *Andariya*. 24 May. https://www.andariya.com/post/The-Hagana-Festival (accessed 1 April 2021).

Mancewicz, A. 2018. From global London to global Shakespeare. *Contemporary Theatre Review*, 28(2), pp. 235–46.

Matarasso, F. 1997. *Use or ornament? The social impact of participation in the arts*. Stroud: Comedia.

Matzke, C. 2013. Performing the nation at the London Globe: Notes on a South Sudanese Cymbeline. In Plastow, J., ed., *African theatre 12: Shakespeare in and out of Africa*. Woodbridge, Suffolk: James Currey, pp. 61–82.

Milner, C. 2016. South Sudanese theatre in 2015. *Sudan Studies* 53, pp. 4–17.

Mitchell, J., Vincett, G., Hawksley, T. and Culbertson, H. (eds). 2020. *Peacebuilding and the arts*. Basingstoke: Palgrave Macmillan.

Mtukwa, T. 2015. Informal peacebuilding initiatives in Africa: Removing the table. *African Journal on Conflict Resolution* 15(1), pp. 85–106.

Murray, P. W. 2018. Citizen's theatre South Sudan: Outcome harvesting evaluation. http://www.transformedia.org.uk/wp-content/uploads/2018/06/Evaluation_Report_Citizens_Theatre_Draft_FINAL-1.pdf (accessed 30 April 2021).

Namubiru, L. 2018. Creatives are stepping up to counter a media clampdown in South Sudan. *Quartz*. https://qz.com/africa/1448939/south-sudan-creatives-use-theater-for-peace/ (accessed 1 April 2021).

Nyaga, B. 2019. South Sudanese artist collective Anataban on a mission to bring lasting peace. *Music in Africa*, 11 January. https://www.musicinafrica.net/magazine/south-sudanese-artist-collective-anataban-mission-bring-lasting-peace (accessed 30 April 2021).

Oakley, D. 2012. Review: Cymbeline, South Sudan Theatre Company (Shakespeare's Globe). *Ceasefire*. https://ceasefiremagazine.co.uk/review-cymbeline-south-sudan-theatre-company-shakespeares-globe/ [ceasefiremagazine.co.uk] (accessed 23 April 2021).

Obasi, N. T., Okpara, C. V., Okpara, F. T., Itiav, V. J. and Gever, C. V. 2021. Effect of theatre for development as a communication intervention strategy on behavioural intentions towards painting, weaving and fashion and design among victims of conflict in Nigeria. *African Security Review* 30(2), pp. 139–51.

Patinkin, J. 2016. South Sudan tribes pursue peace through sport. *Voice of America*, 18 April. https://www.voanews.com/africa/south-sudan-tribes-pursue-peace-through-sport (accessed 30 April 2021).

Potgieter, F. 2016. On intersubjectivity in art and everyday aesthetics. *De arte* 51(2), pp. 3–15.

Price, R. and Ornnert, A. 2017. Youth in South Sudan: Livelihoods and conflict. https://assets.publishing.service.gov.uk/media/5c6eaec3ed915d4a380dda98/203-205_Youth_in_South_Sudan_Livelihoods_and_Conflict.pdf (accessed 30 April 2021).

Radio Tamazuj. 2016. Jonglei celebrates its champion wrestlers. 4 May. https://radiotamazuj.org/en/news/article/jonglei-celebrates-its-champion-wrestlers (accessed 30 April 2021).

Radio Tamazuj. 2017. Man killed in brawl during wrestling match in Jonglei. 18 September. https://radiotamazuj.org/en/news/article/man-killed-in-brawl-during-wrestling-match-in-jonglei (accessed 30 April 2021).

Ranga Shankara. 2012. Shakespeare fest. http://www.rangashankara.org/home/rangashankara/our-festivals/shakespeare-fest/ (accessed 30 April 2021).

Rolandsen, Ø. H. 2011. A quick fix? A retrospective analysis of the Sudan Comprehensive Peace Agreement. *Review of African Political Economy* 38(130), pp. 551–64.

Sixdenier, B. 2017. An interview with AnaTaban: An artists' collective trying to bring peace to South Sudan. *Medium*, 15 November. https://medium.com/politicsmeanspolitics/an-interview-with-anataban-an-artists-collective-trying-to-bring-peace-to-south-sudan-4ad1a0302416 (accessed 30 April 2021).

Solga, K. 2013. Neo-liberal pleasure, global responsibility and the South Sudan *Cymbeline*. In Bennett, S. and Carson, C., eds., *Shakespeare beyond English: A global experiment*. Cambridge: Cambridge University Press, pp. 101–9.

South Sudan Wrestling Bet. 2019. South Sudan Wrestling Bet. https://www.facebook.com/South-Sudan-Wrestling-Bet-106253374093669/ (accessed 30 April 2021).

Srinivasan, S. 2021. *When peace kills politics*. London: Hurst.

Starr Cards. 2016. Harvard-educated wrestling promoter Peter Biar Ajak is South Sudan's Vince McMahon. https://starrcards.com/harvard-educated-wrestling-promoter-peter-biar-ajak-is-south-sudans-vince-mcmahon/ (accessed 30 April 2021).

Stephenson, M. Jr. and Zanotti, L. 2017. Exploring the intersection of theory and practice of arts for peacebuilding. *Global Society*, 31(3), pp. 336–52.

Thomas, E. 2015. *South Sudan: A slow liberation*. London: Zed Books.

Trueman, M. 2012. Cymbeline – review. *The Guardian*, 4 May. https://www.theguardian.com/stage/2012/may/04/cymbeline-globe-review (accessed 30 April 2021).

Tutton, M. 2012. All the world's a stage as Shakespeare goes to South Sudan. *CNN*, 12 January. https://edition.cnn.com/2012/01/12/world/africa/shakespeare-south-sudan/index.html (accessed 30 April 2021).

United States Agency for International Development. 2016. Viable support to transition and stability (Vistas) FY 2016 annual report. https://pdf.usaid.gov/pdf_docs/PA00TQQW.pdf (accessed 30 April 2021).

Vambe, M. T. 2014. Songs that won South Sudan's political independence: A warchild perspective. *Muziki* 11(1), pp. 4–17.

Verjee, A. 2010. *Race against time: Countdown to the referenda in Southern Sudan and Abyei*. London and Nairobi: Rift Valley Institute.

Verjee, A. 2017. South Sudan's high level revitalization forum: Identifying conditions for success. United States Institute of Peace Peace Brief 228.

Verjee, A. 2020. How mediators conceive of peace: The case of IGAD in South Sudan, 2013–15. In Nouwen, S. M. H., Srinivasan, S. and James, L., (eds). *Making and breaking peace in Sudan and South Sudan*. Proceedings of the British Academy 233, Oxford: Oxford University Press, pp. 277–96.

Verjee, A. 2021. Collapse in the capital: The evolution of security arrangements in Juba, South Sudan, 2014–16. *African Conflict and Peacebuilding Review* 11(1), pp. 104–18.

Verjee, A and Vertin, Z. 2021. South Sudan peace process archive. https://www.usip.org/programs/south-sudan-peace-process-archive (accessed 30 April 2021).

Vertin, Z. 2018. *A poisoned well: Lessons in mediation from South Sudan's troubled peace process*. New York: International Peace Institute.

Vice Sports. 2016. Wrestling for peace in South Sudan. https://video.vice.com/en_us/video/wrestling-for-peace-in-southsudan/57bc533c40f990b3503a566e (accessed 30 April 2021).

Voice of America. 2016. South Sudan artists protest civil war with peace campaign. 25 November. https://www.voanews.com/africa/south-sudan-artists-protest-civil-warpeace-campaign (accessed 30 April 2021).

Walkling, S. 2012. Year of Shakespeare: Three Arabic Shakespeares, putting words into our mouths. *Blogging Shakespeare*, 13 June. https://www.bloggingshakespeare.com/year-of-shakespeare-three-arabic-shakespeares-putting-words-into-our-mouths (accessed 30 April 2021).

Wynne-Jones, R. 2012. *Cymbeline*: From war-ravaged South Sudan to the Globe theatre. *The Independent*, 1 May. https://www.independent.co.uk/arts-entertainment/theatre-dance/

features/cymbeline-war-ravaged-south-sudan-globe-theatre-7704215.html (accessed 30 April 2021).

York, G. 2014. South Sudan war disrupts a theatre, inspires a dramatist. *The Globe and Mail*, 7 February. https://www.theglobeandmail.com/news/world/south-sudan-war-disrupts-a-theatre-inspires-a-dramatist/article16760007/ (accessed 30 April 2021).

Young, J. O. 1996. Inquiry in the arts and sciences. *Philosophy* 71(276), pp. 255–73.

Young, J. 2019. *South Sudan's civil war: Violence, insurgency and failed peacemaking*. London: Zed Books.

Zaremba, N. 2018. In South Sudan, an artists' movement for peace catches fire. United States Institute of Peace, 19 January. https://www.usip.org/publications/2018/01/south-sudan-artists-movement-peace-catches-fire (accessed 30 April 2021).

Interviews

1. Jacob Bul Bior Bul, 2 April 2021, online
2. Chris Milner, 7 April 2021, online
3. Ayak Chol Deng, 9 April 2021, online, by text message
4. Nick Zaremba, 15 April 2021, online
5. Angelina Ban, 16 April 2021, online, by text message
6. Joanna Oyediran, 17 April 2021, online
7. Peter Biar Ajak, 19 April 2021, online
8. Anna Rowett, 20 April 2021, online
9. Abit Mayen, 20 April 2021, online
10. Dominic Gorgory, 20 April 2021, online
11. Atem Elftatih and Rebecca Lorins, 20 April 2021, online
12. Joseph Abuk, 21 April 2021, online
13. Don Bosco, 23 April 2021, online
14. Ajang Chol Biar, 23 April 2021, online
15. Michael Achiek Garang, 23 April 2021, online

Street Arts Festival Mostar: Curatorial Agency, Spatial Transformation and *Artpeace* Formation

Lydia C. Cole

'Art has a positive energy everywhere [...]. Because we are a specific city and environment it has a bigger impact [...]. It's changed the infrastructure of public space.' (Street Arts Festival Mostar Organiser 2020)

Street Arts Festival Mostar (SAFMO) is a grassroots festival initiated by Marina Đapić in 2012. The festival has taken place each year since, drawing together local and international artists. Responding directly to the post-war, post-socialist context, the festival intervenes in the layers of abandonment within the city. Inspired by global street artists, festival organisers creatively reimagined abandoned walls and spaces in the city in ways that shape and transform urban space, as well as its legacies of conflict and future use (Carabelli 2020). This chapter examines the curating of street art in urban space in Mostar, asking how the local curatorial agency of organisers and artists challenges simplistic narratives of ethnonational division and reconciliation.

The term 'street art' has traditionally referred to artforms engaged in public space without permission and to a 'countercultural movement' (Ulmer 2017, 492), that disrupts the established rules of public space through the appropriation of its surfaces (Irvine 2012, 235). Street art has an affinity with grassroots organising for change due to its associations with critique in the public space. However, SAFMO is a sanctioned festival which operates with permission from the City of Mostar, as well as building owners where necessary. Contrary to scholars critical of the emancipatory potential of sanctioned street art (cf. Schacter 2014), I suggest that sanctioned street arts, where engaged in broader grassroots struggles for change, have potential for socio-political transformation.

Art and its curating have been seen to play a significant role in spatial transformation. In the chapter, spatial transformation is produced through curatorial agency engaged at the intersection of grassroots struggles for change and arttransformation. To the extent that street art is inherently spatial, its transformative impact is mapped through the mutually constitutive processes of place- and space-making. Mediating the space between grassroots organising and international peacebuilding, curatorial agency within SAFMO engages spatial transformation in ways that enact hybrid forms of socio-political change. My argument builds on aesthetic scholarship that highlights the capacity of the arts to produce space for people to engage with and produce the city (Bell 2009, 139; Carabelli 2018), in ways that enable discussions about the past (Kotecki 2014) and promote cultural exchange within and beyond BiH (Deiana 2020). Within this, street arts have been seen as particularly transformative, in terms of their capacity to spatially represent counter-narratives of a contested peace (Kappler and McKane 2019), and their propensity to materially transform urban space and place (Carabelli 2018; Forde 2019). Building on this work, I am interested in how the curating of SAFMO is engaged within broader peace infrastructures to promote spatial transformation. I suggest that curatorial agency contributes to *artpeace* formation where it is engaged to challenge the status quo of state formation and liberal peacebuilding. Curatorial agency within SAFMO challenges the politics of ethnonational division promoted through elite politics, as well as simplistic understandings of reconciliation which are imposed on grassroots initiatives for peace and materialised through the postwar reconstruction efforts.

Following Kappler and McKane (2019), the city can be understood as a museum where city curators form, transform and contest conflict and peace. In this chapter, I offer a spatial reading of the city as a museum, noting how space and place are 'rebuilt, transformed, occupied' by artists, curators and communities (Björkdahl 2013, 212). Curators may engage from the grassroots or the elite, both of whom seek to curate urban space. Though the practices of grassroots curatorial actors differ in 'form' and 'scope' to those of elites (Kappler and McKane 2019, 6), drawing them together enables the exploration of how space and place are represented, shaped, contested and ultimately transformed through curating. SAFMO engages a range of local curatorial actors who fund, commission, curate and paint murals on public and residential walls. During the festival, artists, organisers and visitors inhabit sites and spaces where murals are placed, producing 'new dynamics' within public space (SAFMO 2021). In the chapter, I explore how and to what extent these dynamics are sustained through spatial transformation, understood as practices of space- and place-making that shape and reimagine Mostar beyond spatial division.

I first provide a brief overview of Mostar as a conflict-affected space, before outlining how curatorial agency can be understood as engaged in *artpeace* formation, demonstrating how arts and cultural actors—and particularly those associated with SAFMO—have navigated Mostar's post-war peace. Second, I show how curatorial agency engages in practices of space- and place-making in Mostar, linking curating to processes of spatial transformation. Third, I trace the curatorial practices of international peacebuilders and city authorities in post-war Mostar. Demonstrating that post-war urban curating often reproduced divisions of the war and focused on large-scale projects of reconciliation, I note that local initiatives for change were often marginalised. The final parts of the chapter turn to consider two sites of SAFMO's curating: Partizan's Playground and Ulica Alekse Šantića (Aleksa Šantić street), arguing that curatorial agency is put toward spatial transformation. Overall, I demonstrate how local curatorial agency—where engaged through wider networks for peace in Mostar—forms and transforms space in the city in ways that challenge its spatial narratives of division and seek to sustain the city for the future.

Mostar: War and the Production of a Divided City

The Socialist Federal Republic of Yugoslavia (comprised of Bosnia and Herzegovina, Croatia, Macedonia, Montenegro, Serbia and Slovenia) disintegrated in the early 1990s. The death of President Josip Broz Tito in 1980 left a political power vacuum, with the ensuing period characterised by rising nationalisms and economic struggles, used by political elites to further nationalist projects (Jovan 2001). In 1991, Croatia, Slovenia and Macedonia declared independence, followed by Bosnia and Herzegovina (BiH) in 1992. This provoked a series of wars of secession across former Yugoslavia. BiH experienced some of the worst violence: over 100,000 people were killed and around 2.2 million people were displaced.

As a formally multi-ethnic city, Mostar's experience of war 'fractured' its urban landscape (Björkdahl and Kappler 2017, 87). The Serb-dominated Yugoslav People's Army laid siege to the city in 1992, occupying the area to the east of the river Neretva and displacing many of its residents. At this time, the Croatian Defence Force and the Bosnian Army joined forces, successfully expelling the Yugoslav People's Army from Mostar in June 1992. However, in May 1993, Croatian paramilitary units began ethnically cleansing the Muslim residents of the city (Calame and Charlesworth 2009, 103). The city was fractured into east and west, with the line of division following the frontline of conflict (Ibid., 103). Many of the city's residents were killed or 'forcibly expelled' (Björkdahl 2012, 8), while others arrived in the city seeking refuge from violence elsewhere. Cultural sites, most infamously, Stari most (Old Bridge), were destroyed in what scholars have come to term *urbicide* (Coward 2008).[1] The city's experience of war set the stage for the 'exhibition' of ethnonational identity (Kappler and McKane 2019, 6), with graffiti performing this division through extremist symbols and messaging

(Bilkic 2018). In what follows, I trace the idea of *artpeace* formation conceptually, while situating the ways that local agency has engaged in peacebuilding in the postwar context.

Curatorial Agency and *Artpeace* Formation

Peace formation is the process by which local actors, drawing on 'contextual knowledge', challenge the status quo of peacebuilding processes (Richmond 2013, 275). Following Shepherd (2011), change is a central component of agency. Then, local agencies use their situated knowledge to navigate complex networks of power to engage in processes of 'social negotiation' to bring about change (Mac Ginty and Richmond 2013, 770). Curating is one site where this social negotiation takes place. In this chapter, I examine how curatorial agency engages in networks of power to negotiate alternative ideas of peace and to bring about spatial transformation.

Curating describes the process through which actors negotiate visibility, making decisions about what can be viewed, as well as how, when and crucially *where* this is possible (Hooper-Greenhill 2003, 7). The curatorial practices of elite and grassroots curators are both subject to negotiation through broader power relations. Where engaged by local actors, curatorial agency can be understood as part of *artpeace* formation. Adapting Björkdahl and Höglund's (2013, 292) notion of frictional encounter—a 'meeting point' between different 'actors, ideas and practice' that shapes and transforms power relations—I suggest that curatorial agencies enact change in and through space. Frictional encounters between curators may result in a range of political outcomes from radical change and the production of new forms of community to the inability to effect spatial change in ways that bring about lasting conditions for peace (Kappler et al. 2023). In the chapter, I trace the process through which curatorial actors meet in space, engaging in social negotiations across 'difference and affinity' (Björkdahl and Höglund 2013, 294). Through frictional encounters between local curators, elite government and international peacebuilders conceptions of space and place are shaped and transformed in Mostar.

Local agency for peace has proliferated in arts and cultural spaces, distancing itself from elite and formal political spaces. This maps on to a broader 'discontent' with the political sphere which is seen as perpetuating the homogenous notions of the ethnonationalism seen during the war (Hromadzić 2013, 268, 270). Spaces conventionally associated with politics are marred by corrupt and nationalist politics (Helms 2013). Indeed, in an interview with Sarajevo-based news outlet *Oslobodjenje*, festival organiser Marina Đapić reflects that she speaks from the 'perspective of life in BiH' rather than entering into the complications of the political sphere (Abadžija 2018). As such, those engaged in struggles for socio-political change have sought alternative channels for engagement.

In BiH, liberal forms of peace were wholly directed from the top-down until 2006. In Mostar, this took form through the European Union Administration of Mostar (EUAM) and the Office of the High Representative (OHR). Funding provided by international peacebuilders focused on democratisation, human rights and institutional governance, often framing civil society as a 'subcontractor' for 'policy implementation' (Kappler 2014, 69). This was particularly notable within reconciliation initiatives which imposed frameworks—particularly ethnic quotas—on their activities (Vogel 2016). Criticising this approach, a representative of a youth centre in BiH reflected: 'we don't want to meet each other, talk about our differences and tolerate each other. We want to meet each other, talk about our similarities and understand each other' (quoted in Ibid., 478). While international peacebuilders gradually shifted toward a more hybrid form of peace which supported, rather than imposed, socio-political change, BiH's peace has restricted opportunities for local dialogue and initiatives (Belloni et al. 2016).

Arts and cultural spaces offer alternative 'visions of peace' through creating space for discussion (Kappler 2014, 145). Challenging the politics of ethnonational division perpetuated by government elites, as well as narrow frames of reconciliation by international peacebuilders, these spaces offer an alternative 'point of departure' (Björkdahl and Kappler 2017, 87). The creation of physical spaces where ordinary people, particularly youth, can meet, talk, share and create has been central to developing alternative visions of peace (Björkdahl and Kappler 2017, 87). Meeting points enable arts and cultural actors to support forms of social negotiation which reach beyond division (Kappler 2014, 129). In this way, artistic agency has been central to processes of questioning the social, political and cultural problems of citizens (Belloni et al. 2016; Zelizer 2003).

Despite attempts to distance cultural spaces from politics, such spaces do not exist separately from liberal peacebuilding. In Mostar, international artists and organisations have supported arts and culture. Organisations like OKC Abrašević were 'built up from the ruins by young people' (Kappler 2014, 133), supported through connections with French artists who travelled to Mostar after the war (Musician 2020). Meanwhile, the Pavarotti Music Centre was established through the initiative of War Child UK and supported by Pavarotti, Brian Eno and U2. Initially focusing on activities which aligned with international framings of reconciliation, including a music therapy programme (Lang and McInerney 1999, 186), over time the centre's aims became more localised. In 2012, responding to the needs of the community, they established a youth Rock School (Mostar Rock School 2021).

Local curatorial actors also engage with international peacebuilders through funding which is often contingent on the ability to relate initiatives within frames of reconciliation. Those operating within artistic and cultural space approach this strategically. An artist working with OKC Abrašević noted how engaging with international funding for arttransformation offered opportunities to organise a degree of independence from elite governmental politics. Artistic and cultural actors have thus been able to shape funding calls to create opportunities for youth engagement. A Sarajevo-based street artist remarked that they had been funded by Schüler Helfen Leben, a German non-governmental organisation (NGO) which aims to support youth engagement with forms of solidarity for peace, to facilitate two street art workshops—one in BiH and the other in Serbia. Though the project 'was based on reconciliation, [...] peace and everything', they also reflected that their main focus was creating space for doing street art, adding that those who were part of the exchange 'were already my friends' (Street Artist 1 2020). Though there are limits to engaging with international peacebuilding frameworks, as we will see later in the chapter, curatorial agency within SAFMO often challenges and re-formulates its agendas 'in a different register' (Richmond 2013, 273).

SAFMO can be situated within this context. The festival was initiated by youth advocate Marina Đapić, who was then the serving representative for OKC Abrašević on Mostar Youth Council, an NGO founded in 2010 by Mostar City Council as a platform for youth. Đapić's engagement with this forum helped to gain permission to paint in Mostar (Festival Organiser 2020). Early on, the festival was supported by United World College and Schüler Helfen Leben. As the festival has grown in reputation, festival organisers have found support through crowdfunding, international embassy funding and more recently, through the Bosnia-Herzegovina Resilience Initiative, which is funded by USAID and implemented by the International Organisation for Migration. Engaging from the grassroots, organisers have found support through structures of international peacebuilding.

Locally, the festival collaborates with organisations and residents. Festival organisers 'recruit' organisations to facilitate parts of the programme where areas of cooperation can be identified (Kesby 2005, 2046), as well as bolster the activities of grassroots initiatives for change. Youth Power (n.d.) have supported the festivals' activities through their Youth Art Movement project which emphasises alternative arts—including street art—as a platform for youth engagement. As will be discussed later in the chapter, LDA Mostar, an NGO which supports citizen engagement with EU integration and democratisation processes, that has supported the festival 'from the beginning', found commonality within themes of youth engagement with cultural heritage (Representative, LDA Mostar, 2019). For its part, IDEAA

Mostar initiated a process of restoration of a disused playground, which also became a space of artistic intervention during the 2019 and 2020 editions of SAFMO. This collaboration shapes the messaging of the festival. Murals supported by LDA Mostar focused on themes of multiculturalism and diversity, while those engaged as part of the restoration of the disused playground tended to feature images which emplaced the playground in Mostar and would appeal to young people who were the intended future users of the playground. Residents support the festival through volunteering their walls for murals (Festival Organiser 2020), through hospitality toward artists such as offering coffee and conversation (Street Artist 2 2020), by guiding interested viewers to nearby murals and through engagement with its activities.

SAFMO also engages with artists. A festival organiser highlighted that over the festival's various editions, they had worked with a mix of 'young artists' from Mostar, 'artists from other cities: like Sarajevo, Tuzla, Banja Luka, smaller cities in Bosnia-Herzegovina', as well as international artists including Aleksandro Reis (Brazil), Ella & Pitr (France), Colectivo Licuado and AlfALfa (Uruguay). This contributes to the aim of facilitating space for 'connection' and 'new friendships' across national bounds (Festival Organiser 2020). For the most part, artists needed to submit a sketch prior to the festival so that organisers could push back on murals which reproduced themes of division (Street Artist 3 2020), as well as share the sketches with residents who had volunteered their walls (Festival Organiser 2020). Local artists engaging in spaces which were part of grassroots reconstruction processes had more autonomy. A graffiti artist working on a mural in the Partizan Playground reflected that the organisers had given them 'freedom to do what they want[ed] to do' and their piece was mostly freestyle on the wall (Street Artist 4 2020).

Curatorial agency in SAFMO navigates the hierarchies of international peacebuilding and state formation processes. Agency is engaged to support artists and residents and importantly, to create spaces of encounter within the city. Distancing themselves from the spaces of elite government, organisers engage strategically with international peacebuilders to support the programme. As a sanctioned festival of street arts, the curatorial agency of SAFMO can be understood as a hybrid form of agency. It challenges the status quo of international peacebuilding and state formation through intervening in spaces which are contested and/or neglected in official reconstruction processes. The next section moves to deepen understandings of space, place and spatial transformation that are at the core of curatorial agency for change.

Curating for Spatial Transformation

Developing Björkdahl and Kappler's (2017) conceptions of place- and space-making, I here aim to show the dynamics of spatial transformation as it is directed through the curating of street art. It is first useful to distinguish between notions of place and space. Place is a situated locale within space: a geographical and material location. Additionally, places are conceptual since they come to be associated with particular subjectivities and ideas of belonging (Björkdahl and Kappler 2017, 18–19). In this way, places are locations where socio-political narratives are produced (Kappler 2017, 133), and thus, can be read. Place can then be understood as a site of encounter between agencies, subjectivities and power relations (Massey 2005; Kappler 2017). Space is the more abstract term, referring to the ideas, concepts and narratives that make places function. In this sense, space is the 'imaginary counterpart' of place (Björkdahl and Kappler 2017, 19). However, space should not be understood as synonymous with place since it is not geographically bound or rooted in the same manner.

In the chapter, I am interested in how agency is engaged to produce and transform place and space, with particular emphasis on the artistic and curatorial practices that work to 'situate it, temporalise it, and make it function' (de Certeau 1984, 117). Drawing on understandings of place and space, I delineate two central, mutually constitutive forms of spatial transformation, place- and space-making, that are driven by curatorial agency. While place-making is conceived as a process through which more abstract ideas of space are given a material presence in a given locale, space-making denotes the process by which place is spatialised, produced within socio-political political discourses that flow beyond the boundedness of a locational place (Björkdahl and Kappler 2017, 25). In what follows, I trace the dynamics of curatorial agency in SAFMO, showing why and how organisers enact spatial transformation.

Curatorial agency in SAFMO is driven through involvement in activist struggles against divisive spatial politics in Mostar. As previously noted, organisers of the festival cooperate with activists and broader peace networks in Mostar and beyond. As such, curatorial spaces of intervention host meetings between a range of socio-politically engaged agencies (Massey 2001). Where curating is engaged in these spatial struggles, they produce sites as 'focal points' for activism and solidarity (Obradovic-Wochnik and Bird 2020, 47), with curatorial agency invested in transforming neglected, forgotten and disused locales in the city.

In this sense, curatorial agency harnesses the spatial aspects of street art. Street art is understood as a practice that is grounded within urban space (Irvine 2012). In this sense, where it 'occurs – or does not occur' (Vogel et al. 2020, 2155), or in this context, where it is placed, provides important insights into the socio-political context where it was written. SAFMO organisers have particularly sought to curate a series of 'open-air galleries' in the city (Festival Organiser 2020), involving the 'spatial clustering' of murals over several editions of the festival (Haworth et al. 2013, 56). It is through this process that the curators of SAFMO aim to materialise abstract ideas of space as encounter. Open air galleries provide a stage for internationally and locally situated artists to meet and connect, while also connecting the residents of Mostar by providing places of connection within the city. In this sense, directed curatorial agency can be used to challenge Mostar's spatial, material and felt divisions.

To this end, curatorial agency draws on the communicative function of street art. The organisers of SAFMO encourage murals that feature a strong, activist message that connects to the (hi)stories of the city (Festival Organiser 2020). Thus, street art within the festival often reflects topics, histories and imaginations within Mostar and beyond (Vogel et al. 2020, 2151), and reveals a range of complex, spatialised identities and meanings in space (Irvine 2012, 237; Vogel et al. 2020, 2153). Stari most has been a key recurring symbol within the festival. As a geographically situated place, the symbol of the bridge has been taken up within broader socio-political discourses. In particular, it has come to signify both the city's 'former coexistence' and the 'divisiveness' of war (Björkdahl and Mannergren Selimovic 2016, 329), as well as international institutional notions of inter-ethnic reconciliation (Forde 2016). The emplaced usage of such symbols contributes to space-making, re-imaging and reimagining notions of space in the city, and shifting socio-political discourse beyond spatialised division.

Street art also has a spatio-temporal element since it intervenes in spaces that have complex and shifting meanings. In this chapter, I refer to such places as palimpsests, a term which captures the ways that narratives of and in space are multiple, layered, often conflictual, coexist in one place and evolve over time (Strange and Kempa 2003, 391). To the extent that SAFMO curators intervene in (formerly) abandoned, ruined and disused sites, these spaces reveal a complexity of meaning within people's experiences and rememberings of the past (Kappler 2017). A core aim of curatorial agency has been seen as place-making through transforming these spaces into spaces for connection and encounter. Through engaging the spatio-temporal aspects of street art to contribute to meaning-making, curators can also contribute to processes of space-making, reshaping relationships to the emplaced past (Kappler and McKane 2019), and to the future. With memory always 'embedded' in space (Ibid., 6), curatorial agency enables the re-curating of meanings, significations and imaginaries of urban space.

Curatorial agency is thus engaged in processes of place- and space-making in ways that contribute to productive forms of spatial transformation. To achieve this, curators of SAFMO intervene in activist campaigns, drawing on the spatial, communicative and spatio-temporal aspects of street art to intervene in a complex, layered and shifting urban landscape. In the next section, I situate the politics of elite curating by international peacebuilders and governmental actors to establish the structural context in which curatorial agencies engage. In doing so, I trace how elite actors have shaped Mostar's 'landscapes of division and unity' (Laketa 2019, 171), reflecting on how scholars and activists have challenged elite forms of urban curating.

International Peacebuilding: Curating Urban Space in Mostar

Since the 1990s, international peacebuilders, as well as city authorities, have curated urban space in Mostar. Responding to the spatial politics of Mostar's wartime division, Mostar became a central focus for international peacebuilders who sought to curate urban space in ways that, it was hoped, would facilitate reconciliation. The EUAM administration played a significant role in this curating, engaging urban planning as peacebuilding after the war (Björkdahl 2012, 11). In 1996, the EUAM implemented the Rome Agreement, a statute for the city which established six administrative districts—three Bosniak and three Croat—and a Central Zone. The Central Zone was imagined as a 'shared, de-politicized public space' (Ibid., 12): a 'physical starting point for a reunited city' (Makaš 2007, 190). However, the boundaries of the central zone were highly contested (Ibid., 188–93), and the administrative districts largely cooperated within ethnonational bounds. Reconstruction in the Central Zone was uneven at best, becoming an 'administrative no-man's land' (Vetters 2007, 199).

Nevertheless, the reconstruction of urban infrastructures was an international priority. After the war, EUAM focused on rebuilding to facilitate the return of refugees and internally displaced persons, with the beneficiaries of rebuilding schemes largely decided by administrative districts (Yarwood 1999, 46–8). This reinforced ethnonational divisions in ways that spatially 'transformed and reconfigured' Mostar (Björkdahl 2012, 11). Apartment blocks in historically ethnically mixed areas such as Alekse Šantića street were particularly badly damaged. However, with limited budgets for repair (Yarwood 1999, 49), and limited elite governmental will, many buildings in the Central Zone remained in ruins.

Cultural heritage was another key focus for urban peacebuilding and was seen as necessary for the reunification of the city and BiH as a whole (Armaly et al. 2004, 9). Stari most became a central focus for international reconstruction efforts and was supported by a large coalition of international institutions including the United Nations Educational, Scientific and Cultural Organisation (UNESCO), World Bank and the Aga Khan Trust for Culture and World Monuments Fund, supported by funds from the Governments of Italy, Netherlands, Croatia, Bosnia and Herzegovina, Turkey and France, as well as the Council of Europe Development Bank and the European Union (Ibid., 7). Formally inaugurated on 23 July 2004, the bridge's reconstruction was intended as a symbol of reconciliation which held the potential to unite Mostar's residents 'as a people once again' (UNESCO 2005, 35).

These forms of international curating have not been without contestation. In the context of Stari most, scholars have criticised the ways that international conceptions of reconciliation have reduced divisions in Mostar to ethnic divisions which could be 'bridged' (Björkdahl and Mannergren Selimovic 2016, 328). Activists have criticised this top-down approach, reflecting on how international elites have prioritised symbolic initiatives with little consultation with local actors for change (Director 2019). Indeed, while, as has been noted, local arts and culture organisations have gained support for their activities through international actors, this support has not always been easy to mobilise, operating on a vastly different scale to large symbolic projects such as the restoration of Stari most (Forde 2016). In this sense, ordinary people in Mostar have both resisted and coexisted with Mostar's 'seem[ing]ly-permanent division' (Carabelli et al. 2019, 117). In the next section, I unpack this dynamic further by introducing two specific sites of spatial transformation: Partizan's Playground and Alekse Šantića street. Tracing the curatorial agency of SAFMO, I show how curating has sought to enact socio-political change at the local level through unsettling ethnonational division and simplistic notions of reconciliation.

Curating and the Sites of Spatial Transformation

Partizan Playground

The Partizan's Playground is a sports ground situated in East Mostar in a residential area close to Stari Most. Through the coordinated efforts of local peace organisations, the space has been a site of place-making in which curatorial agency has been engaged to transform the playground and to reimagine its usage in the contemporary context. A founding commitment of SAFMO was to intervene in abandoned spaces through street art. In 2019, SAFMO worked with other organisations in Mostar to restore the Partizan Playground. The initiative sought to respond to ongoing tensions in the city, which one of the initiating organisations IDEAA Mostar—an organisation established to explore the relationship between urban design and social life in the city—saw as a product of uneven reconstruction and a lack of public and cultural facilities which impacted the cultural life of Mostar. For IDEAA Mostar (2019), this context perpetuated the lack of trust within and between communities and ultimately the situation of division in Mostar. To overcome these tensions, the association sought to identify and rehabilitate spaces for arts and culture.

The Partizan Playground was selected as a site for restoration. Speaking with the director of IDEAA Mostar in 2019, they drew connection between the physical space of the playground and the memory of its past usage, drawing attention to its role as a lively, open space for encounter. During the socialist period, the playground and its adjacent buildings were run by the Partizan society, operating as a cultural hub where youth could practise sports and engage in other arts and cultural activities (Director 2019). In terms of the memory of place, the director's narrative spatialises what Palmberger (2016) has termed ruptured biography. For the older generation who had lived in Mostar during the socialist period, the Partizan Playground had significant memories, but for the post-war generations the site was nothing special—it was simply an abandoned playground (IDEAA Mostar 2021a). Within IDEAA Mostar's approach, the city was understood at the intersections of the built environment, its social use and the memories connected to place: 'the city is what we feel'. For the director, it was important to begin to connect the memory of space with the contemporary context, both through its physical renewal and through engaging people in activity at the site. In doing so, the initiative aimed to connect its past, present and future users (Director 2019). These efforts are disruptive of international framings of the post-war peace which have placed focus on inter-ethnic reconciliation. In this initiative, focus is instead shifted toward connecting stories between generations in place.

In 2019, after gaining permission to work on the plot from the city council, IDEAA Mostar began to develop plans for the renovation. The initial stages involved cleaning and clearing the playground and involved collaboration between Dsrifv Partizan,[2] SAFMO and an international group of architects and volunteers from the local community.[3] Materials to support the renovation were supplied by Baumit.ba. This initial step aimed to transform the playground into an accessible and usable space that could be used by young people in Mostar. Speaking to one of the festival organisers about the collaboration, they argued that it was 'good to work in those places [...] To build something. You never know what might happen there' (Festival Organiser 2020).

Street art was actively engaged in the early stages of the renovation to make the space more appealing to young people. SAFMO supported a workshop hosted by IDEAA Mostar which engaged young people in painting murals at the playground. An international group of architects from Berlin helped to paint the playground, using a traditional Bosnian *ćilim* pattern in blue and yellow, echoing the colours of the BiH flag. As a pattern most often associated with carpets, this pattern can be read as a symbol of comfort and home. In another part of the workshop, led by Zagreb-based artist MANE MEI, the walls of the playground were painted in a brightly coloured, circular pattern. A piece written in the same style reads *'sevap'*, a word of Turkish origin referring to divine reward for a good deed. This again conveys a sense of warmth, along with the hope that the act of clearing, cleaning and painting the playground will enable the continued use and transformation of the site. Driven from the grassroots, the workshop received support from European Cultural Foundation and Baumit.ba.

At the workshop, IDEAA Mostar also hosted a session which invited young people to engage in a creative mapping process to help re-imagine the space and its future usage, with ideas noting its potential as a music space, as a botanical garden and for other artistic and sporting activities.[4] These ideas were then fed into the project 'Partizan in Mostar. Thinking BiH' which set out the framework for the site's rehabilitation (IDEAA Mostar 2019).

In 2020, SAFMO further engaged in the reactivation of the Partizan Playground, curating several collaborative murals, as well as hosting other exhibitions and events at the site as part of the larger programme. The murals created in 2020 were produced by street and graffiti artists from across BiH, many of whom had previously contributed to the festival. One mural was a collaboration between graffiti artists STF Crew and Lack which depicted a futuristic version of Mostar, with an eye rising like the sun over the Neretva. Below this, the artists each sprayed their tags in graffiti lettering. Speaking to one of the members of STC Crew about the mural, they noted that it was important 'to show it [the city] as one single piece' and that it was 'similar from both sides' (Street Artist 4 2020). While the piece echoes the problematic narratives of unity that have become attached to Stari Most, its representation here reappropriates this narrative, with Stari Most coming to stand for a hope that the city will remain united.

The spatial transformation of the Partizan Playground is an ongoing process. The areas surrounding the playground have been made accessible, but the surrounding buildings remain largely in ruin. The curating of street art has been a significant part of the spatial transformation of the Partizan Playground to the extent that the festival organisers direct artistic agency at the site through the festival events. With two years of activity, work continues at the site to connect its past and present and to reimagine it anew. At present, it is possible to say that the mobilisation of a grassroots network for peace has begun a process of curating spatial transformation which has the potential to create the space as a 'place of aggregation, sharing and gathering accessible to all' (IDEAA Mostar 2021b).

Alekse Šantića street

Through curatorial agency, Alekse Šantića street has become one of Mostar's open-air galleries, enacting processes of place- and space-making. Murals have been produced on this street since the establishment of SAFMO in 2012, curated on public walls, the premises of OKC Abrašević and on residential buildings. This curating intervenes in a longer trajectory of multi-ethnic mobilisation in place, with murals contributing to broadening spatial imaginaries beyond simplistic notions of division and reconciliation.

Alekse Šantića street is an urban palimpsest, encompassing multiple layers of dis/connection. As Kuftinec notes (1998, 83), prior to the war, the street acted as 'a main thoroughfare and pedestrian route' into the city. However, during the 1990s, the street acted as a frontline for the conflict, leaving traces of violence which have been 'slow to disappear' (Calame and Charlesworth 2009, 9). Its positioning during the war meant that it was badly bombed and shelled, with many buildings left to ruin. Residents who lived in the apartment blocks were forced to leave their homes, many of whom were displaced within Mostar (Vetters 2007, 201–3).

Following the Rome Agreement in 1996, Alekse Šantića street was designated part of the Central Zone. In the Central Zone, contestations over territorial and shared space stalled much needed reconstruction works. While the EUAM sought to prioritise rebuilding of key infrastructure in this area (Björkdahl 2012, 11–12), many buildings were left in ruin. While rebuilding efforts funded by partisan sources had proliferated in east and west Mostar, residents with homes in the Central Zone were confronted with an 'administrative no-man's land' in terms of responsibilities over rebuilding (Vetters 2007, 199). In 2001, the issue came to a head when one of the Alekse Šantića street apartment buildings was threatened with destruction. A multi-ethnic coalition of residents successfully defended their building. In doing so, they mobilised a larger constituency to fight for their claim to their home (Ibid., 200).

When, in 2004, the OHR issued a statute enabling the administrative reunification of the city, the residents were given renewed momentum. The statute specifically addressed the infrastructural underinvestment in the former Central Zone, with provisions to ensure funding was more fairly apportioned (OHR 2004, Art. 56). In 2005, the Alekse Šantića street residents engaged in a series of protests outside their former homes and the city administration. Forging alliances with other inhabitants who sought to assert their right to buildings located within the former Central Zone, the Alekse Šantića street residents eventually found support for their claim from the local Ombudsman (Vetters 2007, 200).

Alekse Šantića street became a focal point for activism in the city, particularly for those who sought to transform space in ways that reached beyond division in Mostar. The residents' struggle can be located within grassroots efforts to establish shared space within Mostar's Central Zone. The residents' campaign was concurrent with the initiative by the cultural centre OKC Abrašević to establish property rights over the old socialist club on Alekse Šantića street (Forde 2016), with the centre envisioned as a space which would enable forms of meeting and social negotiation beyond the city's ethnic division (Kappler 2014, 129). Inspired by the legacy of multi-ethnic mobilisation, curating by SAFMO on Alekse Šantića street can then be understood as contributing to processes of space-making which emphasise the importance of shared spaces of encounter.

Many of the murals on the street avoid the depiction of potentially contentious topics, particularly those which evoke memories of war and division. Instead, murals often contain images of nature or abstract forms. Discussing the need for positive imagery, one of the festival organisers referenced the residents' struggle. They noted that while the buildings had been reconstructed, the process of rebuilding had largely focused on the outside. They continued that when the residents got their apartments, they needed to invest significantly to make the building into a home: the building was 'only cover, [...] only a façade' (Festival Organiser 2020). One way that festival organisers supported the residents was through curating several murals on the external walls of the apartment buildings. A conversation with one street artist who had painted on Alekse Šantića street in 2020 highlighted the importance of SAFMO's positive curatorial line. Leading up to the festival, the artist discussed their ideas for the mural, noting that most 'connected to the history and to the war and the lack of [...] human understanding' within it. However, the organisers had asked them to avoid these topics since residents were confronted with them on a day-to-day basis. The street artist concluded that residents needed 'something different. They need art [...] that is not putting the pressure on the viewer [...]. Let's just make something beautiful and leave it at that' (Street Artist 3 2020).

The curating of murals on Alekse Šantića street contributes to processes of space-making through reference to significant figures of shared heritage from Mostar and beyond. In this sense, the murals are embedded within wider socio-political and memorial discourses in Mostar. For example, SAFMO has curated two murals which connect to the legacy of Aleksa Šantić—a late nineteenth and early twentieth century Serb writer from Mostar—after whom the street is named. In recent history, Aleksa Šantić has been a celebrated and contested figure within Mostar. While his writings focused on a range of topics including social injustice, nostalgia and Serb language and culture in Mostar, he has been particularly revered for his writings on the city and the Neretva River (Makaš 2007, 316–17). When Mostar came under siege by the figure engaged in the promotion of Serb nationalism, his memory was erased from public space in Mostar (Ibid., 317). During the coalition of the Croatian Defence Force and Bosnian Army, Alekse Šantića street was briefly renamed 'Ricina' in tribute to a former communist leader of Yugoslavia. When the coalition broke down in 1993 when the Croatian Defence Force claimed the west side of the city, the street was renamed 'Dr. Mile Budaka' after a figure within the Ustaša movement, a Croatian fascist organisation active during the Second World War (Kufitnec 1998, 83). The part of the street that remained in Bosnian Army's territory—later forming part of the Central Zone—was returned to its prewar name: Alekse Šantića street (Makaš 2007, 318). In this sense, the street itself also became a marker of division.

In the postwar period, Šantić's memory was rehabilitated. In 2002, Mostar City Council re-erected a monument to Šantić, an initiative which received support from politicians, journalists and residents of Mostar alike. Residents were positive about the statue's return, noting that it was 'tragic' that the statue had been removed and indicating pride in the city's council for the decision to return the monument (Ibid., 320). Today, the memory of Šantić is celebrated in Mostar, with a 'museum, a plaque, a literary festival, a park, [and] a bust' dedicated to him (Ibid., 322). This symbolic return gestures toward the possibility of shared heritage and, for some, indicates hope for a return to a multi-ethnic community.

Two murals that were part of the 2017 and 2019 editions of the festival were connected to the memory of Šantić. In 2019, LDA Mostar provided support for several murals in the festival as part of their contribution to the EU-funded regional project 'CLINK – Cultural heritage linking diversities in Europe'. The project aimed to promote public engagement with cultural heritage, with an emphasis on the exploration and artistic reproduction of cultural heritage (LDA Mostar 2021). The mural was a photo-realistic portrait of Šantić and was painted by Deni Božić, a street artist from Doboj. As a figure who signals the possibility of shared heritage, its placement on this residential building on Alekse Šantića street engages in a practice of space making to the extent that it produces the street as a space that can be viewed beyond wartime division and contestation.

In 2017, Uruguayan street artists Colectivo Licuado and AlfALfa painted a mural on the street (Figure 4.1). Following the artists' commitment to depict themes of 'cultural diversity' and 'stories that belong to the place where we paint' (Colectivo Licuado n.d.), the mural depicts two figures each holding a site of cultural heritage in the palm of their hand. The figure on the right holds Stari Most and the figure on the left holds Tara Kulesi, an Ottoman-era defensive tower on the east riverbank which is now used as the site for the Museum of the Old Bridge. Responding to the image of the mural, some commentators suggested that the figure on the left bore a striking resemblance to Anka

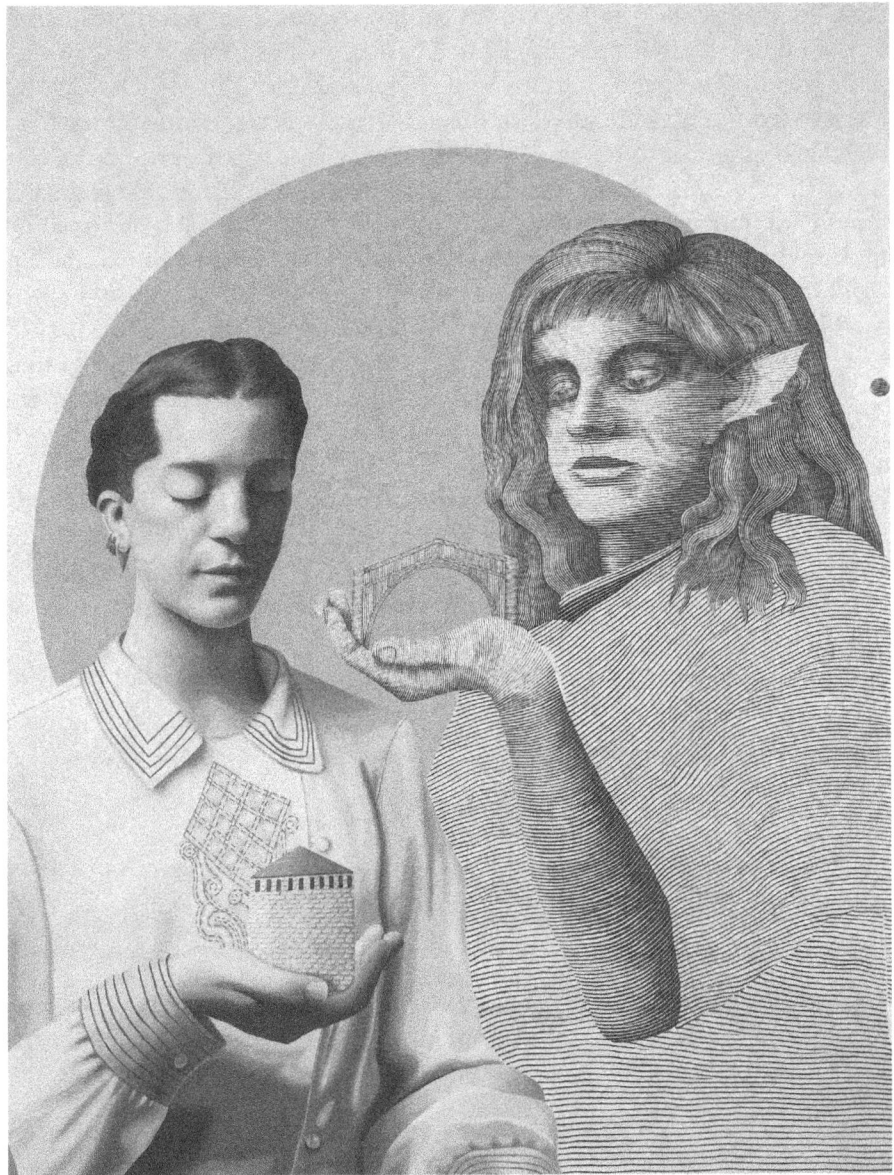

Figure 4.1 Mural by Coletivo Licuado & AlfAlfa (Uruguay). Photo: Lydia
C. Cole, 2019.

Tomlinović, a woman to whom Šantić wrote love poems. Meanwhile, the figure on the right is depicted in AlfALfa's signature style, collaging human and animal-like forms to create mythical beings (Street Art News 2021), and conjures an aquatic aesthetic, linking symbolically to the Neretva River. The composition is suggestive of how both act as custodians of Mostar's heritage.

Drawing connections to the past, the mural suggests a more complex narrative of heritage than those engaged by international peacebuilders.

Continuing to invoke narratives of shared space within Mostar, SAFMO has curated murals which link to the networks of social connection which reach across ethnic and national lines in the city. As part of the 2018 edition of SAFMO, Brazilian artist Aleksandro Reis produced a mural featuring renowned Italian opera singer Luciano Pavarotti (Figure 4.2). As an iconic figure within classical music, Pavarotti is known for his humanitarian work in the Pavarotti & Friends benefit concerts. In 1995, Pavarotti hosted a concert for BiH, with the proceeds donated to establish the Muzički Centar Pavarotti (Pavarotti Music Centre) in 1997. The Rock School that was established by the centre in 2012 can be understood as a shared space in that it facilitates 'social connections across ethnic boundaries', as well as national ones, since its programme now includes international students from the United World College (Forde 2019, 157–60). The aesthetic content of the mural emphasises this internationalised idea of shared space. The background of the piece is made up of the Bosnian-Herzegovinian national flag in yellow and blue with white stars, as well as a depiction of traditional Bosnian weaving patterns, which have been painted in bright colours reminiscent of Brazilian carnival. In this sense, Pavarotti is an

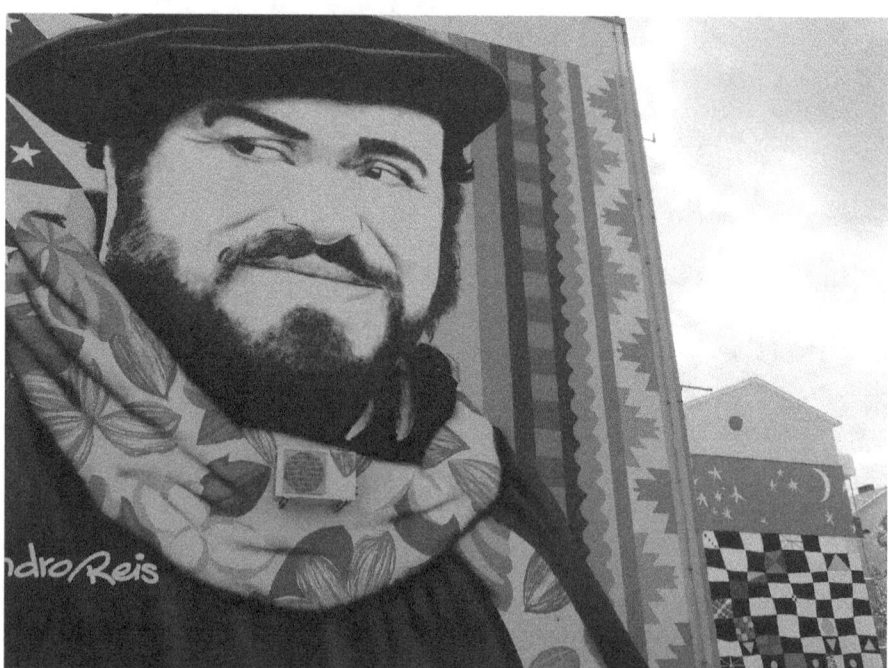

Figure 4.2 Pavarotti, by Aleksandro Reis (Brazil). Photo by Lydia C. Cole, 2019.

international icon associated with ideas of shared space and shared heritage in Mostar.

Viewed cumulatively, curating the Alekse Šantića street area has had the effect of re-making meanings of place and spatial imaginaries in Mostar. The striking, identifiable characters featured within the murals provide ways for residents to circumvent contestations over street names. On this, the organisers reflected how people in Mostar use the visual content of murals as spatial markers: 'They don't tell someone come here in the street of Mile Budaka or whatever. [Instead, they say] Come here to the mural of Pavarotti. Come here to the mural' (Festival Organiser 2020). This effect has been particularly pronounced on Alekse Šantića street, where the murals are curated in such a way as to lead its viewers 'from the bus station [...] to the old city and the west part', offering a 'connection' through the city (Ibid.). Thus, SAFMO organisers curate in ways that reconnect viewers to the past of Alekse Šantića street as a central thoroughfare in the city. In this way, SAFMO not only curate to spatially transform local spaces for art and culture as we have seen in the previous section, but also curate in ways that shift the ideas that are associated with the 'infrastructure of public space' (Ibid.). In this sense, curating at Alekse Šantića street engages in both place- and space-making in ways that re-connect the (hi)stories of the city to its inhabitants.

Conclusion

The curatorial agency of SAFMO embodies the arts' radical potential to effect change, particularly where embedded in grassroots struggles. This chapter has traced the cases of the Partizan Playground and Alekse Šantića street, revealing the ways that curatorial agency has been engaged for spatial transformation. In the case of the Partizan Playground, SAFMO intervened in a grassroots initiative to revitalise an abandoned playground near Stari Most. Having been neglected within the broader international and city rebuilding initiatives, the site was nevertheless significant as a meeting space for youth in the city. Through connecting with the memories of its past use and the users of the space in the present, SAFMO facilitated the site's clearing, street arts workshops and new murals at the playground. In this, curatorial agency was put toward place-making, a process which is still ongoing. At Alekse Šantića street, the curators of SAFMO intervened in multiple layers of history and activism, including contestations over the street's name and the legacy of grassroots multiethnic mobilisation by residents for reconstruction of their homes. Festival organisers sought to curate positive messages on the buildings, particularly those which represent Mostar's shared history. In doing so, SAFMO intervened in a history of multi-ethnic activism on the street, depicting figures of shared and internationalised heritage to reshape its difficult history. The murals on Alekse Šantića street reinforce a more complex notion of commonality in ways that shift everyday perceptions and movement in urban space.

Curatorial agency in SAFMO contributes to *artpeace* formation by transforming spatial politics in Mostar. It aims to curate in ways that foster ideas of space and place as connected, while refusing to narrate connection solely in terms of ethno-national reconciliation. Over time, the festival's curating has become increasingly internationalised, with organisers strategically engaging with international peacebuilding frames, particularly that of democratisation, Europeanisation and reconciliation. Nevertheless, curatorial agency remains grounded in local priorities and activisms to direct spatial transformation. In this sense, curatorial agency hybridises processes of arttransformation in order to create space for local spatial imaginaries within Mostar's status quo peace. SAFMO curators spatially transform the city in ways that create spaces for art and community to flourish.

Notes

1. The term *urbicide* describes the widespread and deliberate destruction of the urban environment (Coward 2008).
2. An association established for the Partizan Playground in 2019.
3. Photos of the action are viewable on the Street Arts Festival Mostar Facebook page, June 4, 2019: https://www.facebook.com/StreetArtsFestivalMostar/photos/2188518067901080 (accessed 8 August 2022).
4. Maps from the workshop are documented on the IDEAA Mostar Facebook page, September 3 2021: https://www.facebook.com/ideaamostar/photos/740473069724437; https://www.facebook.com/ideaamostar/photos/740473063057771; https://www.facebook.com/ideaamostar/photos/740473046391106 (accessed 8 August 2022).

References

Abadžija, M. 2018. Marina Đapić: Političarke su nevidljive. *Oslobodjenje*, 1 August. https://www.oslobodjenje.ba/vijesti/bih/marina-dapic-politicarke-su-nevidljive-382152 (accessed 15 July 2021).

Armaly, M., C. Blasi, and L. Hannah. 2004. Stari Most: Rebuilding more than a historic bridge in Mostar. *Museum International*, 56(4), pp. 6–17.

Bell, C. 2009. Sarajevska zima: A festival amid war debris in Sarajevo, Bosnia-Herzegovina. *Space and Culture*, 12(1), pp. 136–42.

Belloni, R., S. Kappler, and J. Ramović. 2016. Bosnia-Herzegovina: Domestic agency and the inadequacy of the liberal peace. In Richmond, O. P. and Pogodda, S. (eds) *Post-liberal peace transitions: Between peace formation and state formation*. Edinburgh: Edinburgh University Press, e-Book.

Bilkic, M. 2018. Emplacing hate: Turbulent graffscapes and linguistic violence in post-war Bosnia-Herzegovina. *Linguistic Landscape*, 4(1), pp. 1–28.

Björkdahl, A. 2012. The EU administration of Mostar: Implications for the EU's evolving peacebuilding approach. *Australian-New Zealand Journal of European Studies*, 4(1), pp. 2–17.

Björkdahl, A. 2013. Urban peacebuilding. *Peacebuilding*, 1(2), pp. 207–21.

Björkdahl, A. and K. Höglund. 2013. Precarious peacebuilding: Friction in global–local encounters. *Peacebuilding*, 1(3), pp. 289–99.

Björkdahl, A. and Kappler, S. 2017. *Peacebuilding and spatial transformation: Peace, space and place.* Oxon: Routledge.

Björkdahl, A. and J. Mannergren Selimovic. 2016. A tale of three bridges: Agency and agonism in peace building. *Third World Quarterly*, 37(2), pp. 321–35.

Calame, J. and E. Charlesworth. 2009. *Divided cities: Belfast, Beirut, Jerusalem, Mostar, and Nicosia.* Philadelphia: University of Pennsylvania Press.

Carabelli, G. 2018. *The divided city and the grassroots: The (un)making of ethnic divisions in Mostar.* London: Palgrave Macmillan, e-Book.

Carabelli, G. 2020. Grassroots activism in the divided city: Re-appropriating space with art practice in Mostar (BiH). *Sectarianism, Proxies & De-sectarianisation (SEPAD): Interventions,* 5 March. https://www.sepad.org.uk/announcement/grassroots-activism-in-the-divided-city-re-appropriating-space-with-art-practice-in-mostar-bih (accessed 15 July 2021).

Carabelli, G., A. Djurasovic, and R. Summa. 2019. Challenging the representation of ethnically divided cities: Perspectives from Mostar. *Space and Polity*, 23(2), pp. 116–24.

Colectivo Licuado. n.d. Portfolio. https://www.colectivolicuado.com/ (accessed 8 August 2022).

Coward, M.. 2008. *Urbicide: The politics of urban destruction.* London: Routledge.

de Certeau, M. 1984. *The practice of everyday life.* Berkeley, CA: University of California Press.

Deiana, M. 2020. Undoing EU security through the art of failure: Cinematic imaginations in/from the post-Yugoslav space. *Critical Studies on Security*, Online First.

Forde, S. 2016. The bridge on the Neretva: Stari Most as a stage of memory in post-conflict Mostar, Bosnia–Herzegovina. *Cooperation and Conflict*, 1(4), pp. 467–83.

Forde, S. 2019. *Movement as conflict transformation: Rescripting Mostar, Bosnia-Herzegovina.* Cham: Palgrave Macmillan, e-Book.

Haworth, B. T., E. Bruce, and K. Iveson. 2013. Spatio-temporal analysis of graffiti occurrence in an inner-city urban environment. *Applied Geography*, 38, pp. 53–63.

Helms, E. 2013. *Innocence and victimhood: Gender, nation, and women's activism in postwar Bosnia-Herzegovina.* Madison, WI: The University of Wisconsin Press.

Hooper-Greenhill, E. 2003. *Museums and the shaping of knowledge.* London: Routledge.

Hromadzić, A. 2013. Discourses of trans-ethnic narod in postwar Bosnia and Herzegovina. *Nationalities Papers: The Journal of Nationalism and Ethnicity*, 41(2), pp. 259–75.

IDEAA Mostar. 2021a. Partizan Mostar. https://www.ideaa-mostar.com/en/portfolio/partizan-mostar/ (accessed 15 July 2021).

IDEAA Mostar. 2021b. Green design biennale. https://www.ideaa-mostar.com/en/portfolio/green-design-biennale/ (accessed 15 July 2021).

IDEAA Mostar 2019. Partizan in Mostar. Thinking BiH. 19 September. https://www.ideaa-mostar.com/en/partizan-in-mostar-thinking-bih/ (accessed 15 July 2021).

Irvine, M. 2012. The work on the street: Street art and visual culture. In Heywood, I. and Sandywell, B. (eds) *The Handbook of Visual Culture.* London: Berg, pp. 235–78.

Jovan, D. 2001. The disintegration of Yugoslavia: A critical review of explanatory approaches. *European Journal of Social Theory*, 4(1), pp. 101–20.

Kappler, S. 2014. *Local agency and peacebuilding: EU and international engagement in Bosnia-Herzegovina, Cyprus and South Africa.* Basingstoke: Palgrave Macmillan.

Kappler, S. 2017. Sarajevo's ambivalent memoryscape: Spatial stories of peace and conflict. *Memory Studies*, 10(2), pp. 130–43.

Kappler, S. and A. McKane. 2019. 'Post-conflict curating': The arts and politics of Belfast's peace walls. *de arte*, 54(2), pp. 4–21.

Kappler, S., O.P. Richmond and B. Vogel. 2023. Introduction. In Vogel, B., Kappler, S. and O.P. Richmond *Art of peaceformation: Arts-based social movements, blockages and curation.* Edinburgh: Edinburgh University Press.

Kesby, M. 2005. Retheorizing empowerment-through-participation as a performance in space: Beyond tyranny to transformation. *Signs: Journal of Women in Culture and Society*, 30(4), pp. 2037–65.

Kotecki, K. 2014. Europeanizing the Balkans at the Sarajevo Film Festival. *Journal of Narrative Theory*, 44(3), pp. 344–66.

Kuftinec, S. 1998. [Walking through a] ghost town: Cultural hauntologie in Mostar, Bosnia-Herzegovina or Mostar: A performance review. *Text and Performance Quarterly*, 18(2), pp. 81–95.

Laketa, S. 2019. The politics of landscape as ways of life in the 'divided' city: Reflections from Mostar, Bosnia–Herzegovina. *Space and Polity*, 23(2), pp. 168–81.

Lang, L. and U. McInerney. 1999. Music therapy at the Pavarotti Music Centre, Mostar, Bosnia. *Nordic Journal of Music Therapy*, 8(2), pp. 186–7.

LDA Mostar. 2021. CLINK - Cultural heritage linking diversities in Europe. https://www.ldamo star.org/en/portfolio/clink-cultural-heritage-linking-diversities-in-europe-en/ (accessed 15 July 2021).

Mac Ginty, R. and Richmond, O. 2013. The local turn in peace building: A critical agenda for peace. *Third World Quarterly*, 34(5), pp. 763–83.

Makaš, E.G. 2007. *Representing competing identities: Building and rebuilding in postwar Mostar, Bosnia-Hercegovina*. PhD Thesis, Ithaca, NY: Cornell University.

Massey, D. 2001. *Space, Place, and Gender*. Minneapolis, MN: University of Minnesota Press.

Massey, D. 2005. *For Space*. London: Sage Publications.

Mostar Rock School. 2021. Historijat. https://mostarrockschool.org/historijat/ (accessed 15 July 2021).

Obradovic-Wochnik, J. and Bird, G. 2020. The everyday at the border: Examining visual, material and spatial intersections of international politics along the 'Balkan Route' *Cooperation and Conflict*, 55(1), pp. 41–65.

OHR. 2004. Decision enacting the statute of the city of Mostar. 28 January. http://www.ohr.int/ decision-enacting-the-statute-of-the-city-of-mostar/ (accessed 15 July 2021).

Palmberger, M. 2016. *How generations remember: Conflicting histories and shared memories in postwar Bosnia and Herzegovina*. Basingstoke: Palgrave Macmillan, e-Book.

Richmond, O. P. 2013. Peace formation and local infrastructures for peace. *Alternatives: Global, Local, Political*, 38(4), pp. 271–87.

Schacter, R. 2014. The ugly truth: Street art, graffiti and the creative city. *Art & The Public Sphere*, 3(2), pp. 161–76.

Shepherd, L. 2011. Sex, security and superhero(in)es: From 1325 to 1820 and beyond. *International Feminist Journal of Politics*, 13(4), pp. 504–21.

SAFMO. 2021. About Festival. https://streetartsfestivalmostar.com/about-festival/ (accessed 15 July 2021).

Street Art News. 2021. 'The Haretoise' & 'The Ladybug' by AlfALfa in Alberta and Quebec, Canada. 15 January. https://streetartnews.net/2021/01/the-haretoise-the-ladybug-by-alfal fa-in-alberta-and-quebec-canada.html (accessed 15 July 2021).

Strange, C. and M. Kempa. 2003. Shades of dark tourism: Alcatraz and Robben Island. *Annals of Tourism Research*, 30(2), pp. 386–405.

Ulmer, J. B. 2017. Writing urban space: Street art, democracy, and photographic cartography. *Cultural Studies ↔ Critical Methodologies*, 17(6), pp. 491–502.

UNESCO. 2005. The Old Bridge Area of the City of Mostar 15th of July. *World Heritage Scanned Nomination*, 15 July.

Vetters, L. 2007. The power of administrative categories: Emerging notions of citizenship in the divided city of Mostar. *Ethnopolitics*, 6(2), pp. 187–209.

Vogel, B. 2016. Civil society capture: Top-down interventions from below? *Journal of Intervention and Statebuilding*, 10(4), pp. 472–89.

Vogel, B., C. Arthur, E. Lepp, D. O'Driscoll and B. T. Haworth. 2020. Reading socio-political and spatial dynamics through graffiti in conflict-affected societies. *Third World Quarterly*, 41(12), pp. 2148–68.

Yarwood, J. 1999. *Rebuilding Mostar: Urban reconstruction in a war zone*. Liverpool: Liverpool University Press.

Youth Power. n.d. Youth Art Movement - YAM. https://eng.youth-power.org/projects/youth-art-movement-yam/ (accessed 15 July 2021).

Zelizer, C. 2003. The Role of Artistic Processes in Peace-Building in Bosnia-Herzegovina. *Peace and Conflict Studies*, 10(2), pp. 62–75.

Interviews

Director, IDEAA Mostar: Urban House. 2019. 27 September. Conversation.

Festival Organiser. 2020. 25 February, 2020. Mostar, Bosnia and Herzegovina.

Musician. 2020. 6 May. Via Zoom.

Representative, LDA Mostar. 2019. 26 September, 2019. Mostar Bosnia and Herzegovina.

Street Artist 1. 2020. 1 December. Via Zoom.

Street Artist 2. 2020. 12 November. Via Zoom.

Street Artist 3. 2020. 10 November. Via Zoom.

Street Artist 4. 2020. 6 December. Via Zoom.

FIVE

Behind the Image: Exploring Aesthetic Tensions of Peace Formation Through Hip Hop in Medellín

Teresa Ó Brádaigh Bean

'Regarding the issue of violence, we attempted to neutralise it by strengthening the independent musical ascetic of rappers and hip hoppers...' (Salazar 2011)

This statement immediately invites further reflection on the nexus between hip hop as a form of popular culture, community-led peace formation, and government policy for dealing with micro conflicts. The Colombian city of Medellín, once known as the most violent city in the world in the 1990s, has been transformed over the past three decades, gaining an international reputation as a model city for urban and social development and participatory democracy (Hylton 2007; Brand and Dávila 2011; McClean 2015; Brough 2020). Whilst much of the focus has been on the role of public policy and formal political strategies in shaping this change, the role of young community actors, and in particular hip hop movements, in the development of peace has been often overlooked.

This is perhaps because hip hop culture is not obviously or necessarily understood as part of strategies for grassroots peace movements or policies for peace. Firstly, hip hop consists of MCing, graffiti, DJing and breakdancing activities that are not are not considered inherently political in nature. Secondly, hip hop culture is generally produced and consumed by the youth, a demographic category that is not noted for their formal participation in peace formation. Thus, it is often regarded as a youth subculture, a temporary fashion or fad, forming part of a ritual for young people as they transition to adulthood. Watkins (1998), for example, comments on both the uniqueness and inconspicuous nature of hip hop as a movement for social transformation due to these features. However, within the literature, there is an increasing body of work that explores the contribution of popular culture in peace and conflict studies (Bräuchler 2018; McEvoy-Levy 2018; Press-Barnathan 2017; Lundqvist 2020). Indeed, as part of this discussion of what has been termed the cultural turn, McEvoy-Levy notes that there is much more continuity between pop culture, political activism and policy than might be at first assumed.

Thus, building on this development, this chapter will seek to demonstrate why and how hip hop emerged with peace formation in Medellín, whilst also addressing some of the limitations of the movement. The chapter will trace the local conditions that facilitated the evolution of hip hop in the city and explore its role in socio-cultural and political transformation. Here I will contend that hip hop facilitates '*artivism*', in which peace is formed through the creation of alternative spaces, socialisation and identities that subtly and indirectly resist and challenge structures and cultures of violence. This is achieved through socialisation into values of non-violence, tolerance and coexistence as well as exposing children and young people to alternative role models and to image and advocacy for alternative futures. Moving on, the chapter will then argue that the absence of the rule of law, exemplified by the prevailing presence of armed groups in the city and the state's continued co-existence with these groups, has limited the transformational potential of hip hop. To illustrate this, an exploration of the outcomes of hip hop in both formal and informal political spaces will be undertaken, analysing interactions with these centres of power. The chapter will conclude by reflecting on how both institutional and informal centres of power act to limit the effectiveness of hip hop's potential contribution to the processes of peace formation in Medellín and in Colombia.

Context

For over six decades Medellín has been a significant site for Colombia's multifaceted conflicts involving the state, right-wing paramilitaries, left-wing guerrillas as well as narco and criminal actors.[1] However, the 1980s marked the beginning of a critical period for the city punctuated by increasing political instability, the decline in the textile industry in the region and the rising dominance of drug cartels, and criminal and paramilitary groups (Andreas et al. 1991; Salazar and Jaramillo 1992). These conditions coupled with widespread political and institutional corruption and clientelism led to the weakening of the state, most notably in terms of law and order, justice and security (Pécaut 2001; Hylton 2010; Riaño Alcalá 2010; Alcaldía de Medellín 2011; Baird 2012).

The infiltration of 'illegitimate' actors into the state apparatus created the conditions in which the state withdrew from peripheral, poorer areas of the city, such as Comuna 13. Concurrently, these areas were becoming increasingly populated with displaced people fleeing conflicts in rural areas of the province of Antioquía. As a consequence of this rapid and unplanned population growth, coupled with state neglect, these areas became, in effect, an informal city outside of the official local government structures. Moreover, against this backdrop of an absent state and weak rule of law, these areas fell into the hands of illicit, non-state actors. Paramilitary groups, along with drug and criminal gangs, enforced private justice in an atmosphere of lawlessness where authority was imposed by violent force and extortion (Rozema 2007; Alcaldía de Medellín 2011). Consequently, in some communities, self-defence associations emerged to eradicate petty crime and criminal gangs from these neighbourhoods.

During this period, these non-state actors behaved in effect as proxy state actors, providing essential services and executing state functions. For example, the Medellín Cartel provided infrastructure, hospitals, housing, sports facilities, schools and roads in peripheral areas of the city (Salazar 1990; Nieves 1997; Moser and McIlwaine 2004; Riaño Alcalá 2010). Likewise, criminal and drug organisations provided employment in construction (Salazar 1990; Nieves 1997; Moser and McIlwaine 2004; Riaño Alcalá 2010) as well as generating a labour market for hitmen, money laundering, debt collection and arms dealing (Pécaut 2001).

It is important to examine the role of the state as a key actor of violence during this period. In the face of the dominance of violent criminal and political actors such as the Medellín Cartel, the role of the state as a violent actor is often neglected in analysis of the conflict in Medellín in the 80s and 90s (Maclean 2015). However, how the state chose to respond to and facilitate violence is important to understanding how both these forms of violence developed and the fluid nature of the relationship between non-state and state actors. The contradictory positions of the state as a supposed opponent of non-state, criminal violence, a collaborator with non-state actors, such as paramilitaries, and a perpetrator of its own forms of 'legitimate' violence created multifaceted, overlapping and fluid forms and patterns of violence (Bagley 2001; Melguizo and Cronshaw 2001; Civico 2012). Lines between criminal, political and state sponsored acts of violence and legitimate use of force by the state were blurred, presenting obvious challenges in classifying the topography of violence. The collusion between state forces and the right-wing paramilitary group during 'Operation Orión' is an example of the fluidity of these mutually reinforcing dynamics. Operation Orión was part of a series of joint military operations between Colombian forces and paramilitaries to expel left wing guerrillas from Comuna 13 in 2002. The intervention led to the displacements, illegal detentions, disappearance and death of civilians in Comuna 13. Acknowledging these blurred lines between power agents is vital in understanding the emergence, development and trajectory of hip hop. It is these interactions with the various structures and actors and the outcomes of such engagement that this chapter will seek to examine.

The death of Pablo Escobar and the demise of the Medellín Cartel in 1993 fundamentally altered the dynamics of violence in the city. Violence became more fractured, with the emergence of numerous mainly localised gangs. The evolution of the Oficina de Envigado, a protection and debt collection service established by the Medellín Cartel, from a single large structure to a confederation of 200 organisations typifies this dispersal of the structures of violence. Despite the increase in actors, violence became less intense. Homicide rates continued to decline into the 2000s, a trend which remained constant (Medina, Posso and Tamayo 2011; Llorente and Guarín León 2013).[2] This general decline in violence has been attributed to a range of factors, notably, the dispersal of criminal gangs, the disbanding of paramilitary organisations, the expulsion and demobilisation of the Fuerzas Armadas Revolucionarias de Colombia (FARC) and Ejército de Liberación Nacional (The National Liberation Army), as well as pacts between rival gangs, and improved security and police operations (Giraldo-Ramírez and Preciado-Restrepo 2015).

The patterns of violence in the city today have continued on this trajectory. Armed groups operate across the city in complex and sophisticated structures which are entangled in local and national networks of narco-paramilitarism and organised crime.[3] In 2020, it was estimated that there were 15–20 large gangs (*bandas*) operating in collaboration with 350 local gangs (*combos*). Like their predecessors, these actors are engaged in a variety of activities associated with the drug trade and sub-sectors including protection rackets, extortion, forced displacement and recruitment of children and young people into prostitution and gangs. These criminal gangs work in parallel to the state, exercising control in communities and performing state functions such as providing security to businesses, resolving conflicts between neighbours or administering justice (Rozema 2008; Doyle 2016; Blattman et al. 2020). Moreover, the local academic Ángela Garcés Montoya remarked that state actors continue to collude and pay criminal gangs to gain advantages during elections:

> Even the state, behind the scenes, negotiated with them [emerging criminal gangs—Bandas Criminales Emergentes (BACRIM)[4]] so that it would bring calm. Once the elections take place, then violence flares up again. We are calm because everyone is paying. (Ángela Garcés Montoya 2019)

Thus, it is apparent that the decline in violence has not translated into strong institutions, an effective rule of law or good governance. Rather periods of violence can be understood as a part of a strategy of co-existence orchestrated by the state and criminal actors and reflecting the continued entangled and blurring of lines between 'legitimate' and 'illegitimate' centres of power.

A salient and prevailing trend of conflict since the 1970s has been the important role played by young people, both as victims and perpetrators of violence. This is reflected in homicide statistics in which the average age of murder victims in 2018 was 24 years old, with males from lower socio-economic backgrounds from the peripheral areas disproportionately more likely to be affected (Yepes 2018). This enduring demographic feature of the conflict is important in accounting for the emergence and viability of hip hop as a repertoire for peace formation.

Hip Hop: The 'Global Organiser' and Peace Movements of the 1990s

Hip hop arrived in Medellín as a commercial form of popular culture from the United States of America (USA) in the late 1980s/early 1990s. However, there are competing accounts about how this occurred in the peripheral areas of the city. Some local artists attribute the movement of *'Paisas'* (colloquial terms for people from Antioquia province) returning to Medellín with cassettes and magazines from the USA (Alejandro Rodriguez Alvarez 2020), whilst others recall the arrival of television in the peripheral areas and the broadcasting of breakdancing films, such as *Beat Street* as their initial contact with hip hop (El Flaco 2019). Tickner's research supports these assertions, noting that the role of Colombian migration networks in New York and Miami and the availability of mainstream films were key in the development of hip hop in Colombia's major cities (Tickner 2008). These channels also enabled a number of developments in US hip hop to influence the development of hip hop as a force for social mobilisation. Firstly, there was a shift in mainstream hip hop from a purely cultural expression to a call for political and social action, exemplified by Public Enemy's song 'Fight the Power' in 1989, and the work of the progressive rap artist Tupac in the early 1990s. Crucially, in tandem with the mainstream success of 'political rap', this period also witnessed the emergence of local hip hop organisations focused on issues of social justice and poverty.

Concurrently, in Medellín a number of specific local conditions existed in the 1990s that embraced these developments. Emerging in the 1980s, youth street gangs (known as *galladas or pandillas*) developed as a form of alternative socialisation for young males dealing with social exclusion, limited life chances and marginality (Ceballos Melguizo 2000). The groups attempted to navigate a perilous transition to adulthood characterised by blocked social mobility and class-based segregation. Perhaps because of this marginality and lack of economic opportunities, these gangs were easily integrated into the illicit economic ecosystems that emerged as part of the increasing narco trade. This assimilation into criminal activity led to the mass participation of youth in violence (Salazar and Jaramillo 1992), powerfully illustrated by the drastic fall in the age of the majority of homicide victims who, by 1989, were aged 14–20 (Salazar 1990).

Despite this trajectory into criminality, it is possible to argue that the structure of the *galladas* or *pandillas* also lent itself to the development of hip hop as a form of everyday peacebuilding by mirroring this structure of alternative socialisation for youth. Hip hop was able to repurpose these established structures for social relationship and identity building and thus remained within the acceptable and normalised parameters of socialisation. As El Flaco (2019) remarks this leads to blurred lines whereby some young people can initially be simultaneously involved in both social structures:

> The kids now, the teenagers, don't feel like they have to leave their armed groups to be able to get involved in cultural activities. No, they get involved in cultural activities, whilst continuing to earn money with gangs. (El Flaco 2019)

However, he also notes that this becomes increasingly incompatible in the long term as young people become more engaged in hip hop.

Whilst civil society had mobilised to combat violence in the 1970s and 1980s, the early 1990s saw increased levels of participation by civil society actors in addressing this issue alongside a more receptive state. At a national level this was manifested in a new Constitution in 1991, which sought to strengthen checks that underlay the foundations for the Ley de Juventud (Youth Law) in 1996 (Baird 2015, 9). Significantly, this group of religious, education and business groups, at local, regional and national levels, also included youth and cultural organisations. The emergence of NGOs such as arts organisation Nuestra Gente in 1987, youth founded/led Corporacion Regional in 1989 and the Red Juveniles (Youth network) in 1990, are examples of this. Furthermore, increased participation of youth in peace and resistance movements could be read as an urgent response to the increasingly adolescent nature of violence (Márquez Valderrama and Ospina 1999; Fernández et al. 2004; Riaño Alcalá 2010; Alcaldía de Medellín 2011, 2012; Ospina et al. 2011).

The development of these new repertoires to address youth-orientated violence, along with the incorporation of both youth and cultural organisations into a wider peace movement provided a suitable external framework in which hip hop culture could evolve and flourish as a form of *artpeace* formation. *Artpeace* formation draws on different local forms of legitimacy and social art practices grow into the wider peace process quite organically. It is transformative and shapes politics but is also a cultural and social practice in community and local spaces. However, whilst such developments could be interpreted as an evolution of an analytical and diagnostic approach in the face of previous unsuccessful tactics of violence reduction, exploring the social cultural impact of heightened (youth) violence also merits attention.

Jasper's work on the role of emotions in determining mobilisation of social movements provides a suitable framework for this analysis. During what Jasper refers to as 'moral shocks' (Jasper 1997), which he understands as periods of social, cultural and political turmoil, decisions to mobilise and the tactics employed may be influenced by emotional responses and interpretations of such upheaval. The late 1980s and early 1990s saw just such a combination of 'moral shocks' including the highest murder rate in the world and endemic violence penetrating all political and civic spheres, alongside the increasingly adolescent nature of violence, typified by the teenage *sicario* (hitmen) and the Medellín Cartel's bombing campaign against the state. Contemporary literature documenting this period portrays the emotional responses to these events and graphically depicts fear in the city (Rozema 2008; Riaño Alcalá 2010; Alcaldía de Medellín 2011, 2012).

Language is a useful indicator to examine how people understand and respond to their social environment. The mutation of the word *sicario* (hitman) to refer specifically to a young hitman reflects the increasing negative stereotyping and perception of young people in mainstream culture during this period (Ortiz 1991). The use of the phrase '*No nacimos pa semilla*' by youth in the peripheral barrios (officially translated as 'we were born to die' but which could also be translated as 'we were not born to live long') reflects this fear and collective fatalism.

Growing up in Comuna 13 in the 1990s, hip hop MC and producer Alejandro Rodriguez captures this sentiment of the expectation of an early death: 'in Medellín someone who makes it to 40 is really lucky because... there were periods in the war when the majority of deaths were young people' (Alejandro Rodriguez Alvarez 2019). In a similar vein, a series of joint operations between Colombian forces and right-wing paramilitaries aimed at driving out left-wing guerrillas in Comuna 13 created a second moral shock in the early 2000s. As in the previous decade, this 'moral shock' led to the mobilisation of a new wave of youth and arts groups. Notably during this period, in Comuna 13, a network of hip hop groups known as La Elite (from which key hip hop leaders would emerge, as will be discussed later in the chapter) used art as a response to the violence and as a strategy for protection and visibility. A historian at the University of Medellín describes this as follows:

> ...in this period of armed control ... the rappers said if we don't create a network and speak out, then we are going to be killed, disappeared in the 'escombrera'.[5] We have to make ourselves visible like never before and protect ourselves through our music. This was a unique strategy in this area, and it was very effective. (Ángela Garcés Montoya 2019)

Thus, the emergence of hip hop can be attributed to multiple events and strategies that enabled this cultural expression to be integrated into a wider youth and cultural current that mobilised against a backdrop of moral shocks in the 1990s. This is replicated in Comuna 13 as a response to Operation Orión in 2002 and gave birth to a new generation of cultural organisations, including hip hop groups. Having traced the emergence of hip hop in the city of Medellín, the next section will explore how hip hop functions as a repertoire for everyday peace formation.

Hip Hop as an Act of Everyday Peace Formation

Hip hop performs four functions that make it a suitable tool for everyday *'artivism'* amongst male youth and children in Medellín. *'Artivism'* is the notion that art does not merely critique and reflect reality (and in doing so mobilises) but it also imagines, advocates for and tries to realise alternative futures. In the case of hip hop in Medellín, *artivism* can be identified through the following features. Firstly, through the promotion of an alternative form of identity building that aligns with established local versions of 'barrio masculinities'. Secondly, as part of this process, it provides a space for socialisation into a culture of non-violence and co-existence led by positive role models that reimagine alternative futures. Thirdly, it offers pathways for income generation and the possibility of creating sustainable economic and social capital for marginalised youth. Fourthly, because it is a form of popular culture that is aesthetically and socially appealing to children and young people who are at risk of violence and the lure of gangs, hip hop is an accessible and valid form of peace formation.

Emerging in New York as a form of protest and resistance to the increasing ghettoisation and marginality of black youth in the 1970s, hip hop consists of four elements: MCing, break dancing, graffiti and DJing (Rose 1994; Jefferies 2011). These elements became instruments for identity building and a means of understanding and responding to social reality (Tickner 2008). For marginalised, often male, urban youth, hip hop offers an alternative form of communicating messages and pathways to transformation. In the context of Medellín, given the dynamics of violence, direct confrontation or action against powerful state and non-state actors agents is not a viable strategy. In practice, actions are concerned with prevention or resistance to violence rather than direct conformation with violence agents. Therefore, in this context, hip hop provides a subtle mechanism for resistance to dominant discourse or what Tricia Rose terms a 'hidden transcript' (1994). Applying James Scott's (1990) theory on 'hidden transcripts', Rose notes that elements of hip hop provide mechanisms for marginalised communities to challenge social, cultural and political hegemony.

Hip hop has taken on the role as a subtle instrument of defiance. *El Perro*, a graffiti artist and former member of La Elite, from Comuna 13, explains hip hop's 'hidden transcript' is for communicating messages of transformation and resistance to violence:

> ... another concept is how one works within the conflict, and it is the moderation of discourse and what you call things. Because if we are going to tell everyone that we are against the war, opposed to armed groups and these violent processes, you become a direct enemy of these processes. Therefore, you have to change the discourse and change things. We are life, we are hip hop, we are dreams, we are goals, a dignified life. Naming things in that way sounds like opposition, and that isn't a problem for us now. We have learnt to leave a message but not so explicitly. Not so explicitly, but rather more implicit that performs the same function but put another way. (El Perro 2019)

However, his comments also reveal that hip hop as a hidden transcript requires a degree of self-censorship and exploration of the acceptable, and thus can be blocked or limited by powerful agents. Thus, artists have to navigate and establish boundaries in which to frame messages that remain concurrently both visible but hidden. Positioning the message can be challenging as events in 2012 demonstrated when 65 hip hop artists from the network La Elite (El Perro was part of this group) were forced to flee Comuna 13 (Parkinson 2012). A music video they released was allegedly interpreted as a threat by local gangs. Events such as this could be read as instrumental in this process of learning and self-censorship that El Perro refers to in adapting the tone of messages. Thus, the depths of the hidden transcription are dynamic, reflecting the localised nature of conflict at a given time. Indeed, artists from other areas in the city contest the idea of the 'hidden transcript' entirely, noting that rap offers the opportunity to speak frankly without the need to camouflage themes (El Flaco 2019). Equally, Jeihhco of hip hop group C15 also contends that rap lyrics offer valuable insights into young people's opinions on politics and social issues for politicians, the police and parents if they were to listen (Jeihhco 2019).

El Parche: Spatial Transformation Through Hip Hop

The 'hidden transcript' of hip hop is innately visible, manifesting in public spaces and thus can be understood as a collective expression and community activity. These outdoor *parches* (meetups) are significant given the localised nature of violence in Medellín in which public, open spaces have been the sites of micro conflicts. The streets, parks and squares are physical reminders of past violent events and markers of current conflict, manifested most

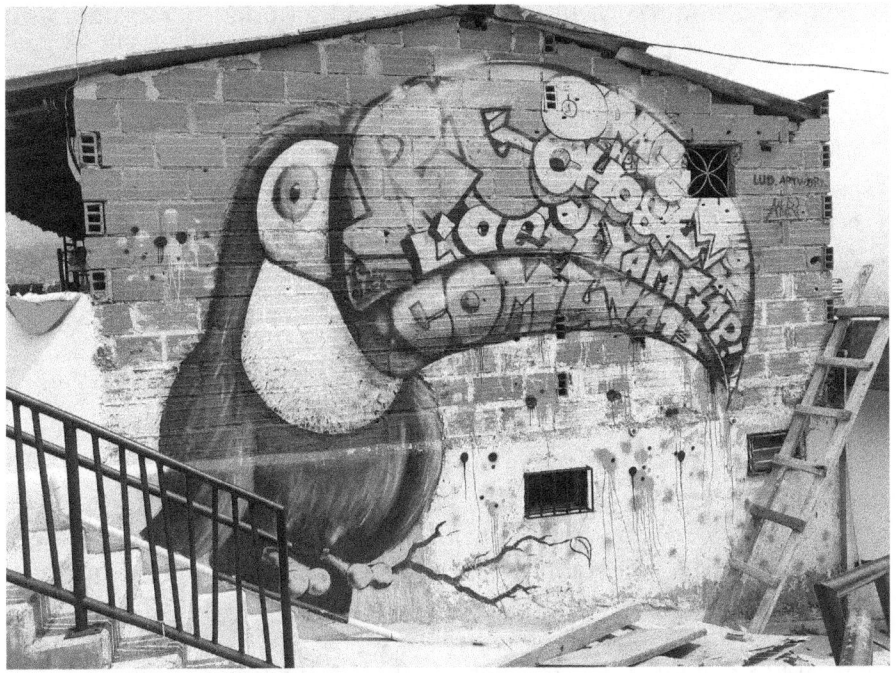

Figure 5.1 Graffiti featured in Casa Kolacho's Graffiti tours in Comuna 13. Photo by Teresa Ó Brádaigh Bean.

notably in invisible borders, the informal, fluid territorial markers that denote control of areas by rival gangs. This is an overt form of collective action in areas savaged by conflict that offers new positive nonviolent meaning to these spaces. As Rose notes, hip hop is an 'open-air community centre' which allows young people to appropriate and transform public space (Rose 1994, 22). In Medellín, the most visible manifestations of the ownership and transformation of public spaces are hip hop schools and graffiti.

Graffiti provides a visual representation of spatial ownership and transformation, depicting individual or collective interpretations of daily life, past experiences or imagined futures. To this end, graffiti may deal with a range of themes, including historical memory, memorials to murdered artists, protests against the government and police forces as witnessed during the 2021 *El Paro* (national strikes) or celebrations of indigenous cultural heritage *Pachamama* (mother earth). Thus, it can be understood as a form of local knowledge production, providing social and political commentary in sites of conflict (Vogel et al. 2020). Graffiti performs a powerful function for marginalised communities as it offers an avenue to challenge imposed negative perceptions of a community and to transmit messages, both within the community as well as acting as a bridge for peripheral neighbourhoods to connect to the rest of the city and the wider world. As a graffiti artist remarked:

> Graffiti has turned into a really beautiful thing because people have expressed them-selves through this medium. It has also been a means by which other people come, they listen to us, it breaks with those norms and they visit us. Graffiti has been a way of connecting the city because it is the first thing you see in the public space where you have an image that says 1,000 words, where we beautify the landscape and it is cathartic for the families. (El Perro 2019)

This is particularly significant for Comuna 13, an area that has been stigmatised as a breeding ground for hitmen and the site of military inter-ventions. The area's reputation as the most violent barrio, coupled with its location on the fringes of the city with limited infrastructure compounded both literally and figuratively its isolation from the rest of the city. Therefore, graffiti has provided an opportunity for new interactions between local resi-dents, people from other more prosperous areas of the city and international tourists evidenced by the influx of visitors to the area. As El Perro notes, the success of Graffiti Tours, a 3-hour walking tour of graffiti in Comuna 13 led by local hip hop artists has transformed the neighbourhood from the most violent to the most visited (El Perro 2019). Thus, in this case, graffiti could be regarded as a medium to challenge enduring negative stereotypes and stigmatisation of communities affected by conflict by offering a channel for encounters with the other. Likewise, graffiti can facilitate a degree of agency in shaping and determining the local landscape, within the constraints of gang control as the Graffiti Tours project demonstrates. Therefore, in the face of such control, graffiti can be interpreted as a form of resistance to this con-trol and a mechanism for spatial transformation.

In the same vein, hip hop 'Eskuelas'[6] are a further manifestation of this spa-tial ownership. Emerging from parches and the interest children and young people took in groups rapping, breaking and graffitiing in public spaces, col-lectives started schools offering training in the four elements of hip hop. The schools offer artistic training for children and young people, free of charge and in the evenings and weekends. Very few hip hop groups have their own premises, and so hip hop collectives usually run their schools in public open spaces, such as parks, recreational spaces or have permission from staff to use playgrounds and classrooms in local schools.[7] One of the best examples of a hip hop school is Crew Peligrosos' 4 Elementos Skuela in Aranjuez which was set up in 1999 by the group and run out of the local high school. The school is run by members of Crew Peligrosos who decide how and what is delivered in the hip hop workshops and they contribute their own resources to run the school. Students at the school have the opportunity to be part of Crew

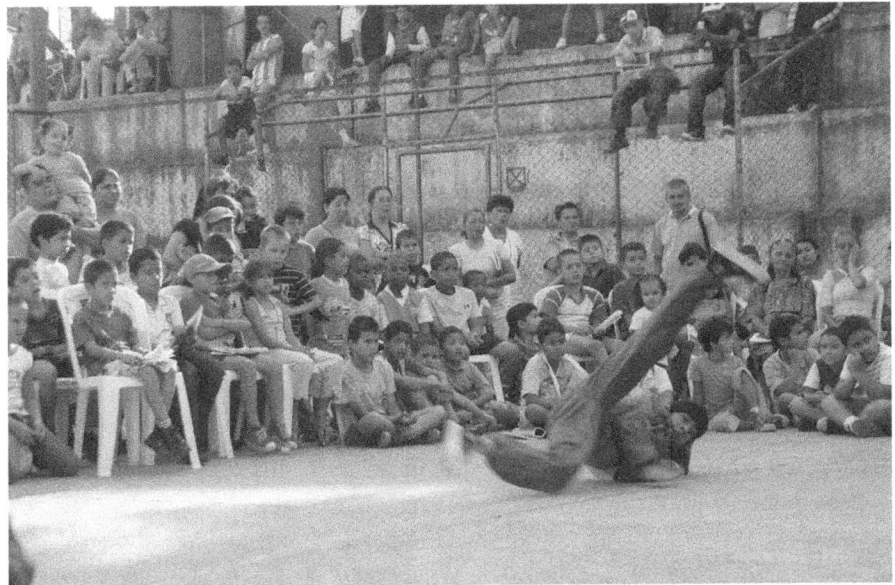

Figure 5.2 Breaking dancing performance in a sports field in Medellín. Photo: Corporación Ciudad Comuna, 2015.

Peligrosos, a well-known hip hop group that has toured Europe and secured partnerships with brands including Red Bull and Adidas. Crew Peligrosos has recently been supported by ABC Foundation in the USA to replicate the school model in other areas of the city (Gordon 2019).

This is not the only example of how institutional actors like the ABC Foundation have sought to replicate the grassroots hip hop school model, thus highlighting the incorporation of hip hop in formal peace formation processes. This is apparent in interventions created by Colombian state agencies such as El Instituto Colombiano de Bienestar Familiar. The project *Territorio de Sueños* was a series of hip hop workshops with children and young people at risk and led by hip hop artists across the country. Equally, hip hop training as a pedagogical tool in projects delivered by the NGO Combos in partnership with the local government in Medellín is further evidence of the co-opting of the hip hop school model by political elites. The incorporation of hip hop into the political elites' repertoires for peacebuilding can be regarded as continuation of *artpeace*building, a neoliberal and established practice of external agencies implementing arts-based interventions in communities as a tool for peacebuilding. El Flaco, MC with hip hop group El Laberinto and workshop facilitator on these projects, highlights the difference between hip hop processes that have been institutionalised and grassroots, unfunded hip hop activities which he referred to as 'illegal' (El Flaco 2019).

The primary difference is the power relations between organiser (the institution), the facilitator (the artist) and the participant (young person). Agenda setting within formal processes often restricts the creative process as institutions dictate how, where and with whom artists work. Hip hop workshops are focused on predefined themes decided by policy and political agendas, with facilitators expected to deliver outputs and results, something which El Flaco regards as rendering the process flawed and unrealistic. In contrast, in grassroots collective-led schools there is a more horizontal structure in which facilitators and participants organically co-create. Artists also have a better understanding of the local context and the dynamics of the barrios where there is the most need for such processes. Thus, aware of the limitations of the formal processes, El Flaco is involved in the running of 'illegal' schools in the city, the ones that do not receive support from formal institutions or NGOs using his own money to buy materials to 'train an army of artists' (El Flaco 2019).

'I Don't do Hip Hop, I am Hip Hop'[8]: Hip Hop as a Culture of Peace

Beyond offering young people the opportunity to develop artistic skills, hip hop culture provides them with what is frequently termed as 'alternative options for life' or 'a dignified life' for young people (Cultura y Libertad 2010; Crew Peligrosos 2014; El Perro 2019). *Artivism* is evident in the development of positive behaviours and competencies. Punctuality, good educational attainment, promoting co-existence and maintaining good relationships with peers and family are requirements for participating in hip hop schools. Moreover, this process of socialisation exposes young people to non-violent role models in the form of hip hop leaders and peers as well as reinforcing values of respect, peaceful co-existence and community in a non-violent space. Furthermore, from a pedagogical perspective hip hop culture can be utilised as an accessible tool to promote awareness of civil and human rights to children and young people.[9]

This educational and social activity is underpinned by a philosophy of non-violence as articulated in The Hip Hop Declaration of Peace. This United Nations-sponsored document outlines the code of conduct and aims of hip hop culture in constructing a global community built on peace and prosperity (Parmar 2009; Malone and Martinez Jr 2010). El Flaco explains how the process of offering alternative ways of life and nurturing codes of non-violent behaviour unfolds with young people who initially participate in both hip hop and gangs:

> We offer healthy alternatives where you can come and voluntarily rescue yourself
> if you want to, without being forced. The more time the kid spends on cultural

activities, the more he sees delinquency as expendable. The kid realises that killing or stealing aren't options, that crime will never be an artistic act or something an artist does. So, they rejected it and lots of people left illegal armed groups because music saved them. But through passive investment, not by giving them money but by saying that this alternative will give you inner peace, security and confidence and externally too that it will give you peace, trust in your family and your surroundings and that is going to improve your quality of life. (El Flaco 2019)

In offering a way of life based on non-violent principles, hip hop culture offers a contrasting value system and code of behaviour to the gang culture of easy money and violence (*plata fácil*). However, cultural norms and codes of behaviour can be concurrently transformative and constraining (Hays 2000; Alexander 2003). Paradoxically, within these parameters of cultural norms, a degree of congruence can be observed between hip hop and gang culture as forms of socialisation, making hip hop a potentially complementary and an alternative mode of socialisation. This is apparent in the fact that young people can either transverse both social structures simultaneously or substitute one for the other. Alejandro demonstrates how these two groups can collide and how as a teenager he could have drifted into a gang like his peers.

It [hip hop] saved my life because in the area where I was raised, in front of my house people became Pablo Escobar's bandits. I grew up with a lad who was a nobody because he had a growth hormone deficiency. He is older than me, but he always looked like a kid, I looked up to him. One day my dad told me not to go out with

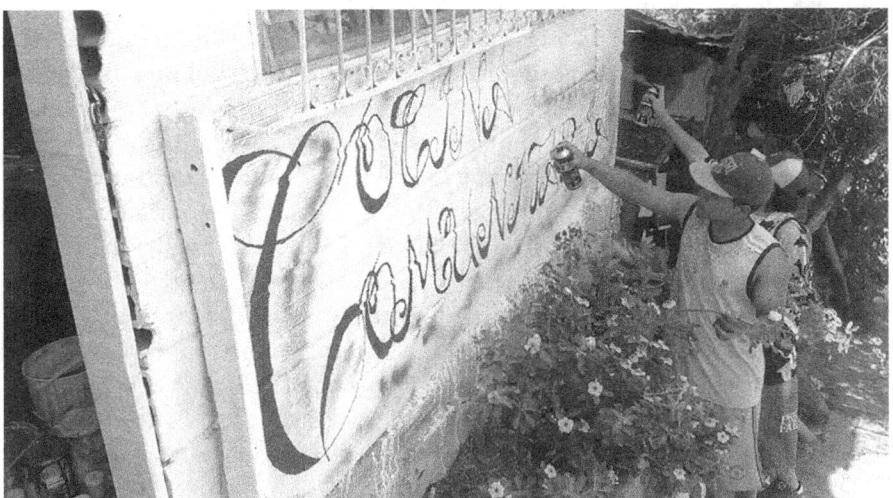

Figure 5.3 Preparations for the opening of a community kitchen in Comuna 13 initiated by hip hop artists during the COVID-19 pandemic. Photo. Alejandro Rodriguez Alvarez, 2019.

him and the others because they had grown up and had become bandits, so my friend, Nelson, told me that we were going to become rappers. (Alejandro Rodriguez Alvarez 2019)

Comparing and contrasting hip hop groups with gangs and locating both within wider local structural conditions is fundamental in understanding how hip hop can act as a nonviolent substitute for social inclusion and an alternative means of achieving social standing amongst (predominantly male) youth. Since the 1980s, poor male youth from the peripheral areas have increasingly experienced limited pathways for decent employment, and social mobility. These obstacles in the way of social inclusion produce minimal life chances and legitimate opportunities for youth, reproducing patterns which have continued to the present day (Riaño Alcalá 2010, 48). Participation in gangs has provided options for economic participation, realising material aspirations and achieving social status and power (Ortiz 1991; Riaño Alcalá 2010, 45–6; Baird 2015). In this way, gangs offer alternative pathways for aspiring to and achieving established local versions of masculinities or what Baird terms 'layered barrio masculinities' characterised by traits of toughness, respect, status and economic power with access to guns, motorbikes and women (Baird 2015).

In many respects, hip hop mirrors the functions of gangs beyond socialisation and identity building; it can offer a space to emulate and achieve these forms of barrio masculinities albeit in a non-violent way. Thus, just as Baird contends that gangs can be regarded as a logical response to social and economic exclusion, hip hop is a variant of this altered logic. Therefore, hip hop can be seen as a non-violent mutation of these embedded alternative structures for young (males) as they transition to adulthood. Furthermore, given the target demographic (children, adolescents and young adults), hip hop is an accessible and subtle form of peace formation. Thus, popular culture is a channel to facilitate engagement with young people as artists involved in the field work attest to initially being drawn to the aesthetics of hip hop and being ignorant of the roots of the movement (Alejandro Rodriguez Alvarez 2019; El Perro 2019; Jeihhco 2019). Indeed, Jeihhco highlights the importance of offering hip hop activities that are fun and engaging, that motivate and keep young people coming back to the school. However, this initial messaging acts as a pathway to a deeper exploration of hip hop as a form of social protest and a global movement for social change. Several artists talked about later understanding hip hop in the context of the civil rights movement in the USA, the Black Panthers, as a global social movement (Alejandro Rodriguez Alvarez 2019; El Perro 2019; Jeihhco 2019) and as an enduring set of principles for adulthood. The next section will seek to chart the outcomes of hip hop movement as it engages with a range of powerful political and social actors at the local, national and international levels by assessing the gains, tensions and limitations that emerge as it navigates this complex terrain.

'Killing Rappers is Bad for Business'[10]: Interactions with Centres of Power

This section will draw on Casa Kolacho/Graffiti Tours as a case study to explore the outcomes of peace formation through hip hop in Medellín. To this end, examining how this organisation has interacted with formal and informal centres of power as a strategy to create social change is required. In doing so, the section will conclude by analysing the limitations of peace formation through hip hop, stressing the need for long term broader social and political changes.

Operation Orión was a key event in the development of hip hop in Comuna 13. In the aftermath, the ACJ-YMCA invited hip hop artists to attend meetings about non-violent resistance, peacebuilding and the history of hip hop (TEDX Talks 2012; El Perro 2019; Brough 2020). It was through these interactions that artists formed La Elite, a network of hip hop collectives, using YMCA offices to organise and develop the network. In 2010, key members of La Elite, Jeihhco and El Perro founded *La casa de la escuela Kolacho*, often referred to as Casa Kolacho. Casa Kolacho offers hip hop workshops and events, as well as a café and a shop selling art and merchandise. The space also runs Graffiti Tours, a historical memory tour, recounting the experience of Operation Orión and everyday life through graffiti. This relationship with an established international NGO is significant in that it opened up channels for participation and visibility in political and cultural transnational networks that other hip hop collectives in the city have not been able to access or engage with limited success. This has translated into gains that have facilitated social mobility, material wealth and status as public figures for a limited number of artists.

The 2000s provided a receptive local political climate for youth-led arts-based peace formation and thus Casa Kolacho was able to leverage its position to build economic, social, political and cultural capital. The election of the first independent mayor, Sergio Fajardo in 2003, followed by Alonso Salazar administrations ushered in a new policy framework with a focus on civil participation and investment in infrastructure with culture and education as key tenets. Cultural expression, including hip hop, was regarded by the Mayor's office as fundamental in repairing the social fabric, and thus the secretary for culture enjoyed large budgets (Bean 2015). Given this, it can be argued that in such an enabling political climate, the movement became emboldened to articulate and make demands on political elites.

Reflecting on this period in the 2000s in which the mayors established a relationship with the hip hop movement, El Perro notes:

> We started to make demands on the state that we have had to do things differently and that we were tired of violence. Fajardo was pivotal and he helped a lot. And then Alonso Salazar also influenced things and then Alonso Aníbal Gaviria, we had a close relationship with them, and we started to demand things differently... (El Perro 2019)

This close relationship meant that co-founders of Casa Kolacho, El Perro and Jeihhco, were visible participants in policy discussions with the *Alcaldia* (Mayor's Office) as well as securing funding for projects such as the *Revolución Sin Muertos* Festival in Comuna 13. Their level of participation and currency in the political arena was evident during a dispute about the removal of graffiti which was met with widespread criticism by artists. As a response, the *Alcaldia* invited artists to discuss the matter, resulting in the creation of designated spaces for graffiti (Martínez Arango 2013; El Tiempo 2013). Furthermore, through these local political networks, Jeihhco and El Perro have gained visible public standing and recognition for their work at Casa Kolacho and Graffiti Tours. This is most evident in mainstream media at both an international and national level with a range of outlets including *The Guardian* (UK), *El País*, *El Mundo* (Spain), and *Clarin* (Argentina) covering their work and personal story. These articles explicitly frame Casa Kolacho/ Graffiti Tours as a site for pacification, a cure for violence and as part of a wider narrative of Medellín's miraculous transformation.

Such messaging in mainstream media has been significant in challenging established stigmas, both of male youth from Comuna 13 and the area itself. Moreover, it has built Comuna 13's reputation for urban art and elevated the status of hip hoppers both within the local community and far beyond. Hip hop artists have gained status within the community and engaging in art is now regarded as a path for opportunities for young people in the barrio (El Perro 2019). As a consequence, the area has benefited from an influx of local and international visitors which has had an important socio-economic impact, with a majority of people making a living from community tourism (El Perro 2019; Naef 2016). Equally, it has also enabled Casa Kolacho to become self-sustaining, opening a new, larger space in 2019 and providing income for 40 families (TeleMedellín 2019; Jeihhco 2019).

Engagement in these networks could be regarded as part of a strategy of cultural diplomacy. Internationally, it facilitates the state's narrative of Medellín's transformation whilst also presenting the state as a legitimate and trusting institution to a local community reeling from the effects of state sponsored violence and continued lack of trust of government institutions.

Furthermore, this strategy has simultaneously offered new avenues for economic participation and social standing for artists in the area. Leading politicians from across Latin America have come to Comuna 13 in the hope of replicating 'the miracle' in their own cities with the work of Graffiti Tours forming part of this narrative of transformation (Correa 2021). El Perro remarks that he advises the Secretary of the Reconstruction of the Social Fabric in San Salvador, El Salvador, offering his insights into youth, art and gangs (El Perro 2019), thus demonstrating the depths of interactions with political elites internationally.

Participation in these networks has also influenced how hip hop artists' position is understood by gangs operating in the Comuna 13: the murder of hip hop artist Duque of Casa Kolacho is an example of this development. Given the media attention and police investigation into the murder, the perpetrator, a 14-year-old boy, was killed on the gang leader's orders for fear of exposing and endangering the gang (Hierro 2016). Thus, associations with these networks have provided a means of disrupting power dynamics in the barrio and artists from Casa Kolacho have a certain currency when engaging with powerful criminal actors. Additionally, Jeihhco also reports that Casa Kolacho successfully negotiated with gangs to avoid paying illegal taxes and extortionate exactions (*vacunas*), thus further illustrating a degree of power afforded within these informal political spaces.

However, this disruption can be regarded as minimal: despite its reputation extending far beyond Medellín and its message of transformation travelling internationally to inform political strategy in other cities, Casa Kolacho's contribution to peace formation is small-scale and confined to a specific locality. Furthermore, participation in these networks can be regarded as temporary, sporadic and vulnerable to changes in political agents and policy strategy. This is evident when comparing levels of participation that leaders of Casa Kolacho enjoyed during the Fajardo, Salazar and Guivaia tenures to their more limited ability to engage with Mayor Federico Gutiérrez (2016–19). Indeed, Jeihhco expresses his frustration about failed attempts to secure concrete outcomes despite several meetings with the mayor (Jeihhco 2019).

Equally, despite the gains achieved through interactions with mayors in the 2000s, he is also critical of their strategies and impact on peace formation. He condemns the investment in infrastructure and the quest for accolades as part of a PR campaign to project Medellín as progressive and transformed whilst children suffer malnutrition, and thousands lack access to basic services like running water. However, it reveals a willingness to engage with formal political actors and indicates a pragmatic and less radical approach is taken in interacting with political elites, acknowledging that change in the city is dependent on such structures. Strikingly, despite having been a key civil society actor in political spaces, Jeihhco rejects the idea of artists becoming involved in politics and is critical of a hip hop artist who ran for office in Bogotá. This appears contradictory as he seeks to influence these political spaces but in a way that can be interpreted as a strategy to engage and lobby, whilst maintaining autonomy from a structure that he considers to be fundamentally corrupt and violent (Jeihhco 2019).

Whilst strides have been made in policy and political strategies to develop participatory democracy, provide a degree of resource and champion youth-led grassroots culture and education programmes, this has been undermined by the state's prevailing inability to uphold the rule of law and continued political instability. The result is a contradictory situation whereby the state largely avoids its responsibilities for addressing violence and takes a superficial approach as evidenced by developing infrastructure projects and funding for culture and education. Therefore, operating within a prevailing context of violence fuelled by the state's extremely weak application of the rule of law, combined with deep structural and social inequality, ensures that organisations like Casa Kolacho have only a limited impact on the fundamental causes of violence and conflict in Medellín.

Such conditions create paradoxes; the success of Graffiti Tours led to the intensification of violence in the barrio as gangs fought to control this lucrative area for extortion. Thus, despite offering socio-economic opportunity for local residents, Graffiti Tours can be seen as a victim of its own success. It is trapped in a system that foments violence and thus the tour propagates the very structure of violence that it seeks to transform. El Perro acknowledges this contraction and the feelings it evokes:

> I have seen that the barrio is heating up again, 28 deaths in a month and if they are arguing or fighting it is over the tour route and I also feel guilty because the creation of a tour is now the reason that people are killing each other. (El Perro 2019)

Conclusion: Between Transformation and the Continuity of Conflict

Medellín today continues to be regarded as an international example of urban and social development, of a city rising from the ashes of its violent past to become a model for innovation and participation (Dávila et al., 2013; Maclean 2015). Peace formation through hip hop among marginalised youth has been woven into this narrative and converted by state actors into an international ambassador transmitting this message of a 'transformed' Medellín.

This is not to suggest that the movement has not altered the landscape of peace and conflict in the city. Indeed, as part of a civic process in the 1990s, it informed and inspired youth policy and citizen participation strategies developed under the Fajardo and Salzar administrations. Equally, to some degree this is also evident at the national level with hip hop being incorporated into state programming for youth. A national hip hop competition for artists committed to promoting hip hop culture as a medium for co-existence, against criminality and drugs being supported by the national police, the US Embassy, the UN and the government of Cali offers an example of this (Alcaldía de Santiago de Cali 2012). Likewise, a recent event organised by the National Truth Commission on the role of hip hop as a mechanism to resist violence, defend human rights, denounce human rights abuses and construct memory also highlights both the acceptance and incorporation of hip hop in the state's narrative of peace formation with youth (Comisión de la Verdad 2020).

However, the outcomes for the movement have been limited and varied: not all artists enjoy the same level of public recognition, economic gains and social standing as Jeihhco and El Perro. For many hip hop artists in the city, like the *gallardos* of the 1980s, social mobility and opportunities for sustainable livelihood remain blocked: for most, employment remains precarious and opportunities limited. A combination of factors could account for varying outcomes, ranging from geographical location, networks, individual artistic talent and the way organisations are structured. For example, Graffiti Tours/Casa Kolacho operates in an area that was affected by the Operation Orión military campaign; thus in the aftermath, and what could be interpreted as part of a state strategy to win hearts and minds, this area received greater investment in infrastructure and institutional attention than other barrios of Comuna 13. The outdoor escalators, large library park and good public transport links serve to illustrate this. Such infrastructure has enabled the influx of visitors with the outdoor escalators and cable cars, becoming a tourist attraction in their own right (Neaf 2016). This sharply contrasts with other areas in Comuna 13 that continue to lack paving and decent transport links.

Furthermore, the political and NGO spotlight on this part of Comuna 13 due to this violent legacy also facilitated interactions between local artists and elites, as well as visits from international politicians including US Senator Jim McGovern. Such interactions, along with the press coverage and collaboration with YMCA, provided new pathways for visibility and support which led to new resources and opportunities. Indeed, Graffiti Tours was initially conceived as a way for local artists to host institutional leaders visiting the barrio.[11] Equally, having been nurtured within an NGO environment, the organisation developed a strong leadership style in Jeihhco and El Perro and processes which facilitated interactions with institutions as they mirrored their hierarchical structures.

Hip hop is a visible network, but individual organisations remain small-scale and vulnerable to the prevailing unfavourable external conditions in which they operate. Whilst the murder rate may have fallen, established structures of violence, patterns of violence and a culture of violence remain. The enduring presence of violent illegal armed actors, their illicit economic system and legitimacy and acceptance in marginal communities in providing security services are clear indicators of this. Coupled with this, chronic poverty and increasing inequality presents as a serious obstacle to the reduction of violence and the growth of social stability. Furthermore, the arbitrary and repressive tactics of the police and ESMAD (anti-riot police unit) during a series of national strikes from 2019–21, including illegal detention, illegal use of force and apparent collusion between police forces and private citizens firing at protesters illustrate the Colombian state's reluctance to protect human rights and uphold the rule of law. Thus, whilst the state has purportedly adopted innovative policies to address inequality and violence, on closer examination, this strategy can be regarded as cosmetic. Mirroring previous state strategies, it is one that is essentially hinged on coexistence and acceptance of illegal centres of power. Thus, the state's transformation process can be regarded as a smoke screen, with large scale infrastructure projects, education and cultural provision seeking to obscure the state's failure to dismantle structures of violence and factors that produce negative peace. This results in the adoption of a largely positive peace strategy typified by civic participation initiatives and investment in infrastructure. Furthermore, such a strategy appears to outsource responsibility for peacebuilding to local communities and grassroots organisations. They are left to address violence through projects often supported by the state through participatory budgeting initiatives.[12] However, this state support does not extend to an enabling environment for peace formation in which structures of violence are addressed. Thus, against this backdrop, hip hop peace formation processes at the grassroots level are faced with a paradoxical and insurmountable situation.

Until the rule of law is established, and illegitimate armed actors no longer control the peripheral areas of Medellín, the impact of hip hop will continue to be limited, regardless of the important gains made locally, by a system that cultivates violence. However, this is not to suggest that hip hop as a tool for peace formation is redundant. On the contrary, in the context of youth violence, it has the potential to undertake a variety of peace formation functions, notably 'artpeace formation' and 'artivism'. Hip hop is an initial and accessible channel for the participation of children and youth in peace formation processes due to its embedding a culture of peace and protecting and promoting human rights as a philosophy for life in adulthood. This has not only shaped cultural and social practice in Comuna 13 and the wider city but also influenced political strategies and policy. However, as Jeihhco shrewdly observes, in the case of Medellín: 'They have spent more time changing the image than the reality' (Jeihhco 2019).

Notes

1. For a detailed analysis of armed actors in Medellín, see Melguizo and Cronshaw (2001).
2. With the exception of spikes in 2008/2009, partly the result of a power vacuum created by the capture and extradition of high-profile figures such as Don Berma.
3. For further details see Posso, Palacios and Perafan (2020).
4. BACRIM is a term coined by Colombian Intelligence Services, Police and Military to describe armed criminal groups that emerged in the context of the process of disarming, disbanding and reintegrating United Self-Defence Forces of Colombia (AUC) in 2003.
5. La Escombrera is a landfill where armed actors are suspected of burying hundreds of bodies.
6. As part of the hidden transcript, the spellings of words are altered.
7. Observations during field research visits to various hip hop schools from 2010–19.
8. Quote from TEDX Tigre (2014).
9. Visit to various hip-hop schools in Comuna 1, Comuna 6, Comuna 13, and Comuna 15 in 2010, 2011, 2013 and 2019.
10. This quotation is from Jeihhco (2019).
11. El Perro, Graffiti artist and Co-founder of Casa Kolacho/Graffiti Tours, interviewed by Miguel Barreto, Medellín, 17/07/2019.
12. This is an initiative in which 5 per cent of the annual budget is allocated for projects voted for and developed by local residents.

References

Alcaldía de Medellín. 2004. *Plan de Desarrollo 2004-2007 "Medellín, Compromiso de toda la Ciudadanía"*. https://1library.co/document/1y918vwq-proyecto-plan-desarrollo-Medellín. html (accessed 15 May 2021).

Alcaldía de Medellín. 2009. *Medellín: La transformación de una ciudad.* https://aciMedellín.org/wp-content/uploads/publicaciones/libro-transformacion-de-ciudad.pdf (accessed 15 May 2021).

Alcaldía de Medellín. 2011. *Plan de Desarrollo Cultural de Medellín 2011–2020.* https://bibli otecasmedellin.gov.co/wp-content/uploads/2015/07/Plan_de_Desarrollo_Cultural_de_Medellin_2011-2020.pdf (accessed 4 November 2022).

Alcaldía de Medellín. 2012. *Plan Integral de Seguridad y Convivencia 2012–2015.* https://www.medellin.gov.co/irj/go/km/docs/pccdesign/SubportaldelCiudadano_2/PlandeDesarrollo_0_1/ProgramasyProyectos/Shared%20Content/Imagenes/2015/PISC.pdf (accessed 4 November 2022).

Alcaldía de Santiago de Cali. 2012. Continúan abiertas inscripciones para concurso de hip-hop Tu voz cuenta, 15 June. https://www.cali.gov.co/cultura/publicaciones/46254/continan_abier tas_inscripciones_para_concurso_de_hiphop_tu_voz_cuenta/ (accessed 15 May 2021).

Alexander, J. C. 2003. *The meanings of social life: A cultural sociology.* Oxford: Oxford University Press.

Bagley, B. 2001. Drug trafficking, political violence and U.S. policy in Colombia in the 1990s. http://www.mamacoca.org/junio2001/bagley_drugs_and_violence_en.htm (accessed 15 May 2021).

Baird, A. 2012. Negotiating Pathways to Manhood: Rejecting Gangs and Violence in Medellín's Periphery. *Journal of Conflictology*, 3. 10.7238/joc.v3i1.1438.
https://www.researchgate.net/publication/269780019_Negotiating_Pathways_to_Manhood_Rejecting_Gangs_and_Violence_in_Medellín's_Periphery (accessed 15 May 2021).

Baird, A. 2015. Swimming against the tide: Youth policy and contexts of chronic vio-lence in Medellín. In Filzmaier, P. Plaikner, P., Hainzl, C., Duffek, K. A. And Daniela

Ingruber, D. (eds). *Jugend und Politik. Generationendialog oder Gesellschaftskonflikt.* Wien: Facultas-Verlag.

Banes, S. 2004. Breaking. In Forman, M. and Neal, M. A. (eds). *That's the Joint! The Hip-Hop Studies Reader.* New York: Routledge.

Barker, G. T. 2005. *Dying to be men: Youth, masculinity and social exclusion.* New York and London: Routledge.

Bazerli, G., Bean, T., Crandall, A., Coutin, M., Kasindi, L., Procter, Robert N., Rodger, S., Saber, D., Slachmuijlder, L. and Trewinnard, T. 2015. Humanitarianism 2.0. *Global Policy Journal.*

Brand, P and Dávila, J. D. 2011. Mobility innovation at the urban margins, *City*, 15(6), pp. 647–61.

Blattman, C., Duncan, G., Lessing, B., Tobón, S. and Mesa-Mejía, J., P. 2020. Gobierno criminal en Medellín: panorama general del fenómeno y evidencia empírica sobre cómo enfrentarlo. Nota de Política CIEF No01, 21 de octubre de 2020. https://www.eafit.edu.co/escuelas/economiayfinanzas/cief/Documents/gobierno-criminal-Medellín.pdf (accessed 15 May 2021).

Bräuchler, B. 2018. The cultural turn in peace research: Prospects and challenges. *Peacebuilding*, 6(1), pp. 17–33, DOI:10.1080/21647259.2017.1368158.

Brough, M. 2020. *Youth power in precarious times: Reimagining civic participation.* Durham, NC: Duke University Press.

Ciudades Defensoras de los Derechos Humanos. https://ciutatsdretshumans.cat/es/defensoresas/jeison-castano-jeihhco/ (accessed 15 May 2021).

Civico, A. 2012. 'We are illegal, but not illegitimate.' Modes of policing in Medellín, Colombia. *Political and Legal Anthropology Review.* 35(1), pp. 77–93.

Comisión de la Verdad. 2020. El hip hop ha ayudado a narrar la violencia. https://comisiondelaverdad.co/actualidad/noticias/hip-hop-ha-ayudado-a-narrar-la-violencia-comision-verdad-colombia (accessed 15 May 2021).

Correa, S. 2021. *La transformación de la comuna 13 de Medellín inspira intervención urbana en Ciudad de México,* Alcaldia de Medellín, 12 January. https://www.Medellín.gov.co/irj/portal/Medellín?NavigationTarget=contenido/8812-La-transformaci%C3%B3n-de-la-comuna-13-de-Medell%C3%ADn-inspira-intervenci%C3%B3n-urbana-en-Ciudad-de-M%C3%A9xico (accessed 15 May 2021).

Brand, P, Coupé, F, and Dávila, J. D. 2012. Medellín: contexto institucional y cambio de paradigma urbano. In *Movilidad Urbana y Pobreza: Aprendizajes de Medellín y Soacha, Colombia.* London: Development Planning Unit, University College London and Universidad Nacional de Colombia, pp. 47–58.

Ceballos R. 2000. Violencia reciente en Medellín: una aproximación a los actores. *Bulletin de l'Institut français d'études andines* [online]. 29(3), ISSN: 0303-7495. https://www.redalyc.org/articulo.oa?id=12629306 (accessed 15 May 2021).

Crew Peligrosos 2014. *4 Elementos Skuela* [Video]. https://www.youtube.com/watch?v=jgBTpIdHCQw (accessed 15 May 2021).

Cultura y Libertad 2010. http://culturaylibertadMedellín.blogspot.co.uk (accessed 15 May 2021).

Doyle, C. 2016. Explaining Patterns of Urban Violence in Medellin, Colombia. *Laws*, 5. 10.3390/laws5010003

El Tiempo. 2013. Habrá debate en Alcaldía de Medellín por borrar grafitis de homenaje. *El Tiempo*, [Online] 26th November. http://www.eltiempo.com/archivo/documento/CMS-13222714 (accessed 15 May 2021).

Fernandez, C., Garcia-Duran, M. Sarmiento, F. 2004. Alternatives to war: Colombia's peace processes. http://www.c-r.org/accord-article/peace-mobilisationcolombia-1978–2002 (accessed 15 May 2021).

Fernando, S. 1994. *The New Beats: Exploring the Music, Culture and Attitudes of Hip-Hop.* New York: Anchor/Doubleday.

Giraldo-Ramírez, J. and Preciado-Restrepo, A. 2015. Medellín, from theatre of war to security laboratory. *Stability: International Journal of Security & Development*, 4(1): 34, pp. 1–14.

Gordon, O. 2017. Behind the 'Medellín miracle': Why the smart kids are going to hip-hop school, *The Guardian* [online], 20 November. https://www.theguardian.com/cities/2017/nov/20/Medellín-miracle-hip-hop-school-gangs (accessed 21 August 2023).

Gordon, O. 2019. The Hip Hop school taking on Medellín's mean streets. *Struggles from Below*, 4 October. https://www.strugglesfrombelow.com/the-hip-hop-school-taking-on-Medellíns-mean-streets (accessed 15 May 2021).

Gould, D. B. 2004. Passionate political processes: Bringing emotions back into the study of social movements. In Goodwin, J. and Jasper, J. M. (eds). *Rethinking social movements. Structure, meaning and* emotions. Lanham, MD: Rowman & Littlefield Publishers.

Hays, S. 2000. Constructing the centrality of culture-and deconstructing Sociology? *Contemporary Sociology*, 29 (4), pp. 594–602.

Hierro, L. 2016. Casa Kolacho: La violencia se cura con hip hop. *El País* (online), 30 June. https://elpais.com/elpais/2016/06/23/planeta_futuro/1466698760_170228.html (accessed 15 May 2021).

Hylton, F. 2007. Medellín's makeover. *New Left Review*, 44, pp. 70–89.

Hylton, F. 2010. Students as spies: The deep politics of U.S.-Colombian relations. *NACLA*, February 8. https://nacla.org/news/students-spies-deep-politics-us-colombian-relations (accessed 21 August 2023).

Jasper, J. M. 1997. *The art of moral protest: Culture, biography, and creativity in social movements.* Chicago, IL: University of Chicago Press.

Jefferies, M. P. 2011. Thug life: Race, gender and the meaning of Hip-Hop. Chicago, IL: The University of Chicago Press.

Llorente, M. V. and Guarín León, S. 2013. Colombia: éxitos y leyendas de los 'modelos' de seguridad ciudadana: los casos de Bogotá y Medellín. En C. Basombrío, *¿A dónde vamos? Análisis de políticas públicas de seguridad en América Latina.* Washington DC: Woodrow Wilson International Center for Scholars.

Lundqvist, M. 2020. Nep-hop for peace? Political visions and divisions in the booming Nepalese hip-hop scene, *International Journal of Cultural Studies*, 24(3), pp. 454–69.

Malone, C. and Martinez Jr, G. 2010. The organic globalizer: The political development of hip hop and the prospects for global transformation. *New Political Science*, 32(4), pp. 531–45.

Martínez Arango, R., 2013. En acuerdo con la Alcaldía, Medellín tendrá una ruta unificada de grafitis. *El Colombiano* [Online], 27 November. https://www.elcolombiano.com/historico/en_acuerdo_con_la_alcaldia_Medellín_tendra_una_ruta_unificada_de_grafitis-AAEC_271540 (accessed 15 May 2021).

Márquez Valderrama, F. and Ospina, M. 1999. *Programa Casas Juveniles: pensando a la juventud de una manera diferente.* Medellín, Colombia: Corporación Región.

Maclean, K. 2015. *Social Urbanism and the Politics of Violence: The Medellín Miracle.* Basingstoke: Palgrave Macmillan.

McEvoy-Levy, S. 2018. *Peace and Resistance in Youth Cultures: Reading the Politics of Peace Formation from Harry Potter to The Hunger Games.* London: Palgrave Macmillan.

Medina, C. & Posso, C. & Tamayo, J. A. 2011. Costos de la violencia urbana y políticas públicas: algunas lecciones de Medellín. *Banco De La República.* https://www.banrep.gov.co/docum/ftp/borra674.pdf (accessed 15 May 2021).

Melguizo, R. C. and Cronshaw, F. 2001. The evolution of armed conflict in Medellín: An analysis of the major actors. *Latin American perspectives*, 28(1), pp. 110–31.

Moser, C., and McIlwaine, C. 2000. *Violence in Colombia and Guatemala: Community perceptions of interrelationships with social capital.* International Conference on Crime and Violence: Causes and Policy Responses. 4–5 May, Bogotá.

Naef, P. 2016. Touring the 'comuna': Memory and transformation in Medellín, Colombia. *Journal of Tourism and Cultural Change*, 16(2), pp. 173–90.

Nieves, R. J. 1997. Colombian cocaine cartels: Lessons from the front. *Trends in Organized Crime*, 2(4), 36–9.

Ortiz, C. 1991. El sicariato en Medellín: Entre la violencia política y el crimen organizado. *Análisis Político*, 14, pp. 60–73.

Ospina, H. F., Muñoz, M., S. and Castillo, J. R. 2011. Red juvenil de Medellín: Prácticas de desobediencia y resistencia al patriarcado y al militarismo. https://core.ac.uk/download/pdf/35215549.pdf (accessed 15 May 2021).

Parkinson, C. 2012. Bandas criminales se lanzan contra raperos en Medellín. *El Nuevo Herald* [(online] 27 December, https://www.elnuevoherald.com/noticias/mundo/america-latina/colombia-es/article2019834.html (accessed 15 May 2021).

Pareja, M. 2019. Arte para vencer la violencia: Así es el Graffitour de la Comuna 13 de Medellín. *El Mundo*, 27 July. https://www.elmundo.es/viajes/espana/2019/07/27/5d135938fc6c83504f8b458a.html (accessed 15 May 2021).

Parmar, P. 2009. *Knowledge reigns supreme: The critical pedagogy of Hip-Hop artist KRS-ONE*. Rotterdam and New York: Sense Publishers.

Pécaut, D. 2001. La tragedia colombiana: Guerra, violencia, tráfico de droga. *Revista Sociedad y Economía*, no. 1 (September). https://www.redalyc.org/pdf/996/99617827006.pdf (accessed: 15 May 2021).

Posso, G. C., Palacios, C. J. V. and Perafan, L. G. 2020. Informe sobre Grupos Armados. *Indepaz*. http://www.indepaz.org.co/wp-content/uploads/2020/11/INFORME-GRUPOS-ARMADOS-2020-OCTUBRE.pdf (accessed 15th May 2021).

Press-Barnathan, G. 2017. Thinking about the role of popular culture in international conflicts. *International Studies Review* 19(2), pp. 166–84.

Riaño Alcalá, P. 2010. *Dwellers of memory: Youth and violence in Medellín, Colombia*. New Brunswick, NJ, and London: Transaction Publishers.

Rose, T. 1994. *Black Noise: Rap Music and Black Culture in Contemporary America*. Hanover, NH: University Press of New England.

Rozema, R. 2007. Paramilitares y violencia urbana en Medellín, Colombia. *Foro Internacional*, XLVII (3), pp. 535–50.

Rozema, R. 2008. Urban DDR-Processes: Paramilitaries and Criminal Networks in Medellín, Colombia. *Journal of Latin American Studies*, 40(3), 423–52.

Salazar. A. 1990. *Born to die in Medellín*. London: Latin America Bureau.

Salazar, A., and Jaramillo, A. M. 1992. *Medellín: Las subculturas del narcotráfico*. Bogotá: Cinep.

Schloss, J. G. 2009. *Foundation: B-boys, B-girls and hip-hop culture in New York*. Oxford: Oxford University Press.

Scott, J. 1990. *Domination and the arts of resistance: Hidden transcripts*. New Haven, CT: Yale University Press.

TEDX Medellín. 2012. *Revolución sin muertos*. 3rd April. [Video]. http://www.youtube.com/watch?v=CjOFGkIu5so (accessed 18 September 2014).

TEDX Tigre. 2014. *Revolución sin muertos*. [Video]. http://www.youtube.com/watch?v=EVHtP2o2QzA (accessed 18 September 2014).

TeleMedellín. 2019. *La Casa Kolacho estrena nueva sede en San Javier [Noticias]* [Video] https://www.youtube.com/watch?v=sVoxNhag99Q (accessed 15 May 2021).

Tickner, A. B. 2008. Aquí en el Ghetto: Hip hop in Colombia, Cuba, and Mexico. *Latin American Politics and Society*, 50(3), pp. 121–46.

Vogel, B., Arthur, C., Lepp, E., O'Driscoll, D. and Haworth, B. T. 2020. Reading socio-political and spatial dynamics through graffiti in conflict-affected societies. *Third World Quarterly*, 41(12), pp. 2148–68.

Vulliamy, E. 2013. Medellín, Colombia: Reinventing the world's most dangerous city. *The*

Observer, 9 June [Online]. https://www.theguardian.com/world/2013/jun/09/Medellín-colombia-worlds-most-dangerous-city (accessed 15 May 2021).

Watkins, S. C. 1998. *Representing: Hip Hop Culture and the Production of Black Cinema*. Chicago, IL: University of Chicago Press.

Interviews

Alejandro Rodriguez Alvarez, MC, Old Guns and Music Producer at La Embajada Cultural, Comuna 13, interviewed in Medellín and via Zoom 16/07/2019, 20/02/2020 & 08/02/2021.

Angelo, Hip Hop artist, interviewed in Medellín 16/07/2019.

Ángela Garcés Montoya, historian, University of Medellín, interviewed by Miguel Barreto in Medellín 16/07/2019.

El Flaco, MC and Hip Hop workshop facilitator, interviewed in Medellín 20/07/2019.

El Perro, graffiti artist and Co-founder of Graffiti Tours/Casa Kolacho, interviewed in Medellín 17/07/2019.

Jeihhco, MC, C15 and Co-founder of Graffiti Tours/Casa Kolacho, interviewed in Medellín 17/07/2019.

SIX

Artivism, Peacebuilding and the Antipolitics of Music in Congo

Peer Schouten

This chapter explores the multifaceted, entangled and sometimes contradictory politics of art in the contemporary Democratic Republic of the Congo (DRC), by situating its 'artivist' scene within a discussion of the increasing influence of international non-governmental organisations (NGOs) in the art scene, survival as a quintessentially Congolese art and art as a form of survival in Congolese society. I use 'artivism' both as an emic Congolese term for a loose network of activists and artists in diverse scenes and an analytical term to denote a hybrid between art and activism, between societal critique and aesthetics practised by this network of artists (cf. Lye 2018). As we will see, Congolese artivists engage in partly overlapping and partly separate—even competing—initiatives such as minor and major art festivals, exhibitions, concerts, stand-up comedy, local music production, installations in the public sphere, art classes and forms of activism more narrowly understood. The chapter first discusses the work of these artivists as a form of situated political engagement. It will show how key artists place their work in material and contextual conversation with questions of conflict and underdevelopment that define everyday life in contemporary Congo. Second, it discusses the fraught relations between Congolese artivism and international peacebuilding efforts, by exploring the contention within the artivist scene around the influence of NGOs seeking to deploy art as a 'weapon of peace'. Finally, the chapter seeks to speak back to the overarching theme of the book by discussing whether and how the synergies produced by different manifestations of artivism in eastern Congo can be understood as a 'peace formation'.

The chapter is based on 25 preliminary interviews conducted with artists, activists and people involved in cultural organisations in Goma, eastern DRC; a handful of diaspora artists based in Belgium but still active in Congo's art scene; a few academics and international NGO staff working with artistic engagement; and background knowledge derived from 10 years of research and engagement in Goma.

Context

Goma is a town of about one million inhabitants situated in eastern Congo's North Kivu province, right at the border with Rwanda. Because of its location, it is a vibrant trade and humanitarian hub, home to rebel leaders, politicians, mineral smugglers and the highest density of Land Cruisers in the country. While until the 1980s Goma was a backwater tourist town, the genocide in Rwanda in 1994 turned it into an epicentre of disaster, home to millions of Hutu refugees from Rwanda, followed by an influx of aid workers and quickly after also Rwandese soldiers (Hendriks and Büscher 2019). It became the staging ground for a Uganda and Rwanda-backed uprising (ADFL) that toppled Mobutu in 1996–7, and has remained a central node in subsequent waves of civil war and rebellion in eastern Congo until today.

While eastern Congo is not technically 'at war', in terms of an interstate or civil war over a defined political stake, there are over 120 rebel groups currently active (Stearns and Vogel 2021) and armed violence is a daily occurrence across the broad region. Militarisation and violence are normalised, and many people have adapted to and developed entrenched interests in the absence of stability (Schouten 2021). Thus, as in other contexts, what happens in eastern Congo challenges an all-too-neat dichotomy between war and peace that structures theories of peacebuilding and conflict transformation.

But conflict and emergency are not the only defining characteristics of the boom town that Goma is. Moving around in Goma means navigating a cacophony of music, blasting from cars or the generator-fuelled blown-out speakers of small boutiques that line the busy streets. At least since the 1960s, Congo—or Zaire, as it was called between 1967 and 1997—has been a musical giant, producing a continuous stream of artists reinventing the rumba and other endemic music styles. Indeed, besides illegally mined minerals, music is Congo's biggest export product (White 2000), making people move in clubs around the continent. As the superstar Fally Ipupa put it, 'Congo feeds the musical planet' (La-Croix 2020). Celebrating, in Goma and elsewhere in Congo, means going dancing. Popular culture—in its musical incarnation—is thus a fundamental part of everyday experience for Congolese. Yet, as we will see next, most Congolese music has—consciously or unconsciously—functioned as an escape from an everyday life suffused with politics and suffering, as Achille Mbembe (2005; cf. Seymour 2012) has observed.

Music as the Politics of Suspension

It is a very interesting question to ask what constitutes 'emancipation' in a context like Congo. It would be easy to tell a story in which emancipation would revolve around the continued battle to gain independence from oppression, via a struggle for more just or representative institutions. Most people know about the horrors that took place in the private colony of King Leopold II between 1885–1908, which was perversely called the Congo Free State. In the period that the Belgian state took over administration of the Congo (1908–60), colonial oppression weakened in brutality but increased in pervasiveness, mediated as it was by a vast infrastructural apparatus (Schouten 2014). Independence in 1960 was followed by five years of civil war and intervention, which ended when the West settled on backing Mobutu as a 'beacon of stability' in Central Africa. Cold War anxieties in the West meant that donors were all too happy to keep Mobutu afloat during his 32-year rule, shutting their eyes to how he only intensified political oppression, to the extent that Zaire—as he renamed the country—turned into both a model autocracy and a model kleptocracy. Today still, as we will see below, many Congolese believe there is a concerted effort by outside powers to divide eastern Congo and gain control over its resources. But, as we will also see, in most of the popular culture of Congo these issues hardly play a role.

There is another take on emancipation that seems more relevant. In a context in which power pervades all, in which the state is as weak as it is repressive (cf. Aretxaga 2003), and poverty and misery are widespread, it might be that what can otherwise be seen as downright, even hedonistic musical entertainment and celebration are in fact a form of resistance, in that they temporarily vacate a space of politics and empty it for pure enjoyment. Congolese are avid consumers of concerts, and in downtown Goma it is always possible to hear an all-night party going on somewhere. Indeed, it might be surmised that in contexts of protracted misery and conflict the very production of something which is expressly not political but only beautiful and enjoyable is the highest form of artistry and resistance to that condition; and that artistry expresses itself through the capacity to be able to temporarily suspend that condition for an audience. The famous *sapeurs* of big urban areas have translated that anti-political ideal into an embodied performance via luxury fashion which celebrates excess and 'bling' (Bazanquisa 1992). Indeed, the highly popular dance music of Congo and its 'celebration of celebration' only becomes conceivable as a form of embodied agency and resistance (Covington-Ward 2016; Mbembe 2005) if placed in the context of endemic suffering and the dangers associated with political expression in the (militarised) public sphere (cf. Chabal 2009; De Boeck 2015; Gondola 1999). If war and the overbearing weight of politics and poverty is the normal condition, then paradoxically, it might be necessary to look for the subversive in the production of a 'moment' and 'space' purposefully devoid of any political content; if 'necropolitics' (Mbembe 2003) is the order of the day, then, as the Congolese choreographer DeLaVallet Bidiefono puts it, by expressing the desire to live, 'art is the only form of resistance' (*Le Monde* 2017). Contrary to other settings in Congo (de Heredia 2017) or other countries—in which art has been analysed as a conscious everyday form of resistance[1]—the cathartic potential of Congolese musical experience resides in its ceremonial rupture of everyday misery—in an experience almost just as ritualised as that other collective purging institution, the church (cf. De Boeck 2005).

Second, and flowing from the first, given widespread poverty and adversity, 'emancipation' for many artists in Goma simply means advancing in life. As will be discussed further below, there is a lot of public discussion about the role of NGOs in Goma's art scene, and it has become an important public trope for artists to assert their independence of NGO influence. But a big proportion of the artists I spoke to, privately voiced scepticism towards this public posturing. Just to cite one artist who preferred to make this comment off the record:

> if I can make it by 'selling out' to the NGO world, or simply by producing art that will be consumed by western audiences, I am able to emancipate in a personally very meaningful way. (Interview 14, 2020)

Another artist stated, 'Art is to make a living; if people anywhere—Europe, Japan—buy it, all the better! Like for all artists anywhere, there's nothing wrong with making a living' (Interview 3, 2019). Perhaps more than in some other contexts, money is power in Congo, and emancipation means getting rich; it is a way to obtain power—whatever the way. Thus, again, notions of personal or collective emancipation cannot be analysed outside of the context within which they operate.

Extraversion in a Theatre State

Does art intervene in the Congolese public sphere, or does it mobilise in the designated, and recognised by the state, confined sphere of artistic expression? And if not, what prevents it from doing so? As indicated before, public life is suffused with politics, to the extent that despite Congo's alleged state weakness, collective action in urban areas is considered subversive and consistently met with violent suppression. This also constitutes the most straightforward barrier to the emancipatory potential of art in Congo: as a legacy carried over from colonial times, the 'public space' in Congo is often a stage, a site of scripted interaction between art 'from above' and a public. Performances in the public sphere in Congo were a key tool of power for Mobutu, whose programme of cultural *authenticité* hinged on a 'society of spectacle' (White 1996): what was called *animation politique* entailed mass music and dance performances that were carefully staged by, and subservient to, his rule (see image below). Indeed, Mobutu was fond of saying that

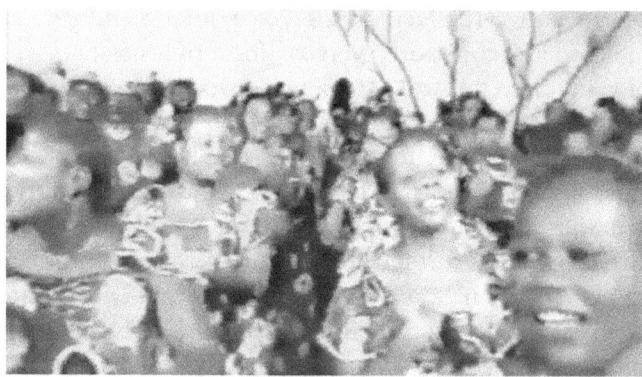

Figure 6.1 Still from a video of dance during one of Mobutu's public events. Source: author VHS of recorded TV show, 1970s.

'happy are those who sing and dance', and even at the height of crisis, his public appearances were always accompanied by 'happily' dancing *citoyens* (see Figure 6.1, cf. White 2007). Even the most famous of Zaire's legendary rumba singers could not escape this, and had to 'sing the praise of power' (White 2014), that is, sing songs specifically to support Mobutu.

Today, Congo still has some trappings of what Clifford Geertz famously called a 'theatre state' (Geertz 1980), in which the ritual and scripted performance of statehood is central to the production of the spectacle of power and the political subject as a 'big man'. Consequently, public performance is heavily politicised and policed. To organise a performance or meeting in public space, one has to apply for many permissions that will be scrutinised by all matter of political and security agents, and carefully surveilled by the police. 'Even today, public space isn't public', the photographer Sammy Baloji observed in an interview with the *New York Times*, 'it's a space of constant confrontation' (in Mitter 2019). Indeed, in eastern DRC, public space is highly political, it is a space where power is always imminent and always feels under threat (Ndijo 2005). As a result, the artists I talked to told me they would think twice before calling their work 'political'. Politics has a bad name: it means being willing to engage in a murky field best kept at bay; and if one does make political claims in Congo, one is likely to end up in jail, or worse. The rapper Bob Elvis sang *Dégage* ('leave') to urge former president Joseph Kabila to give up power and was abducted by security forces. Performance artist Precy Numbi was arrested shortly after with three others when they artfully protested the violence in Beni and Kasai (Interview 4, 2019; Interview 19, 2020). All of the artivists, when asked about how free they feel to perform publicly, recalled similar events and cautioned that engagements in the public sphere are closely scrutinised by the regime—for public space is its stage.

Also, as a legacy of the subservience of culture to power, musicians have to have important patrons, and are embedded in patronage networks. The biggest music stars have contracts either with the brewery Bralima (which brews the staple beer Primus) or its competitor Brasimba, and show this beer on stage each and every time; they align with specific political candidates, and have to sing their names as well as those of rich people who pay for being mentioned, at the end of songs (Van Reybrouck 2011). Many of the artists I talked to indeed confided they felt compelled to tread carefully the relations of power in Goma and nationally, to avoid stepping on the toes of the powerful and be sure to publicly compliment their benefactors to ensure future work. In a context where art is not a salaried job or a sector with public funding, artists are dependent on their patrons.

This leads naturally to the second important blockage to art as a weapon of peacebuilding voiced by my interlocutors. One local culture organiser described NGO-funded songs as 'music for food' (Gesthuizen 2013). One consultant and academic, in an interview, suggested that international NGOs have simply joined the field of powerful patrons, whose praise Congolese artists now have to sing uncritically.[2] This sits within a larger critique of aid in Congo, where one strand has been to reproach Congolese government officials from staging a 'masquerade' to western donors—publicly performing compliance with reforms while subverting them in practice (Trefon 2011)— and another strand has instead critiqued the aid industry of retaining top-down control over programmes that claim to support bottom-up initiatives by local civil society (de Heredia 2017; Vogel 2016). The Congolese theatre state, then, does not only stage power and pomp towards its citizens, but is much more sophisticated, because it also performs yet another play for international donors. Such critiques should be understood in a context in which aid organisations are a crucial element in the political economy of urban hubs such as Goma, with the resources they bring through programming and operational expenses profoundly impacting on local markets, giving rise to what Karen Büscher and colleagues have called 'humanitarian urbanism' (Büscher et al. 2018). The ambition to capture some of the wealth that NGOs dispose of has given rise, among a portion of urbanites in Goma, to a kind of 'mimetic desire' (Girard 2005) to stage themselves in 'fundable' terms. As a result, and despite the fact that art—both the consumption of popular culture by urbanites and the métier of producing art—have certain inherent emancipatory features, it nonetheless seems as if there is a kind of obligatory outward role that artists have to perform in which they script adherence to larger claims to social transformation, emancipation and thinking, and approaching society differently. If popular singers from Kinshasa also adopt a war-like discourse in giving titles to their albums, in eastern Congo the pervasive trope of peace in art seems to be a more direct outgrowth not of

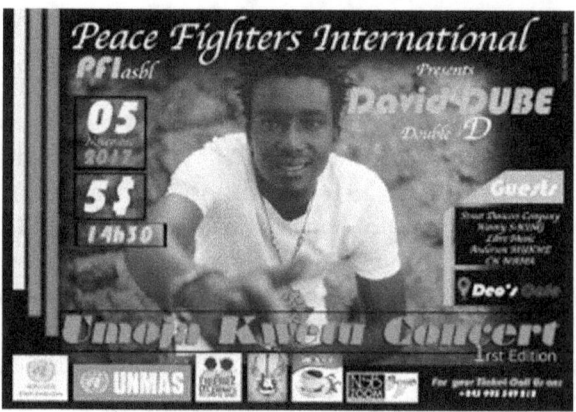

Figure 6.2 Event poster for concert by 'Peace Fighters International'. Source: flyer in author possession.

war—which has been around since the 1990s—but more of the NGO-isation of funding for arts. It is not uncommon to find artists calling themselves *Peace Fighters International* (as in the image below) or other names that might equally be appropriate for a private security company—just like how the alphabet soup of rebel group acronyms (there are currently over 120 armed groups in eastern Congo) seems to be pulled straight out of the United Nations' lexicon of good governance.

Indeed, activism is part and parcel of how Goma artists profile themselves. In Goma, according to the painter Justin Kasareka, 'to be an artist is to be an activist' (Ozy Media n.d.). However, often, very quickly these discourses become vague and rather empty of direct and explicit linkages to concrete kinds of transformatory action that their work engages in. It seems that for many, the very act of being an *artiste* somehow radiates transformation. This discourse is particularly pervasive when artists engage with western audiences: it seems a function of this extraversion that a kind of mutual mimetic desire has been built up around art as filling this space of potentiality around transformation, in which both are locked. NGOs and activists from the outside have shown so often they expect artists to be engaged politically, that Congolese artists have adopted this discourse and activate it automatically when approached by a potential western patron. Indeed, part of the reason the Amani (Swahili for 'Peace') Festival is drawing so much international attention, is simply in its name, linked to the setting of Congo. Apart from this marketing, it is little more than a terrific festival with pop music, some performances, and a lot of beer.

The rapper Blackman Bausi from Goma (about whom we will talk more later), in a recent public outcry, pleaded to the President that 'we don't want "amani" to be a festival, we want real peace in eastern Congo' (Blackman

Bausi 2020). By extension, Congolese artists who operate without NGO financing have questioned the actual peace impacts of transformative art projects that are part of hybrid international and local peace formations. As one theatre maker said about peace theatres in villages, 'they take place in post-conflict contexts, shake up a lot of emotion among people, but then they (expat NGO workers, *red*) leave again feeling they've achieved something. But people just go back to their normal lives!' (Interview 12, 2020).

Beyond questioning the effectiveness of art-based peace interventions, the role of NGOs is a fault line of contestation in Goma's art scene. For example, the people of Yolé Africa, an artist collective engaged in social transformation, are vocal about being independent of donor and NGO funding and denounce what they see as the disproportionate role of NGOs as a corruption of the Congolese art scene. Indeed, Chérie Rivers Ndaliko, the executive director of Yolé Africa, published a book subtitled *Music, Film, and Charitable Imperialism in the East of Congo* in which she attacks this NGO-art-culture explicitly (Ndaliko 2016). The main bone of contention is that the deployment of art by NGOs makes art and artists simply a mouthpiece for NGO programmes and breeds a generation of artists (which, true, have been largely born into an NGO-d Goma) who cannot think of undertaking something without NGO funding, just like musicians have to be sensitive to the whims of the economically powerful.

On the one hand, from the perspective on emancipation outlined above, the politicisation of art's content as is now current in Goma might be met with weariness, as it threatens to have politics colonise yet another life-field. Yet, in terms of the potential for political transformation, temporarily suspending power-relations, of course, does not mean challenging them structurally. It is not as if the celebration of enjoyment is a gradually expanding space which incrementally vacates life-worlds from misery and politics. In the most vivid illustration, I have marvelled in *ngandas* (bars) where some nights I found rebel leaders dancing together with the army officers they would continue fighting the next day; and like the powerful churches, the Congolese celebration of enjoyment might be interpreted as a Marxist 'opium', in that it makes people endure their misery by offering them temporary exit from it, a politics of suspension that enables one to stay in touch with a sense of humanity.

The broader stake here is that popular culture becomes a vehicle for outside agendas, like when outside ideas become the main driver of the production of culture. Or, as Achille Mbembe posited it in an interview, 'it seems to me, the function of art in Africa is precisely to free us from the shackles of development both as an ideology and as a practice' (Mbembe 2009). In the context of African politics, this outside-orientedness has been called 'extraversion' by Jean-Francois Bayart (2000), and it is perhaps a productive lens to apply to the art scene as well. Typically, at the entrance of the UN base in Goma a few artists always sell their work, work with a specific expat taste in mind: African masks (often imported from another African country), paintings of exotic scenes and tropical sunsets, and, most playful, white UN jeeps fashioned out of recycled tins. Most people from the Goma art scene do not consider these forms of 'commercial' art as real art.

Of course, all art is in some way produced with an external audience in mind, but it is a matter of excessive degree if the main mobilising drivers of a local art scene are external agendas, tastes and sources of finance. Indeed, if one recalls that, as Van Beurden (2013) argues, the collection of 'art' objects from Congo was thoroughly entwined with the colonial construction of the 'primitive' and the civilising mission, then this critique attains a deeper layer of significance—and cautions against attempts to appropriate African art for critical agendas devised elsewhere, perceived as slipping into a postcolonial reiteration of this colonial situation (see Ponzanesi 2015 for discussion). Indeed, throughout history Congo has often appeared as a 'stage' or 'object' within performances from the outside: a harvesting site, a meaning-making place for other audiences and agendas—from Joseph Conrad to Renzo Martens, Congo is used as a mirror.

It has become an important positioning device for Yolé Africa and other cultural actors in Goma to claim to be independent of NGO funding and agenda-setting. As one associate of Yolé put it in an interview, 'NGOs pretend you can just make problems—conflict, disease—disappear by singing, painting or performing them' (Interview 11, 2020). Indeed, in her review of 'humanitarian theatre' in Rwanda, Burundi and eastern Congo, Le Lay (2021) argues that NGOs adhere to a 'theory of change' in which local theatre is deployed to effectuate catharsis, a change of behaviour, by internalising the message of the performance. Besides the risk of retraumatising people, she points out that while such expectations are built on Boal's *Theatre of the Oppressed*, he in fact opposed catharsis as a tool to have people adapt to structural contexts and as a mechanism that diffuses the possibility for real revolution. Indeed, given the criticism around NGOs as the new loci of power in postcolonial contexts (Ferguson 2005), NGOs might be argued to fill the role of theatre director left vacated by Mobutu, in consciously using theatre as propaganda to arrive at an alien vision of order. It is for this reason that Ndaliko posits that aid-funded art in Congo is haunted by 'Mobutu's ghost' (2020), because it is subject to the same problematic relation to power as cultural production was in Mobutu's Zaire. But this is only if one is theoretically generous to NGOs, that is, if one attributes them Foucauldian powers (Koddenbrock and Schouten 2015); it is also possible to instead see a very limited impact of NGOs in steering the 'conduct of conduct' in eastern Congo. At least, the ambition is not lacking. Indeed, for scholars who have cautioned against the militarisation of aid, the donor focus on 'the role that arts and cultural programmes can play as part of a spectrum of interventions linking culture, security and development' or urge us 'to devise new theories of change which use arts and culture to support security and stability outcomes' (British Council 2019, 4) can only be approached with a certain apprehension.

Nonetheless, these criticisms of NGOs reflect a broader Congolese mistrust of 'the West'. Congolese often suspect that the US, France, Belgium or 'the West' more broadly are secretly engineering Congo's exploitation (of minerals), and are very critical of the presence of the UN, which costs a fortune but has led to few visible 'peace dividends'. About once every year a UN compound gets attacked by a protesting angry mob, desperate with the inaction in response to widespread violence, and some international health workers lost their lives in the Ebola response, which also involved attacks against health centres (Insecurity Insight 2020). At the very least, the discussions in the Goma art scene around the role of aid in art represent a healthier form of 'friction' (Tsing 2005) between the global and local, productive of the shape of art to come as people in the network mature and negotiate their positionality in the arts as a field (in the Bourdieuan sense of the word).

The Emergence of Politically Conscious Art in North Kivu

Yet, conflict-ridden eastern Congo has increasingly seen a grassroots movement emerge that positions itself outside of discussions on aid and dependency. While North Kivu was not formerly known for artistic expression—most Congolese intellectuals and artists concentrate in Kinshasa and Lubumbashi, and Goma lacks a similarly vibrant newspaper and public culture—over the last ten years, things have changed quickly. The town has seen a veritable boom in increasingly visible and vocal civil activism and grassroots art. Goma and later Beni became home to a vibrant scene of politically conscious young bloggers, rappers, DJs, plastic and performance artists, photographers, cultural centres, activists, stand-up and theatre makers and cultural organisers.

When asking about the emergence of this art scene, I roughly get two explanations. On the one hand, people point to a new political awareness that took hold after 2011, when Joseph Kabila was re-elected, and that intensified as he delayed elections between 2016 and 2019. In 2011, the group La Lucha (short for *'Lutte pour le Changement'*, fight for change) emerged here, demonstrating a different form of political activism premised on what its militants call *la luchologie*, a set of principles to keep the movement nonviolent, horizontal and non-partisan (Interview 24, 2021).[3] In its essence, La Lucha mobilises around collective action to denounce and resist abuses by the Congolese state, starting with students forcing the provision of water and electricity at the University of Goma through public demonstrations. It has since organised issue-based gatherings or demonstrations, involving youth and groups of civil stakeholders affected by the issue. Because the movement is not led by anyone it is impossible to 'decapitate' the movement by arresting its leaders. La Lucha also renounces funding from political parties or NGOs, on the premise that it may compromise their independence. La Lucha has since developed into a protest movement to reckon with, with chapters in urban centres around the country. In Goma, the particular style of La Lucha seemed to have spawned a contagious form of political awareness that spread among urban youth, leading bloggers, rappers, cultural organisers and theatre-makers to develop a stance called 'artivism', which we will discuss below.

On the other hand, people point to the humanitarian sector. Starting in the early 2000s, Search for Common Ground debuted peace theatres in the region (Search for Common Ground 2014), but it was really only about five years back that more donor funding became available for cultural activities. The idea behind the NGO-sation of art was not that art can bring peace, but that cultural activities can help in post-conflict reconciliation, trauma healing, conflict prevention and awareness-raising around all matter of developmental issues (Slachmuijlder 2011).

Both benefit from a third, not explicitly articulated, factor that I argue is important as well. Since Goma became a hub of humanitarian activities in the 2010s, there has been a notable 'gentrification' in Goma, with increasing numbers of hipster cafes, bars and other global phenomena showing up in Goma, probably emerging to cater to the interface of the stable flow of young expat workers passing through Goma and the local elite and middle class that has managed to emerge despite—or because of—two decades of conflict, illicit resource extraction and humanitarian emergencies (see Thomas and Vogel 2018, for similar dynamics in another context). Indeed, twenty years of professional, economic and social interaction between humanitarians and Congolese in Goma has left its marks on the town. Goma's clubs have menus and DJs that cater to the tastes of African and Caucasian expats; cultural activities have adopted different, decidedly Western, forms, such as festivals and the opening of exhibitions in galleries accompanied by wine and DJs.

Despite the existence of multiple cultural centres where different subgroups congregate, it is still a fairly intimate scene where everyone knows everyone, which is why it is possible to consider it a single 'network' or 'community of practice', joined by a shared interaction with the flow of cultural activities and activism. Among my interlocutors from within this group, the idea that art can transform society by offering individuals change is widely shared. It concerns the idea that art offers a venue of life alternative to being engaged in conflict—in its simplest version, by busying oneself with something that is not war, one is contributing to peace; by offering art education—teaching music, theatre and so on—to youths, one is offering them an outlet to channel their energies and emotions that is positive. This is what drives the centres where volunteers assist the youth in creative activities such as painting and theatre.

The Art of Débrouillardise

But there is a final form of Congolese artivism that critically engages societal questions in a distinct way, by putting to use the debris that signifies the ruins of past development promises and transforming it into probing question marks. This is best reflected in the artists that were featured in *System K* (2019). This group of artists places scrap waste and survival at the centre of its work, as entry points to key determinants of the life conditions that make up contemporary Congo. The country is about the size of Western Europe but has only 2000km of paved road, while the Belgians left behind their colony as one of the most industrialised in Africa. Infrastructural dilapidation since independence (1960) went hand in hand with economic and institutional decay, leaving Congolese to fend for themselves (Schouten 2021). This has become such a pervasive art that Congolese quip that 'fend for yourself' (*débrouillez-vous*) is the fifteenth, informal, article of their constitution, which in reality only has fourteen articles (de Villers et al. 2002). The art of fending for oneself comprises the capacity to creatively make do with—or despite— the conditions one finds in place.[4] As Bob White, the anthropologist of Congolese music, put it, art can help make sense of everyday life, and in the ruins of past developmental promises that Congo is, everyday creative solutions for survival become a form of art (White 1999, 167). Thus, in reassembling and repurposing the debris of past infrastructures and technologies, the BoZaR group prompts us to consider everyday acts of survival as art, and their art as being a mirror of the broader Congolese art of fending for oneself. Mirroring how youth gangs define themselves as *bana désordre*, 'children of disorder' (De Boeck 2009), Freddy Tsimba of the BoZar group explains in the movie that 'Our work feeds on chaos, given that we are a population constantly inventing new ways to survive'.

Tsimba is a sculptor shuttling between Goma, Kinshasa and Brussels who assembles his work out of bottle caps, trash, machetes and pretty much everything and anything he can amass in large quantities. One of his installations is a small house assembled from machetes (a weapon of choice in Congo's conflicts); he also makes statues from bullet shells. His work thus provokes questions about what these materials do and can do. Whereas bullets and machetes are used for destruction of human lives, by fashioning homes out of them, he shows these very same raw resources, and the energies used to apply them, could equally create homes. At the same time, standing in a house made of machetes, one asks oneself, is Congo, my home, made of deadly technologies? His work also provokes a meditation on the global political economy and lifecycle of the mineral resources that Congo has been providing since colonial times. It is to be remembered that Congo is one of the biggest producers of copper in the world, and that much of that copper has been used over the decades to produce bullets and other technologies of war. By working the debris of discarded tools fashioned out of these materials, Tsimba restages such everyday waste as political materials emblematic of Congo's predicament.

Precy Numbi, another member of the same family, creates his Robot Sapiens Kimbalabala out of old car parts (see Figure 6.3), and in placing these artforms in public space, Precy and other BoZar luminaries bundle and thus acutely bring to the forefront of consciousness the absences of functioning infrastructures. To understand this as *political* critique, it is necessary to understand a bit of the historical context of that moment in time, around 2018. Former President Joseph Kabila's electoral campaign of 2006 had hinged on a 'revolution of modernity' that comprised 5 *chantiers* or pillars: transport infrastructure, employment, education, water and electricity, and health provision. Yet, years after, few in eastern Congo have seen any of these pillars of modernity, instead being confronted with the progressive dilapidation of roads and other infrastructures and a proliferation of armed groups (De Boeck 2011). In working with the debris of past infrastructures, implicitly, the BoZar school evokes the failure of the 'revolution of modernity' that was former president Kabila's main electoral promise. Indeed, this loose collective of artists labels its work as 'artivism', a hybrid between art and activism, between societal critique and aesthetics.

System K and the artists it features have received rolling accolades in the international press, who have hailed it as a haunting portrait of the incredible street art boiling in Kinshasa, Congo's capital; its protagonists are portrayed as making arts in, and for, the streets of Congo. Yet despite the image conveyed in the film, Precy explained that in reality these artists hardly ever intervene in the public sphere, and instead want to be taken seriously as professional artists, instead of being framed as an exotic third world 'street' version of art. Furthermore, as explained, Congo's public spaces are heavily policed, and public events such as demonstrations can only be staged after official approval from government offices, including the security services. As a result, politically critical street artists would quickly end up in jail for fuelling unrest. Instead, the performances of the BoZar group usually only enter public space as part of western-heavy festivals and galleries, where the social critique of their work finds eager traction. By contrast, their work is not received in Congo with the kind of eager embrace that popular music

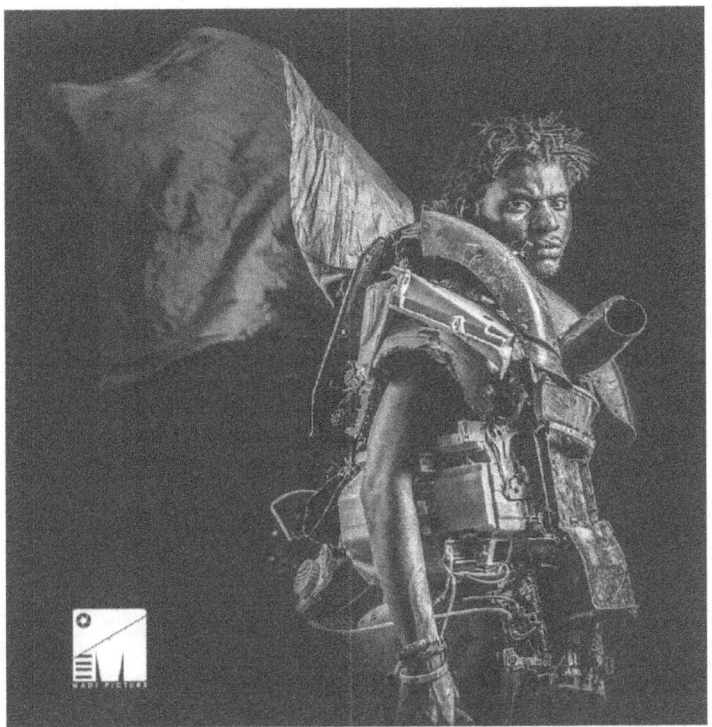

Figure 6.3 Precy Numbi aka Kimbalambala, or, 'the terminator of Kinshasa'. Image courtesy of the artist.

receives. In that sense, this circle of artists holds cultural capital *outside* Congo more than inside it.

However, an important part of the group of artivists retains a strong local focus and popularity. Idinco Delcat, a young musician from Beni, is one of them. He is an active member of La Lucha, meaning he commits to independence from political ties or NGO funding, and most, if not all, of his reggae songs have a strong political message. Take his song 'Etat de Chaises' (State of Chairs). It reflects critically on the state of siege announced by the government in the east of the country to give the army leeway to deal with the proliferation of armed groups. In his lyrics, Idinco (sometimes also spelled Idengo) criticises the government for using the pretext of the state of siege to suppress civil activism, with the refrain going like this:

State of Chairs:
Dictatorship, violence
Civil Society? Buried Alive!
Human Rights? Buried Alive!
Pressure Groups? Buried Alive! (Idinco Delcat 2021)

He was arrested early 2021 after releasing a song called 'Crooked Politicians', listing politicians by name—including the president—as crooks. After his subsequent release from prison, he produced a new song, 'mad government', a happy, uplifting melody accompanied by lyrics calling the president crazy, his entourage crazy—the whole government crazy: 'they don't work, they don't care!' Another sunny reggae tune starts with sweet voices chanting, *Oo-ooh, pays de prisonniers* ('oo-ooh, country of prisoners'), and continues with an explanation of how everyone in Congo is captive—youth, mothers, fathers, by swindling politicians, by neighbouring countries, by bad political agreements, but the politicians themselves are also imprisoned, held captive by ties and logics they cannot escape. In Goma, the rapper Blackman Bausi also weaves social and political criticism through his lyrics, taking on the very notion of power ('kiti' in Kiswahili) and its pursuit as an evil haunting his country (Blackman Bausi 2019). Blackman Bausi and Idinco Delcat are very popular among the urban youth in Beni and Goma, and their music circulates widely on social media.

Conclusion

As the 'artivists' portrayed in the film *System K* ask, 'Where does art begin? And where does it end?' If popular culture is the subject of investigation in relation to peace formation, it is important to question the gate-keeping effects of an implicit focus on one narrow form of cultural expression to the detriment of others.[5] Indeed, popular culture as under discussion here is a decidedly urban phenomenon, produced and consumed by people with a definite physical and cultural distance from the rural areas where most armed groups concentrate. Ultimately, if the emancipatory potential of artivism resides in allowing collective action and sense-making by mobilising cultural symbols, then popular art should perhaps be analysed on the same plane as church meetings—which are accompanied in Congo with as much popular music as concerts—or even the work of prophets and healers (Blier 1993). For the seances of these symbolic entrepreneurs arguably matter even more for how collectivities in Congo make sense of war, poverty and indeed mobilise behind political alliances and collective forms of action. In fact, in Congo's past—recent and deep—messianic movements, sects and other spiritual aspects of cultural life played a constant and definitive role in mobilising resistance and revolt against oppression, real and perceived.

That said, I have hoped to argue how Congolese popular music is already a vital political force in that it helps constitute temporary zones of exception, where celebration subverts the suffocating pervasiveness of politics and strife in everyday life. To the extent that collective musical celebration temporarily brackets conflict and power, it can be considered a meaningful vernacular 'infrapolitics of peacebuilding' (Richmond 2013). Moreover, a wide array of more explicit forms of politically vocal art exists in eastern Congo—some which seek to cater to or are funded by international NGOs, and others which wish to set themselves apart from what they see as the corrupting influence of donor dependency. It is among the latter—which encompasses artivists linked to the collective La Lucha as well as the BoZar group portrayed in *System K*—that the most creative, critical and thought-provoking cultural interventions engaging questions of peace and underdevelopment are produced. These are not the results of external peace interventions, and often the protagonists actively position themselves against foreign agenda-setting, but that also means artivism matures in conversation with programmatic artistry and finds inspiration in artistic and resistance movements in other contexts. They are not hidden or disguised but instead seek as much visibility as possible, domestically and internationally.

Notes

1. For example, Farzana (2017), and other contributions to this volume.
2. However, in a context of political repression where art has historically been expected to be a channel for the expression of power, Congolese artists have a long history in devising their own artistic 'weapons of the weak', that is, ways of being subversive that remain under the radar of those in power. Since colonial times, Congolese singers have practiced *mbwakela*, that is, expressing critique in a convoluted, coded, indirect and subtle way (Pype 2020, cf. White 1999). In subsequent work, I hope to explore this cultural technique of subversion more.
3. In this, it sets itself apart from other civil activist groups like Veranda Mutsanga in Beni and Butembo, which doesn't shun violence to achieve its goals nor political ties.
4. Congolese also call this capacity to navigate the chaos of everyday life *matematik* (De Boeck 2015), prompting the writer In Koli Jean Bofane to write an excellent novel entitled *Mathématiques congolaises*.
5. Indeed, the question throws up the famous point by Gallie (1956) that art is an 'essentially contested concept'. There was a debate in the 1980s and 90s about the distinction between art and culture, and thus the appropriateness of aesthetic or anthropological interpretations of artworks/cultural objects. This discussion is highly apposite with regards to the question of the political transformative power of cultural expression in postcolonial contexts (Clifford 1988; Kirshenblatt-Gimblet 1991).

References

Aretxaga, B. 2003. Maddening states. *Annual Review of Anthropology*, 32, pp. 393–410.
Bayart, J. F. 2000. Africa in the world: A history of extraversion. *African Affairs*, 99(395), pp. 217–67.
Bazanquisa, R. 1992. La Sape et la politique au Congo. *Journal des africanistes*, 62(1), pp. 151–7.
Blackman Bausi. 2019. BLACKMAN BAUSI KITI (OFFICIAL VIDEO) with English translation. *Youtube*, 27 April. https://www.youtube.com/watch?v=zH3rVDluXDg (accessed 22 August 2023).
Blackman Bausi. 2020. Blackman Bausi s'adresse au président de la RDC. *YouTube*, October 20. https://www.youtube.com/watch?v=Qz_tAklhY3Y# (accessed 22 August 2023).

Blier, S. P. 1993. Truth and seeing: Magic, custom, and fetish in art history. In Bates, R., Mudimbe, V. Y. and O'Barr, J. (eds), *Africa and the disciplines: The contributions of research in Africa to the social sciences and humanities*. Chicago, IL: University of Chicago Press, pp. 139–66.

British Council 2019. The art of peace: The value of culture in post-conflict recovery. London: British Council.

Büscher, K., Komujuni, S. and Ashaba, I. 2018. Humanitarian urbanism in a post-conflict aid town: Aid agencies and urbanization in Gulu, Northern Uganda. *Journal of Eastern African Studies*, 12(2), pp. 348–66.

Chabal, P. 2009. *Africa: The politics of suffering and smiling*. London: Zed Books.

Clifford, J. 1988. On Collecting Art and Culture. *The Predicament of Culture*. Cambridge, MA: Harvard University Press, pp. 215–51.

Covington-Ward, Y. 2016. *Gesture and power: Religion, nationalism, and everyday performance in Congo*. Durham, NC: Duke University Press.

De Boeck, F. 2005. The apocalyptic interlude: Revealing death in Kinshasa. *African Studies Review*, 48(2), pp. 11–32.

De Boeck, F. 2015. 'Poverty' and the politics of syncopation. *Current Anthropology*, 56(S11), S146-S158.

de Heredia, M. I. 2017. *Everyday resistance, peacebuilding and state-making: Insights from 'Africa's World War'*. Manchester: Manchester University Press.

de Villers, G., Jewsiewicki, B., Monnier, L., and Dibwe dia Mwembu, D. (eds). 2002. *Manières de vivre: Economie de la "débrouille" dans les villes du Congo/Zaïre*. Tervuren/Paris: CEDAF/'lHarmattan.

Farzana, K. F. 2017. *Memories of Burmese Rohingya refugees: Contested identity and belonging*. New York: Palgrave Macmillan.

Ferguson, J. 2005. Seeing like an oil company: Space, security, and global capital in neoliberal Africa. *American Anthropologist*, 107(3), pp. 377–82.

Gallie, W. B. 1956. Art as an essentially contested concept. *The Philosophical Quarterly*, 6(23), pp. 97–114.

Geertz, C. 1980. *Negara: The theatre state in nineteenth-century Bali*. Princeton: Princeton University Press.

Gesthuizen, T. 2013. Congo's hidden cultural hub. *The Guardian*, March 13. https://www.the guardian.com/world/2013/mar/13/congo-cultural-hub-goma (accessed 22 August 2023).

Girard, R. 2005. *Violence and the sacred* (P. Gregory, trans., 2nd edn). London: Continuum.

Gondola, C. D. 1999. Dream and drama: The search for elegance among Congolese youth. *African Studies Review*, 42(1), pp. 23–48.

Hendriks, M. 2019. 'My life is like a movie': Making a fiction film as a route to knowledge production on gang political performances in Goma, DR Congo. *Journal of Extreme Anthropology*, 3(1), pp. 57–76.

Hendriks, M. and Buscher, K. 2019. *Insecurity in Goma: Experiences, actors and responses*. London: Rift Valley Institute.

Idinco Delcat. 2021. ETAT DES CHAISES BY DELCAT IDINCO 2021 officiel vidéo Beni drc. *YouTube*, 7 June. https://www.youtube.com/watch?v=fEAVy15ROks (accessed 22 August 2023).

Insecurity Insight. 2020. Attacks on Health Care During the 10th Ebola Response in the Democratic Republic of the Congo. November. Geneva, Switzerland: Insecurity Insight.

Kirshenblatt-Gimblet, B. 1991. Objects of Ethnography. In: Karp, I. and Lavine, D. S. (eds), *Exhibiting Cultures: The Poetics and Politics of Museum Display*. Washington: Smithsonian Institution Press, pp. 386–443.

Koddenbrock, K., and Schouten, P. 2015. Intervention as ontological politics: Security, pathologization, and the failed state effect in Goma. In Bell, C., Bachmann, J. and Holmqvist, C. (eds), *War, Police and Assemblages of Intervention*. London: Routledge, pp. 183–203.

La-Croix. 2020. Fally Ipupa: "le Congo nourrit la planète musicale". *La-Croix*, December 15 https://www.la-croix.com/Fally-Ipupa-Congo-nourrit-planete-musicale-2020-12-15-1301 130236 accessed 01-09-2022 (accessed 22 August 2023).

Le Lay, M. 2021. Performing for peace and social change in Africa's Great Lakes Region. *Theatre Research International*, 46(1), pp. 23–38.

Lye, A. Y. 2018. Les nouveaux défis du métier d'artiste en République Démocratique du Congo. *Artl@s Bulletin*, 7(1), pp. 12–17.

MacGaffey, W. 2000. Aesthetics and politics of violence in Central Africa. *Journal of African Cultural Studies*, 13(1), pp. 63–75.

Mbembe, A. 2003. Necropolitics. *Public Culture*, 15(1), pp. 11–40.

Mbembe, A. 2005. Variations on the beautiful in the Congolese world of sounds. *Politique Africaine*, 4(100), pp. 69–91.

Mbembe, A. 2009. African Contemporary Art: Negotiating the Terms of Recognition. Interview of Vivian Paulissen with Achille Mbembe. *Africultures*, December 1. https://africultures.com/afri can-contemporary-art-negotiating-the-terms-of-recognition-9030/ (accessed 22 August 2023).

McPherson, G., Mamattah, S., Moore, D. A., Cifuentes, G., and Moualla, Y. 2018. *A Review of the Contribution of Arts & Culture to Global Security and Stability*. Glasgow: University of Western Scotland.

Mitter, S. 2019. On the Frontier, the Lubumbashi Biennial Makes Art from Obstacles. *The New York Times*, 3 December. https://www.nytimes.com/2019/12/13/arts/design/lubum bashi-biennial.html (accessed 22 August 2023).

Ndaliko, C. R. 2020. Mobutu's Ghost: A Case for the Urgency of History in Cultural Aid. In Ndaliko, C. R. and Anderson, S. (eds), *The Art of Emergency: Aesthetics and Aid in African Crises*. Oxford: Oxford University Press.

Ndaliko, C. R. 2016. *Necessary noise: Music, film, and charitable imperialism in the east of Congo*. New York, NY: Oxford University Press.

Ndaliko, C. R., and Anderson, S. M. 2019. *The art of emergency: Aesthetics and aid in African crises*. New York, NY: Oxford University Press.

Ndjo, B. 2005. Carrefour de la Joie: Popular deconstruction of the African postcolonial public sphere. *Africa*, 75(3), pp. 265–94.

Ozy Media. n.d. The defiant Congolese city daring to resist a dictator. https://www.ozy.com/ around-the-world/the-defiant-congolese-city-daring-to-resist-a-dictator/85951/ (accessed March 1 2022).

Ponzanesi, S. 2015. The postcolonial cultural industry: From consumption to distinction. *Frame*, 28(2), pp. 9–30.

Pottier, J. (2007). Rights violations, rumour, and rhetoric: making sense of cannibalism in Mambasa, Ituri (Democratic Republic of Congo). *The Journal of the Royal Anthropological Institute*, 13(4), pp. 825–43.

Pype, K. 2020. Stones thrown online: The politics of insults, distance and impunity in Congolese polémique. In Budka, P. and Bräuchler, B. (eds), *Theorising media and conflict*. Oxford: Berghahn Books, pp. 237–54.

Richmond, O. P. 2013. Peace formation and local infrastructures for peace. *Alternatives: Global, Local, Political*, 38(4), pp. 271–87.

Schouten, P. 2014. *Private security companies and political order in Congo: A history of extraversion*. PhD thesis, University of Gothenburg, Gothenburg.

Schouten, P. 2021. *Violence and fragmentation in Congo's political marketplace*. London: LSE CPR Working Paper #30.

Search for Common Ground. 2014. Participatory Theater in DR Congo. March 25. https://www. sfcg.org/participatory-theater-in-dr-congo/ (accessed 22 August 2023).

Seymour, C. 2012. Ambiguous agencies: Coping and survival in eastern Democratic Republic of Congo. *Children's Geographies*, 10(4), pp. 373–84.

Slachmuijlder, L. 2011. Setting the stage for peace: Participatory theatre for conflict transformation in the Democratic Republic of Congo. In Nagler, M. N., and Pilisuk, M. (eds), *Peace Movements Worldwide, Vol. 3*. Santa Barbara, CA: Praeger.

Stearns, J. & Vogel. C. 2021. *The landscape of armed groups in eastern Congo*. New York: Kivu Security Tracker.

Steyerl, H. 2020. Aesthetics of Resistance? Artistic Research as Discipline and Conflict. *Transversal Texts*, https://transversal.at/transversal/0311/steyerl/en (accessed 22 August 2023).

System K. 2019. Dir. Barret, R. Film. Les films en vrac.

Thomas, J., and Vogel, B. 2018. Intervention gentrification and everyday socio-economic transactions in intervention societies. *Civil Wars*, 20(2), pp. 217–37.

Trefon, T. 2011. *Congo Masquerade*. London: Zed Books.

Tsing, A. L. 2005. *Friction: An ethnography of global connection*. Princeton, NJ: Princeton University Press.

Van Beurden, S. 2013. The value of culture: Congolese art and the promotion of Belgian colonialism 1945–1959. *History and Anthropology*, 24(4), pp. 472–92.

Van Beurden, S. 2015. The art of (re)possession: Heritage and the cultural politics of Congo's decolonization. *The Journal of African History*, 56(1), pp. 143–64.

Van Reybrouck, D. 2010. *Congo: Een geschiedenis*. Amsterdam/Antwerp: De Bezige Bij.

Vogel, B. 2016. Civil society capture: Top-down interventions from below? *Journal of Intervention and Statebuilding*, 10(4), pp. 472–89.

White, B. 2000. Soukouss or sell-out? Congolese popular dance music as cultural commodity. In Haugerud, A., Stone, P. M., Little, P. D. (eds), *Commodities and globalization: anthropological perspectives*. London: Rowman and Littlefield.

White, B. 2014. Singing the praises of power. In Gandy M. and Nilsen, B. (eds), *The Acoustic City*. Berlin: Jovis.

White, B. W. 1996. L'incroyable machine d'authenticité: L'animation politique et l'usage public de la culture dans le Zaïre de Mobutu. *Anthropologie et Sociétés*, 30(2), pp. 43–63.

White, B. W. 1999. Modernity's trickster: 'dipping' and 'throwing' in Congolese popular dance music. *Research in African Literatures*, 30(4), pp. 157–75.

White, B. W. 2014. Listening together, thinking out loud: Popular music and political consciousness in Congo-Zaire. *MUSICultures*, 41(2): pp. 54–74.

SEVEN

Travelling Arts and the Syrian Revolution: Reshaping Peace Formation through Artivism

Azadeh Sobout

'The nation that is able to transform its commitment into art, can rise again, whenever it wants.'

Jaber al Azmeh-Syrian artist (Al-Khoury, 2012).

The last two decades have witnessed a growing academic interest in studying the nexus between arts and peacebuilding (Ayindo 2008; Bergh and Sloboda 2010; Cohen 2005; Cohen et al. 2011; Varea 2011; McCarthy 2007; McClain 2012). Practitioners have increasingly been 'using' art as a peacebuilding instrument and several studies have explored 'appropriate' ways to 'utilise the arts as a tool for peacebuilding' (Premaratna 2018, 2; Tselika 2019, 10; Brightman 2022, 7). This chapter takes a critical approach to the liberal peace tradition and argues that artists in the context of post-war Syria have engaged with art not as a tool for peacebuilding, but as a political strategy and as an intellectual and critical intervention.

Despite the wealth of literature exploring the relationship between art and peace, few scholars have provided an empirical analysis of the ways in which arts initiate peacebuilding (Cohen et al. 2011; Zelizer 2003; Reich 2012). Mainstream peacebuilding processes are framed within conflict resolution and management discourse with less attention to the voices and experiences from the ground (Mac Ginty 2010, 156). Similarly, the theory and practice of peacebuilding is largely dominated by approaches that focus on institution building, democratic procedures, abstract rights and neoliberal development (Premaratna 2018, 3). Few studies have explored the contribution of arts during the war in Syria (Ghanem 2019), Image politics and the art of resistance in Syria (Sacrani, 2013), Creativity and Resilience in the Syrian Revolution (Cooke 2018), Syrian refugee art (Espiritu and Duong 2018), Street Art in Revolutionary Syria (Baranko 2020) and art therapy intervention for Syrian Refugee Children (Ugurlu et al. 2016). However, less attention has been paid to the role of arts in constructing a framework for critical thought and political action. Bank (2020) is one of the few scholars to have written about 'commitment and critique in Syrian art'. Drawing on her research in Syria and later among displaced Syrian artists in Berlin, she elaborates artists' efforts in redefining their role in Syrian society as they form a new understanding of an engaged and aesthetically innovative art. This chapter intends to contribute to this conversation. First, by exploring the contribution of activist art to initiation of grassroots peacebuilding strategies, and second, by revisiting the creative experience of communities displaced and affected by the Syrian war through the lens of peace formation. To understand the potential contribution of everyday artistic activities to peace formation, it is necessary to introduce the concepts of artivism and peace formation and to discuss their theoretical and practical implications.

In the past decade there has been a growing interest in the concept of artivism. Sandoval and Latorre (2008) coined the term, linking art and activism in academic research. Raposo defined artivism 'as a cause and social claim and simultaneously as an artistic rupture', formed through 'proposing alternative scenarios, landscapes and ecologies of fruition, participation and artistic creation' (Raposo as cited in Guerra et al. 2020, 8). In Aladro-Vico, Jivkova-Semova and Bailey's view, the power of artivism lies in its ability to highlight 'injustices and social inequalities through a set of languages, images, metaphors, alternatives, seeking to generate events that break the structure of conventional communication' (Guerra et al. 2020, 9). For Mourão, artivism 'is the most radical, interdisciplinary and risky vanguard of artistic action in reality', an active art which 'subverts established norms and standards'. Mourão also underlines the connection 'between *artivism* and the practices of occupying public space, the relationship between *artivism* and the emerging social movements' (Mourão as cited in Guerra et al. 2020, 9).

An overview of the academic literature on artivism and aesthetico-political activism underlines a dynamic relationship between creativity and processes of political agency. The literature also consolidates 'social criticism and political activism' as key components of artistic activism, placing emphasis on 'the political dimension and social responsibility of art and artist' (Guerra et al. 2020, 33). Since the existing academic literature on artivism is limited, this study will also consult some of the theoretical perspectives found on activist art, protest aesthetics, aesthetico-political activism and aesthetico-political action. In the view of philosopher and art theorist Boris Groys (2014, 1), the role of art activists is not to criticise the art system or its underlying political and social conditions, but 'to change these conditions by means of art—not so much inside the art system but outside it, in reality itself'. The central role of aesthetic-political activism is questioning the established venues of 'representation and creating mechanisms capable of constructing new narratives' (Guerra et al. 2020, 24). In this sense, aesthetico-political activism is viscerally linked to the creation of alternative representation and discourse, 'making possible the emersion of voices, thoughts, and looks historically silenced' (Guerra et al. 2020, 24). Having explored the concept of artivism, I now move to discuss its connection to peace formation in everyday settings.

Richmond (2013, 276) defines peace formation as 'relationships and networked processes where indigenous or local agents of peacebuilding … find ways of establishing peace processes and sustainable dynamics of peace'. Peace formation is shaped through critical forms of agency that rise in 'everyday settings' (Richmond and Mitchell 2011, 327). These everyday settings move beyond the formal structures of 'civil society' and engage with the 'local-local' (Richmond 2009, 325), the hybrid space that demonstrates 'the existence and diversity of communities and individuals that constitute political society beyond' the liberal conceptualisation of civil society (Richmond 2010, 667). Peace formation engages with deeper layers of the local where local individuals and communities 'develop political strategies … towards the state and towards international models of order… engaging with needs, rights, custom, individual, community, agency and mobilisation in political terms' (Richmond 2010, 670).

Shedding light on the local actors and forms of agency that are unique to the hybrid context of Lebanon, peace formation offers a lens to explore whether the contribution of artists has facilitated processes that enhance the capacities required for peace. Richmond's conceptualisation of peace formation (2013, 2016) helps us to rethink the potential of localised agency in developing innovative methods of political expression, deconstruction and replacement of power hierarchies that replicate unequal structures. Simultaneously, I adopt the lens of 'critical localism' (Mac Ginty 2015) to address the local-local 'as heterogeneous and capable of agency' (Lopez 2017, 12) and remain conscious of the interplay of vertical and horizontal power relations, power dynamics and interaction between top-down actors (Mac Ginty and Richmond 2013; Richmond 2010). This conceptualisation engages with the 'local-local' as a critical tool, while recognising the existing transnational and transversal connections. It highlights the agency, autonomy and resilience of local actors and organisations, while not undermining their need for assistance. The concept of peace formation enables this study to explore the spaces and diverse dynamics of local agency, shedding light on the needs, goals and aspirations of local actors while examining their relationship with the state and with donors, as well as with their transnational networks.

Converging with this perspective, I root my theoretical proposal in a detailed discussion of the work of artists displaced and/or affected by the war in Syria. To advance a broader theoretical framing on the connections which constitute the relationship between artivism and peace formation, I elucidate two key contributions of activist art relating to 1) art as an intellectual and critical practice and 2) art as a form of social and political critique. In this sense, I approach the arts on two levels. First, thinking of the arts as an alternative way of understanding the Syrian revolution and its legacies, I investigate them as a mode of intellectual criticism and an alternative mode of discourse production. Second, engaging with the arts as a revolutionary practice, I explore how for many artists 'doing' art has been an act of revolution, creating a stage where individuals and communities come together, and new political possibilities and social relationships are formed. Furthermore, I examine how different artists have engaged with the 'local-local' as a critical tool for social and political change in the context of the relationship between artivism and peace formation (Richmond 2013, 276). In addition, in order to understand the impact of artivism on peace formation, this chapter engages with three of the four concepts proposed by Duncombe: 'Imminent Cultural Shift' which transforms the way people think or talk about an issue; 'Imminent Material Impact', achieved through a visible change in law or policy; and 'Ultimate Material Result' which leads to long-term tangible structural change (Cooper 2021, 4). The chapter will conclude with a discussion on the blockages preventing local artistic initiatives from forging peace formation despite their potential.

Research Approach and Methodology

While it is true that the arts can facilitate a creative process of bringing people together, fostering the communication and skill building for children and healing the collective traumas, my focus in this chapter is to go beyond this interpersonal level and engage with art as a place of production of political critique, methods and intervention. My intention with this chapter is to advocate for a shift away from thinking about arts as a 'tool' of peacebuilding and toward them as an active process that works politically in and of itself. In other words, this paper does not speak about the 'use' of art for political action rather about *doing* art as a political action.

The analysis offered in this paper is based on intensive field study conducted between April and June 2019 in Lebanon, and between March and April 2021 over Zoom. The field trip revolved around visiting creative spaces, art galleries, street arts, refugee camps and cultural organisations in Beirut, Tripoli, Saida, Tyre and Beqaa Valley. With the focus on the art that has emerged since the beginning of the Syrian revolution, over 70 'active interviews'[1] were conducted with independent artists, creative practitioners and NGO professionals in addition to some government funded organisations on the intersection of arts and peacebuilding. To understand the hybrid space of the local-local and forms of everyday agency, I combined ethnographic methods with semi-structured interviews while reflecting on the existing academic literature, artists websites, NGO reports and media.

In conducting the interviews, I used a narrative methodology. I invited artists to tell their story of their artistic journey with reference to the Syrian revolution and its consequent social and political implications (for example, displacement, refugee rights and transnational solidarity). While artists shared about the journey of their artivism, I explored how peace formation and artivism have influenced each other and interact. The interviews were held in places that were meaningful to the artists, the places of their dwelling or at the site of their artistic production. I visited artists in their homes, inside the refugee camps or at their studios as a way to facilitate the flow of conversation in a more meaningful and active way. During the interviews, I examined the sources of inspiration which shaped each artist's art. I also looked at things like 'critical moments' that may have shaped each artist's thoughts or feelings on the issues discussed. Moreover, I moved beyond the conventional interview method in which one person asks and the other responds. As such, I proactively engaged and exchanged my ideas in conversation, turning the interview session into a site of co-construction of knowledge and ideas.

Travelling Arts and the Syrian Revolution

The Syrian Revolution led to a surge in spontaneous and organised forms of intellectual and artistic expression in the region. It is widely believed that the arrival of artists from Syria transformed the art scene in Lebanon. For instance, Ayman Nahle (2019), Lebanese film maker remembers the time when dozens of art galleries were being opened on a single street in Beirut. Abdullah AlKafri (2019), the award-winning Syrian playwright, theatre director and cultural activist based in Beirut also recalls how the arts from Syria 'brought ... fresh blood to Lebanon at the time the country was struggling with depression'. Interviews depict that for some of the artists the move to Lebanon brought an opportunity 'to (re)establish new artistic devices' to exercise their creative abilities (Meerzon 2012, 2). For many, if displacement was not the start of their career, it was certainly a driving force behind their engagement in a collective creative process that reinforced and corroborated their aesthetic-political activism. Recounting from his own experience, Zorba (2019) says:

> Many artists in Syria were not artists in the beginning but for them art became a means of expression, resistance and revolution ... while the government denies there was any revolution the artists' work express it, through their work you can see the revolution.

While most artists interviewed consider their art as an act of inspiration, critique, memorialisation and revolution, none of them reclaimed the existence of their arts as 'pure' artistic creation. For many artists, displacement has brought a creative opportunity to be connected to the Syrian Revolution in exile. Seeing arts as part of the wider revolution discourse, artists have demonstrated that 'revolution as an effort to change, to gain dignity and equality, freedom of opinion and expression' lies at the core of their work (Pearlman 2016, 21). AlKafri (2019) asserts that 'art can help [in] creating a space for the voices of the revolution, the voices of ordinary people who tell their stories'. Milad Amin describes the role of the artist as 'revolutionary', as one disrupting the status quo and claiming transformation through acts of re-imagining, re-making, resisting and critiquing. In Karam Nachar's view (in Syrian Revolution: A History from Below 2020), 'revolution is not only about who is being in power but also about the change in our relationship'[2] to religion, gender dynamics and power structures. Dima Nachawi (2019), a Syrian illustrator, storyteller and clown, refers to the capacity of art in redefining social relations and different ways to be revolutionary. For her, the act of creation is an exercise in meaning-making within a revolution and itself a revolutionary practice.

Reflecting on the movement created by arts, Serene Dardari (2019), the Syrian founder of the Chams Network,[3] recounts that prior to the war, travel was possible only for artists from elite backgrounds who could afford to attend international exhibitions. Lebanese, Syrian, Palestinian and Yemeni artists worked in isolation from one another. Dardari further points out that 'the war has created a more cosmopolitan Syrian people ... so many Syrian artists are travelling and sharing their stories' (2019). Several artists have acknowledged that the stability of public arts institutes and art academies in Syria provided the cornerstone for the blooming art which later travelled and continued with the revolutionaries to their new spaces. In Dardari's view, the relative freedom exercised in Lebanon offered displaced artists an opportunity to express themselves freely—an opportunity which was non-existent in Syria. It was in this context that the Syrian arts travelling to Lebanon resulted in the explosion of various artforms and a blooming art scene. Rethinking the similar experience of artists who have travelled to other parts of the world, she notes:

> Their arts have been travelling with them ... I don't know if these travelling arts would come back and explode to something bigger in Syria in long term, but I hope for this art becoming a foundation we can recreate Syria with again. (2019)

Dardari (2019) introduces the metaphor of the voyage to describe the transfer of arts from Syria to Lebanon and across the globe. Her above-quoted notion of travelling as a concept closely resembles Edward Said's notion of travelling theories. As Said argued:

Theories ... journey both in space and in time—and they are marked by each place and by each historical constellation through which they travel. En route, they are continually shaped and reshaped according to the local conditions of production, reception, transmission, and—not least—resistance. (In Frank 2009, 61)

Dardari's remark provokes us to think how travelling arts are affected by their journeying as they move from one environment to another; the art will change, and gets transformed, a process that raises important methodological and interpretive questions about the impact of arts on the wider social and political context. What is interesting from the perspective of 'travelling art' is its impact on grassroots struggles, creative resistance and the experimental engagement with new forms of collectivity and solidarity in the new context. The artist is thus not only a creator, but also a traveller, moving 'between familiar and alien traditions and cultures', creating new forms of trans-local/national solidarities and alternative forms of political association (Lloyd 2015, 2).

Mehdi Yehya, the Lebanese artist and co-founder of Peace of Art, a music academy in Beqaa Valley, recounts how the war in Syria affected the inter-community dynamic in Lebanon. Prior to the war, there were a lot of inter-relations and marriages between Sunni-Shia communities in the Beqaa villages, but the conflict in Syria had a detrimental impact on this relationship. For many Lebanese, the war in Syria has revived the memories of the Civil War in Lebanon (1975–90), opening the wounds of the past. Referring to the intertwining of histories and oppressions in the region, Yahya notes: 'what is happening in Syria is not just a Syrian or Palestinian issue but also a Lebanese issue'. Ayman Nahle (2019), the Lebanese filmmaker, refers to the history of shared oppression as a driving force for emergent collectivities in Lebanon. In his view, one of the key reasons Syrian artists found freedom and opportunity for self-expression in Lebanon is because both Lebanese and Syrians have a common history of oppression by the Syrian regime, for many Lebanese lost family members to the Syrian army during the 29 years of Syrian occupation of North Lebanon (1976–2005).

While the Syrian displaced population in Lebanon exceeds 1.5 million people today, the conflict in Syria has also forced many Palestinian refugees previously living in Syria to flee to Lebanon in search of safety. Lebanon currently hosts at least 479,537 Palestinian refugees (UNRWA 2022) most of whom have been displaced more than once in their lifetime. In the same context, the legacy of the Lebanese civil war and Israeli military invasions (1982, 1996, 2006) continues to sustain the internal displacement of many Lebanese communities from South and Mount Lebanon, most of whom have found a home in proximity to Palestinian refugee camps in Beirut. Furthermore, the recent displacement of Armenians from Syria to Lebanon, a century after their survival from the 1915 genocide has extended the continuum of displacements in the region.

This perpetual state of displacement experienced by Palestinians, Armenians, Syrians and many Lebanese is deeply reflected and reproduced in the collaborative work of artists, leading to the formation of a shared aesthetic between different communities in Lebanon. It is against this background that the political aesthetic created following the Syrian Revolution is not only limited to the creative work of Syrians but artists from diverse communities who continue to contribute to the art of and about Syria through different mediums and platforms. Reflecting on the strong solidarity between artists from various backgrounds, AlKafri (2019)[4] and Dardari (2019)[5] both assert that despite the existence of structural racism against refugees in education, health and employment sectors, incidence of racism is rarely encountered in the art sector. Drawing on this introduction, the following section examines how the 'travelling arts' from Syria is transformed and shaped in Lebanon.

Art as an Intellectual and Critical Practice

The interviews demonstrate that artists contributing to the art of and about Syria in Lebanon have created a multi-disciplinary space for the exchange of knowledge, strategies and participatory research. Through engaging with arts as a form of intellectual expression they have formulated an alternate knowledge of the understanding of Syrian revolution, war and displacement. Abdullah AlKafri (2019) articulates the paradigm shift that emerged in the work of many artists in the years following the uprising:

> We felt there is a need to move from creating artistic initiatives toward development of a cultural policy where artists and cultural practitioners are seen as main players in the future of Syria.

Questioning the absence of art and culture in high level discussions such as the EU conference on 'Supporting the future of Syria and the region', AlKafri (2019) urges for the need to engage with artists and cultural practitioners in activities that support the reform of cultural legislation and infrastructure in the region. With a critical approach to the role of arts and culture in times of crisis, AlKafri (2019) along with a few other artists founded Ettijahat-Independent Culture.[6] The organisation was born from the belief that culture and arts constitute the backbone of a society, and the role of artists and cultural practitioners is 'to bring the question of art and culture to the table and to prove that art and culture have a major role in the future of Syria as a country experiencing transition' (AlKafri 2019). It is in this context that instead of investing their efforts on initiating artistic activities, Etthijahat engages with

individual artists and collectives to create momentum for the debate and formulation of new cultural policies in a bottom-up manner—an effort which
leads to long-term tangible structural change or 'Ultimate Material Result'
(Cooper 2021, 4).

Several artists have linked the post-war reconstruction process with the
power of imagination, highlighting the view that artists enable conflict-
affected societies to move beyond the existing paradigms by finding new
creative solutions to the conflict. Mirroring Roland Bleiker's claim that works
of art 'can lead us to see the world in a new light and rethink assumptions
we have taken for granted' (2018, 3), many artists believe that their work
provides the social, political and aesthetic imagination needed for the future
reconstruction of Syria. Reflecting on her creative illustrations of the Syrian
landscape and war-torn cities, Dima Nachawi (2019), Syrian illustrator,
storyteller and clown, demonstrates how artistic engagement facilitates the
re-imagining of social relationships and hence contributes to the visioning
of new futures. In this context, art could be seen as a vital societal element
rather than an activity incorporated into peacebuilding initiatives. Artistic
organisations such as Etthijahat 'do not promote arts-based peacebuilding
initiatives but offer spaces of encounter and dialogue between artists and
communities affected by war through the creation of a common artistic production of high aesthetic quality' (Marcuello-Lopez 2017, 2).

For a country that is yet to be rebuilt, 'the focus on art and culture is a way
to achieve social change for the future and to engage in a process of state
building' (AlKafri 2019). In AlKafri's view, artistic creation is an attempt
at state formation from below, which is achieved not only 'through strategies focused on governance institutions and processes' but also through
rebuilding the relationship between communities and cultural institutions
(Richmond and Pogodda 2016, 15). In the same vein, Etthijahat has developed long-term collaboration between Syrians and other communities in the
region and seeks to focus on 'the art from Syria' instead of 'Syrian art' (AlKafri
2019). In one of their projects titled 'Tota Tota', Etthijahat provided Syrians,
Palestinians and Lebanese participants training in theatre production with
an opportunity to co-create a play in collaboration with a theatre collective.
The play was performed in several cities and refugee camps in Lebanon, as
AlKafri asserts:

> This is something very important for us: working for Syrians doesn't mean that we
> work only with Syrians. Through our work, we are hoping to bring about a different
> discourse about Syria. (Interview with AlKafri in Al Sharq n.d., 3)

The example of Etthijahat demonstrates the development of a cultural model
and artistic framework that supports critical interventions and culture-related

research in conflict and transitional contexts. AlKafri (2019) elucidates that the majority of artists involved with Etthijahat are *'artivists*, those who combine art with activism and are active on all sides and geographical locale'. The work of these artists could be understood as a conscious effort in creating a common space for communities as they work together to move toward a consensus on the most important priorities emerging from the current social and political circumstances. Part of this effort lies in the recognition that artistic interventions can offer a way into understanding the complex reality, as they help to broaden the possibility of what can be seen, what can be thought and what can be done in times of political transition.

Zayraqoun[7] is another initiative which engages with the arts in a critical manner. The collective was founded by Rami Chahine and a group of activists in 2020. Zayraqoun's creative engagement is organised in a form of performance and parade depicting 'the surreal journey of a group of nomads, as they move from one transformative experience to the other in a circus of songs, music, dance rituals and games' (Chahine 2021, 71). Explaining the motive beyond the collective's choice of parade as an artform, Chahine asserts that parade is a metaphor of constant movement, finding resonance with the (dis)placement of many communities in the region. 'It is also a metaphor of a journey to reach and come together, celebrating the possibilities and dreams of true co-existence'. The multidisciplinary performance and parades also challenge the notions of public space and collective creation as participants gather 'to explore their individualities through play, exchange of skills and stories which are then shared with the society at large in the streets across Karantina neighbourhoods' (Ibid.). The streets chosen for the rehearsal and parade are in the most marginalised areas of Beirut where internally displaced Lebanese, Syrians, Palestinians and other migrant groups co-inhabit. Casting a critical look at the role of arts in peacebuilding and the way it is currently appropriated in humanitarian programmes, Chahine (2021) notes:

> I am inspired by Johan Huizinga's notion of 'art' as the essence of human beings. Art embodies our values, rituals and culture. Art is not a tool for humanitarian action, it is our essential culture. The artist's mission is to create a material that pushes the societal culture to question itself and reconstruct it from new.

As a multimedia artist, Chahine sees art as a creative and critical means of reaching out to society, transforming its culture and politics. Chahine's articulation of art as the essence of the human being resonates with the holistic approach promoted by Serene Dardari (2019). Casting a critical eye on the current post-conflict development and humanitarian programmes, she argues that art should be placed at the core of such programmes and not seen as a single and stand-alone activity. Pointing to UNESCO's conceptualisation of art as an essential element for human development, Dardari describes her efforts in integrating art and humanitarianism at an informal school in north Lebanon. Providing education to Syrian children by creating an art-based educational syllabus, she stresses the need for the arts 'to be seen as a vital and basic human need'. Reflecting on the same approach, AlKafri (2019) challenges the utilitarian and didactic view of international funders and agencies on the role of arts:

> International funders see art as a tool for gathering people, for healing traumas and providing capacity building and training workshops, but not as a critique and creator of a new social and political order. As an organisation, we don't get involved in conversations that define art as a means to provide psycho-social support. For the same reason we don't get involved in peace building projects developed by international NGOs.

It is in the same context that he notes 'We don't use art, we do art, responding to the needs of artists and communities. Achieving art is not using it' (AlKafri in Marcuello-Lopez 2017, 8).

Engaging with Art as a Site of Discourse Production

In response to the official narratives of the Syrian war which have been selectively recorded, manipulated and suppressed, artists and activists have initiated a combination of creative and political practices to reclaim 'the right to truth'. Several artists have highlighted the production of counter-narratives and alternative models as the central contribution of their art. In the words of Milad Amin (2019), the Syrian artist and film maker, the Syrian revolution more than anything is a 'war over narratives'. Amin describes how the regime's narrative defined revolutionaries as Islamist and extremists while there were leftists, artists and ordinary people at protests. Speaking of his engagement in arts and documentary work, Amin explains that, for him, art is a creative way to challenge the meta-narrative of both the Syrian regime and international forces. Highlighting the intrinsic link between documentary work and the truth, he notes:

> I produced a movie to stay in history, to counter the forgetfulness and challenge the dominant narrative that wants to take over. This is our history. This is our pain, and we cannot forget it. All those people who have run away—the 8 million displaced, cannot forget. This is our cause, our land, our pain. We tell it and we screen it. Our documentary of what was happening in Syria in 2014 had more than 10 million YouTube viewers. I think we are winning this war because we are telling the truth. (2019)

Engaging with art as a site of discourse production, the Lebanese filmmaker Ayman Nahle (2019) stresses deconstructing the 'narrative of Syrian revolution which has been fabricated by international politics and the Syrian regime'. Working on memory, objects and sounds, he engages with archive as a method of social change. His documentaries amplify the voices of those most affected by providing an avenue for introducing their narratives. In *Now: End of Season*[8] he deconstructs the experience of displacement by placing the everyday struggles of refugees in a political context. Through his choice of voices and characters he demonstrates what is happening to those refugees is not 'humanitarian' but political. These artistic engagements demonstrate the multiple ways in which it is not only possible to deconstruct the narrative of war in Syria but also to create the basis for political visibility of refugees and thereby place the forced displacement of millions of Syrians in a larger historical and political context.

Originally from South Lebanon and born during the Civil War, Nahle (2019) reinterprets legacies of the Lebanese Civil War through the lens of Syrian revolution. In his art he connects experiences of struggle and survival within and between communities and creates archival infrastructures that connect legacies of the past struggles and victims of today's oppression. To him, art and documentary making are not about a new creation, they are about re-creation of shared struggle and shared history. By engaging with art as a critical force, artists such as Nahle have disrupted the dominant humanitarian and political narratives. Casting a critique on the dominant discourse of the 'refugee crisis' and the tendency of homogenising individuals by the migration regimes in Europe, AlKafri echoes similar views. Supporting the work of individual artists as a counterstrategy to the mass homogenisation of Syrian people, he highlights the role of the arts in challenging the existing stereotypes about Syrians:

> Syrians are mainly seen as refugees and this image has the connotation of someone being totally displaced and powerless, a connotation which is not fair nor appropriate. Ettijahat strives to challenge such discourses, discourses that see people 'as just refugees'. They are displaced, and legally they might be refugees. But they are not just that. (Interviewed in Al Sharq n.d., 2)

Being reduced to mere categories and experiencing dehumanisation under this discourse the individuality of refugees is lost. For AlKafri (2019), the contribution of the arts is to reverse this dehumanisation and recognise the agency and activity of those frequently marginalised or excluded, the process which in Berents view forms the foundation of peace formation (2015, 1). Shedding light on the same discourse, Nahle (2019) questions the tendency of international organisations in developing numerous trends on 'refugee arts' and 'refugee artists':

In the context where communities are very proud of their ethnic and cultural backgrounds and do not associate their identities with their displaced status, this language has created a refugee, non-refugee binary. In Lebanon they are called Syrians, Palestinian Lebanese[9] and Palestinian Syrians.[10] They are not refugees.

The artistic initiatives have also opened spaces of resistance and critical imagination. The work of Salim Assi, a Palestinian mural artist from Lebanon, depicts the vital role that the Palestinian artists have played in documenting the devastating effects of the war on Syria's Palestinian refugee population. Assi's art bears witness to the tragic history of Palestinian displacement and highlights the moral responsibility of viewers in ending the perpetual cycle of violence and rightlessness. Challenging the concept of art for peace, Assi asserts: 'I don't make art for peace or for building bridges. As a Palestinian artist, I can say it in another way: Give me my rights first and then I will lead the peace across the world' (2019). Reconstructing resistance through art, Assi's artistic practice challenges the colonial definition of peace which sustains the status quo, injustice and rightlessness. In this sense, his art practice is viscerally linked to the creation of alternative representation and discourse, bringing visibility to peace formation and an understanding of peace from below.

The narrative on the Syrian Revolution often tends to simplify what actually is a complex and varied reality on the ground. In this multifaceted context, the arts can function as an alternative lens through which we understand the multi-layered experience of diverse communities affected by war and conflict in Syria. The central role of aesthetico-political activism for many artists departs from Duncombe's notion of 'Imminent Cultural Shift' as they question the established venues of representation and create 'mechanisms capable of constructing new narratives' (Guerra et al. 2020, 2, 2024). These artistic initiatives have visualised the human consequences of war in ways which might resist or complicate the official representations of peace and conflict that underpin the dominant narrative.

Art as a Form of Social and Political Critique

This section explores whether arts-based interventions have been able to interact with and change other political spaces around them. Schwarzman argues that for art to promote transformation it has to differentiate 'between art that is about politics, and art that is political (Schwarzman as cited in Benjamin 2003). 'It is not enough for art to represent a political event for others to observe. It must also provide a context within which others can take action' (Schwarzman as cited in Purcell 2009, 114). The focus of this section is therefore on the art that creates a context for political action. Founded in

2012, Utopia works in war-torn neighbourhoods of Tripoli, the city which has suffered from protracted political violence, high rates of unemployment and poverty. The deep-rooted conflict between the Bab al-Tabbaneh and Jabal Mohsen neighbourhoods can be traced back to the time of the Syrian occupation of North Lebanon and the Tabbaneh Massacre of 1986, when more than 1,500 people from the majority Sunni area of Tabbaneh were killed by the Syrian Army. The Syria street connecting the poor areas of Tabbaneh and Jabal Mohsen is marked by the ruins of civil war. The first clashes between the two areas started at the time when the majority Alawaite community of Jabal Mohsen sided with the Syrian regime and the tension escalated with the start of the war in Syria. Throughout the last decade, the area has witnessed many movements and communal tensions with increasing numbers of Syrians seeking refuge in the poverty-stricken neighbourhood.

One of the early initiatives of Utopia was the *This Is Lebanon Project* (2014) in which the future visions of Lebanon were captured from the perspectives of youths in the community. Right in middle of the conflict, a group of young artivists re-appropriated the war-torn cinema of Al-Andalus which was closed during the Civil War and turned it into a haven for fighters. Recalling the experience, Shafiq Abdur Rahman (2019), programme manager of Utopia states: 'By re-appropriating the Cinema, our aim was not only to rebuild the cinema as a space, but also as a concept'. For artists, rebuilding the Al-Andalus was a way of reimagining their neighbourhood through the reconstruction of its only cinema. Today, the reappropriated cinema has turned into a safe space which serves as the only socio-cultural centre in the area. This re-appropriation demonstrates how artivists have made a political use of a war-torn space by repurposing it and converting it to a theatre for promoting social cohesion.

In Utopia, theatre artists have created a space of activism in the margins, a space in which and through which communities can act. One of the most influential interventions developed in the area is the Flash Mob and Street Theatre. The project was initiated by engaging with youths and women from different communities living in the area. Abdu Rahman (2019) recalls the time when social workers went to streets and invited the youth to come and join a movie night. Soon the cinema club became a hub for many young people from Tabbaneh and Jabal Mohsen who joined interactive theatre workshops while engaging in conversations over sectarian issues, issues affecting child protection inside families and communities and discrimination faced by refugees. Under the instruction of a theatre artist, the participating youth initiated a flash mob project where the young performers would get a chance to express their ideas and thoughts through creative and non-violent actions.

The flash mob creates a scene based on a particular social issue (child marriage, domestic violence and so forth) in the street, turning the public space into a stage where young artists perform a provocative story as a real-life event. Unaware of the event being a performance, the public viewers intervene in the scene as actors. For instance, intervening to defend a woman who has experienced domestic violence, or a child exploited as a labourer on the street. The flash mobs provide the artists and the public viewers with the possibility of collective engagement in an interactive social context. Following every flash mob, a group discussion is organised where the public audience is invited to share their views about the topic of the performance. The flash mob therefore provides a space for learning, reflecting and relating to critical social issues. The theatre club in Utopia therefore has become part of a wider social discourse that engages with marginalised communities who use their own bodies to foster collective action and social change.

Chadi Nachabe (2019), the co-founder of Utopia, recalls the time when through a street flash mob and media support, the neighbourhood campaign succeeded in gaining financial assistance for people from Tabbaneh and Jabal Mohsen to repair their war-torn houses. The flash mob happened outside the government building during a cabinet meeting and eventually led to the approval and transfer of the funding to house owners in ten days. Utopia's work has had an immediate impact on the lives of communities through a visible change in law or policy, thereby its contribution can be understood as 'Imminent Material Impact', to use Duncombe's term (Cooper 2021, 4).

In a different context, Farah Wardani (2020) discusses how the theatre work of Laban has contributed to shaping political agency, solidarity and resistance. Founded in 2009, Laban was the first playback theatre in Lebanon that used ideas from the Theatre of the Oppressed as a bridge to peacebuilding work. At the beginning of the war in Syria, Laban created a space for expressing less heard narratives and brought them into the communal discourse. As a theatre practitioner and founder of Laban, Wardani (2020) notes that for many Lebanese these playback sessions provided their very first experience of listening to communities displaced from Syria:

During those sessions we heard more about politics than we had ever found in the news. Many Syrians, Palestinians and Lebanese found a safe space in our studio, they felt they had a voice to speak and to be heard. During the playback, the audience would share stories about a certain issue. The actors would then come up with a short play that depicts the essence of the shared stories. Afterward the audiences would build this story along with the actors or advise the direction and ending of their wish. This type of theatre gives the participants a voice, a chance to shape and tell a story. In this way, people become visible through the re-telling of their stories and the re-imagining of their testimonies.

Wardani remembers how the attendants of the playback came back with changed opinions on Syrian and Palestinian people, their causes and sufferings. The playback could thus be read as an attempt to create 'Imminent Cultural Shift' as it challenged racist political ideologies and created inclusive social imaginaries (Duncombe in Cooper 2021, 4). At the heart of Laban's work is the struggle for equal recognition and visibility which chimes with Jacques Rancière's emancipatory politics. For Rancière, politics begins when those formerly 'denied a place in the social order' assert for themselves the exercise of power and entitlement of inclusion (Rancière as cited in Huzar 2018, 11). Laban's peacebuilding through theatre has transformed public venues into platforms where those who have been marginalised are involved to take control of their narratives by acting as co-players and becoming the creator of the theatre. The example of Utopia and Laban demonstrates the capacity of artists to articulate social responses against former taboo subjects like violations of children rights, domestic violence and discrimination against refugees.

Similar to Nchabe and Wardani, Mehdi Yehya the co-founder of the Peace of Art (PoA) explains how the first and the only Fine Arts Academy in Beqaa Valley has provided a space for interaction between youths from different backgrounds—Sunni, Shia, Druze, Christians and the newly arrived refugees from Syria (2019). Today the Syrian refugees are estimated to constitute half of the population of the Beqaa. In a region with high levels of unemployment, poor infrastructure and armed violence, this demographic change has led to further tensions between the local and Syrian communities. In 2014 and at the time the area was severely destabilised by the Islamic State of Iraq and Syria (ISIS), PoA started the 'Art Against Discrimination' project. The ongoing initiative has brought together more than 100 young people from around the Beqaa Valley with refugees from both Syria and Palestine, to partake in a series of artistic and civic training, with the aspiration to transform the culture of violence and discrimination into acceptance, development and freedom.

Recalling the many challenges faced by PoA in its early years, Yehya notes how artists from different nationalities travelled to Beqaa Valley to compensate for the absence of art and music teachers in the area. Through their creative engagements in a highly militarised space, these artists introduced a new thread of artivism as well as a site of resistance, which allowed them to mobilise action, solidarity and change. In Yehya's view, the foundation of PoA more than anything was an effort to find a solution against the growing sectarian tensions while addressing other forms of structural violence, militarism and inequality. Turning artistic initiatives into an everyday space of activism, PoA's everyday artistic initiatives have transcended ethnic division and generated political solidarity across different communities in the region. The work of artists in creating transnational solidarity in supporting the oppressed and marginalised groups reinforce the Sartrean view of art as a form of 'political engagement' and reiterates the fact that artistic engagement produces different kinds of politics (Papastergiadis 2014, 8).

Blockages and the Limits of Travelling Art

In this section, I examine some of the barriers artists and grassroots interventions have faced in sustainable political and social transformation. Following the Beirut Blast in 2020 and amidst the ongoing economic and political crises, Lebanon's cultural organisations and long-established artistic infrastructure struggle to survive. With diminishing funds, smaller organisations are finding it hard to sustain themselves and due to the change in the political discourse which has diverted the attention on Syria to return of the refugees, supporting creative expression as part of the processes of democratisation and change is no longer a priority. The situation has left many formerly active arts and cultural initiatives under-funded and at the risk of closure. Having to rely on international sources to fund artistic initiatives, many artists have pointed to the challenges within the funding infrastructures. Nachawi (2019) finds her identity as an artist to be compromised in dealing with these funding requirements. Challenging the current refugee rhetoric within the funding criteria she notes:

> Since my departure from Syria, art has become a key component of my life, a way to project my identity and fight against stereotypes. I see myself as an artist not a Syrian refugee. But if you don't present yourself as a 'refugee', you will be less attractive to some donors.

Nachawi (2019) consciously flags up the uncritical adoption of the term 'refugee' in labelling people, in her view most humanitarian and international funding bodies have only focused on the experience of 'displacement' and neglected all other aspects of the lives of people who have been displaced. This emphasis has also affected the creative work of artists as they are driven towards topics dictated by the funding agencies (for instance artworks about war, seeking asylum and politics). Challenging the rhetoric of 'artists as peace maker' and the view that sees art as a tool for social and political change, Nachawi (2019) asserts:

> Art does not change but aspires. I do not see peace building as the responsibility of the artist. As an illustrator I am there to aspire and as a clown, I am here to bring smile on people's face but I do not wish to take the burden of peace building on my shoulders. I see myself as a change maker through aspiring people and motivating them to have hope in a better future.

Nachawi's testimony demonstrates how art can drive aspiration in a deeper sense, as a way 'to stir up reflection, to provoke … (and) to challenge power by providing alternative models' (Tolan 2015). Drawing on conversations with artists, this chapter recognises that artistic initiatives are unlikely to be a sufficient factor in creating an effective change in the dynamic of the conflict unless they are part of a more holistic approach to social reconstruction and political change. Artists have pointed to 'social criticism and political activism' as key components of their artistic engagement, placing emphasis on building alliance, critical thinking and decolonising the education system (Silva, Guerra and Santos 2018, 33). As Dardari (2019) points out:

> The art created at grassroots has a limit in creating change and cannot transform until it is moved to a strategic level … artists need to create coalitions … they need to integrate their social activism with a political message … integrating art with development, art with economics, art with politics and art with critical theory. We need to see more integration of art in education and for this we need to decolonise the education system.

During the interviews several artists highlighted the tension around the conceptualisation of peace by international agencies and the way art is being co-opted into international projects. Following the Syrian war, most funding bodies required the local NGOs to incorporate 'conflict resolution' and 'reconciliation' training into their programmes. All too often, the starting points of this training were related to Western concerns of security and terrorism, rather than an effort to reintegrate affected communities by helping them to preserve their own cultural identities. Mehdi Yahya (2019), co-founder of Peace of Art problematises this top-down practice of peacebuilding and explains how Peace of Art has succeeded in constructing a grounded conception of peace that proves to be more practical than the international NGOs 'good practices':

> There is a tendency in Lebanon not to talk of 'peace', for a community which has survived civil war talking about peace would suggest we are not in peace. In designing our workshops, we rethink our societal contexts. We provide young people with possible scenarios enabling them to subconsciously think about complex tensions. We creatively engage with youth in music classes on discussion about conflict, coexistence and peace without referring to peace.

Mirroring the same view, Stephanie Twigg the Arts Manager of the British Council Syria recounts that in the early days of the revolution, a lot of funded projects were developed on the security perspective looking at people as perpetrators and treating victims of violence as a threat, which created mistrust between people working in funding programmes and local artists. Twigg recalls how, through resistance of artists, the programming focus of many international organisations eventually changed from security-driven peace towards a human security approach to peacebuilding, while the shift highlights the autonomy of local actors to 'renegotiate, ignore, engage with, disengage from and exploit the liberal peace' (Mac Ginty 2010, 104).

Further conversations with artists demonstrate that the international organisations' focus on 'empowering the local organisations' is embedded in the idea that local peace practices lack autonomous capacities for peacebuilding and promote the idea that peace needs to be built through 'capacity development' programmes provided by international agencies. This view is resisted by artists as it conceives local communities as powerless and non-autonomous actors. Similarly, many artists have emphasised that art should be part of the broader process for justice because creative expression is not only important for establishing peace but also to challenge injustice. This is particularly highlighted in conversation with Moataz Dajani, Jerusalemite artist, cultural activist and educator to whom peace as driven by international peace industry denotes normalisation and acceptance of status quo (2019).

Conclusion

Through close analysis of collaborative and collective art practices in Lebanon, the chapter has engaged with notion of *artpeace* as a way of highlighting traces of local peace formation that have emerged in response to shifting political conditions following the Syrian Revolution. Conceptualising how artivism can create spaces for local agency and transformation, the chapter has illustrated how peace formation can occur through 'travelling arts' and movements of ideas and aesthetics. Drawing on the power of artivism in highlighting injustices and social inequalities, it has also underlined the work of artists in 'widen(ing) the sphere of the political' as they consider 'the agency of those excluded or marginalised ... through action and voice' (Berents 2015, 18).

Reflecting on the idea of 'peace formation' (Richmond, 2013), the chapter sheds light on the potential of grassroots art-based initiatives in creating safe and supportive spaces for marginalised and displaced communities, enabling them to share their personal and political experiences, strategies and tactics to create positive change. Similarly, it has discussed how artists have engaged 'the deeper layers of the local', promoting alternative strategies for political expression and creating spaces for critical agency and intervention (Mac Ginty 2010, 104). Drawing on the way artists have facilitated reconstruction of social relationships and mobilising political communities, the chapter has elucidated the way artists have transcended sectarian and national borders, striving to cultivate reconciliation, social cohesion and transnational solidarity.

By engaging artists through their aesthetic and intellectual concerns, the paper has identified the contribution of the arts to a number of critical interventions. It has demonstrated the role of the arts in continuing and sustaining revolutionary ideas and politics. It has explored how art has provided an alternative lens through which we can understand the multi-layered experience of diverse communities affected by war and displacement in Syria. It has shed light on the crucial work of art in forming critique of the dominant humanitarian paradigm and developing a new political discourse for post-war reconstruction. Finally, the arts have functioned as a form of collective empowerment for the Syrian people and other communities affected by the ongoing war and displacement in the region.

Notes

1. 'Active Interviews' transform interviewers from 'subjects' into 'constructors of knowledge' in collaboration with the interviewee (Ritchie 2011, 13).
2. Conversation with Karam S. Nachar, Syrian writer and academic, during the webinar The Syrian Revolution: a History from Below (2020).
3. The Chams Network (Sun in Arabic) is a youth-led, nonprofit community organisation which designs and implements small to medium scaled initiatives that have a positive social impact, empower marginalised individuals and raise awareness on issues specifically related to girls and women's socio-economic rights.
4. The award-winning Syrian playwright, theater director, and cultural activist based in Beirut (2019).
5. The creative founder of the Chams Network (2019).
6. Further information about the organisation can be found at: https://www.ettijahat.org/
7. Further information about Zayraqoun can be found at Zayraqoun-Development workshops and games Hunters and birds https://vimeo.com/473624324, Rehla Ila – Zayrakoun https://youtu.be/7Z4EJvt6NjY and the Zayraqoun website: https://cargocollective.com/Zayraqoun/
8. The documentary can be accessed at: https://vimeo.com/145747524
9. Palestinians who took refuge in Lebanon since the occupation and dispossession of their lands in 1948.
10. Palestinians who took refuge in Syria since the occupation and dispossession of their lands in 1948.

References

Al-Khoury, T. 2012. Places and Bodies in the Arts of Arab Revolutions. *Majallat al-Dirasat al-Filastiniyya*, Issue 90 – Spring. https://www.palestine-studies.org/en/node/38059 (accessed 18 November 2022).

Al Sharq. n. d. Syrian art and social change: Art helps us rethink the future of the country. https://www.disorient.de/files/1702_ettijahat-en-final.pdf (accessed 05 June 2021).

Ayindo, B. 2008. Arts approaches to peace: Playing our way to transcendence? In Hart, B. (ed.), *Peacebuilding in traumatized societies*. Boulder, CO: University Press of America.

Bank, C. 2020. *The contemporary art scene in Syria: Social critique and an artistic movement*. New York: Routledge.

Baranko, E. 2020. Visualizing participatory politics: The communal power of street art in revolutionary Egypt, warring Syria, and divided Lebanon. CMC Senior Theses. 2492. https://scholarship.claremont.edu/cmc_theses/2492 (accessed 22 August 2023).

Benjamin, W. 2003. *Understanding Brecht* (New Edition). London: Verso. https://www.csus.edu/indiv/o/obriene/art206/Readings/Walter_Benjamin_-_The_Author_as_Producer.pdf (accessed 20 November 2022).

Berents, H. 2015. An embodied everyday peace in the midst of violence. *Peacebuilding*, 3(2), pp. 1–14.

Bergh, A. and Sloboda, J. 2010. Music and art in conflict transformation: A review. *Music & Arts in Action*, 2(2), pp. 1–16.

Bleiker, R. (ed.). 2018. *Visual global politics*. London: Routledge.

Brightman, M., 2022. *Drawing the line: a Media Analysis of the Relationship Between Art and Peacebuilding and Conflict Resolution in Colombia* (Doctoral dissertation). https://dalspace.library.dal.ca/handle/10222/81598 (accessed 20 November 2022).

Chahine, R. 2021. *Collective Creation Games*, 3rd edn. Lebanon: Aaley Publication.

Chahine, R. 2020. Zayraqoun-Development workshops and games Hunters and birds [Online]. https://vimeo.com/473624324 (accessed 20 November 2022).

Cohen, C. Varea, R. G., Walker, P. O., Milosevic, D. and Mulekwa, C. 2011. *Acting together I: Performance and the creative transformation of conflict: Resistance and reconciliation in regions of violence*. New York: NYU Press. https://doi.org/10.2307/j.ctt21pxmd8 (accessed 20 November 2022).

Cohen, C. 2005. Creative approaches to reconciliation. In: Fitzduff M. and Stout C. (eds), *The Psychology of Resolving Global Conflicts: From War to Peace*, Vol 3. Westport, CT: Greenwood, pp. 69–102.

Cooke, M. 2018. Reimagining the Syrian revolution. *ASAP/Journal*, 3(2), pp. 269–78.

Cooper, J. 2021. 'No soy un activista, soy un artista': Representations of the feminicide at the intersections of art and activism. *Bulletin of Latin American Research*, 41(3), pp. 344–58.

Danko, D. 2018. Artivism and the spirit of avant-garde art. In Alexander, V.D., Hägg, S., Häyrynen, S. and Sevänen, E., *Art and the Challenge of Markets Volume 2. National Cultural Politics and the Challenges of Marketization and Globalization*. London: Palgrave Macmillan, pp. 235–61.

De Genova, N. and Roy, A. 2020. Practices of illegalisation. *Antipode*, 52(2), pp. 352–64.

Espiritu, Y. L. and Duong, L. 2018. Feminist refugee epistemology: Reading displacement in Vietnamese and Syrian refugee art. *Signs: Journal of Women in Culture and Society*, 43(3), pp. 587–615.

El Khechen, M. 2021. Rehla Ila – Zayrakoun / Zoukak's Theatre Mentorship Program and Production [Online]. https://www.youtube.com/watch?v=7Z4EJvt6NjY (accessed 20 November 2022).

Frank, M. C. 2009. Imaginative geography as a travelling concept: Foucault, Said and the spatial turn. *European Journal of English Studies*, 13(1), pp. 61–77.

Ghanem, M. 2019. Stories Untold: Art from Syria. *New England Journal of Public Policy*, 31(1), p. 6.

Groys, B. 2014. On art activism. *E-flux*, 56, pp. 1–14. http://www.e-flux.fflom/journal/on-art-afltivism/ (accessed 20 November 2022).

Guerra, P., Hoefel, M. D. G., Severo, D. O. and Sousa, S. 2020. Women on the move: Contributions to the aesthetic-political activism approach of Brazilian migrant women. *Mémoire (s), identité (s), marginalité (s) dans le monde occidental contemporain*. Cahiers du MIMMOC, 21.

Huzar, T. 2018. *Themes of Visibility in Rancière, Butler and Cavarero*. PhD Thesis, University of Brighton.

Lloyd, M., 2015. Travelling theories. *Redescriptions: Political Thought, Conceptual History and Feminist Theory*, 18(2) https://journal-redescriptions.org/articles/abstract/10.7227/R.18.2.1/ (accessed 20 November 2022).

Lopez, A. L. 2017. Local peacemaking trajectories and hybrid peace: Tracing knowledge, capacity and agency in conflict-driven areas. PhD Thesis, Universiteit Antwerpen. https://medialibrary.uantwerpen.be/oldcontent/container2143/files/Prize/Lopez_Dissertation.pdf (accessed 21 November 2022).

Mac Ginty, R. 2010. Hybrid peace: The interaction between top-down and bottom-up peace. *Security Dialogue*, 41(4), pp. 391–412.

Mac Ginty, R. 2014. Everyday peace: Bottom-up and local agency in conflict-affected societies. *Security Dialogue*, 45(6), pp. 548–64.

Mac Ginty, R. 2015. Where is the local? Critical localism and peacebuilding. *Third World Quarterly*, 36(5), pp. 840–56.

Mac Ginty, R. and Richmond, O. P. 2013. The local turn in peace building: A critical agenda for peace. *Third World Quarterly*, 34(5), pp. 763–83.

Marcuello-Lopez, M. 2017. Syrian art in Beirut: Breaking boundaries and restoring hope. https://www.semanticscholar.org/paper/Syrian-art-in-Beirut-%3A-Breaking-boundaries-and-hope-Marcuello-Lopez/8c18def853caaa20ce7e8c40051134b412eeca45 (accessed 21 November 2022).

McCarthy, P. 2007. Peace and the arts. In Webel, C. and Galtung, J. (eds), *Handbook of peace and conflict studies* (Vol. 7). London: Routledge.

McClain, L. M. 2012. Artistic suggestions for peaceful transition in Northern Uganda: What youth are saying. *African Conflict and Peace Building Review*, 2(1), pp. 152–63.

Meerzon, Y. 2012. *Performing exile, performing self: Drama, theatre, film*. London: Palgrave Macmillan.

Nahle, A. 2015. Now: End of Season. [Online]. https://vimeo.com/145747524 (accessed 20 November 2022).

Papastergiadis, N. 2014. A breathing space for aesthetics and politics: An introduction to Jacques Rancière. *Theory, Culture & Society*, 31(7–8), pp. 5–26.

Pearlman, W. 2016. Narratives of fear in Syria. *Perspectives on Politics*, 14(1), pp. 21–37.

Premaratna, N. 2018. *Theatre for peacebuilding: The role of arts in conflict transformation in South Asia*. Cham: Palgrave Macmillan.

Purcell, R. 2009. Images for Change: Community development, community arts and photography. *Community Development Journal*, 44(1), pp. 111–22.

Reich, H. 2012. The art of seeing: Investigating and transforming conflicts with interactive theatre. https://berghof-foundation.org/library/the-art-of-seeing-investigating-and-transforming-conflicts-with-interactive-theatre (accessed 21 November 2022).

Richmond, O. P. 2009. Becoming liberal, unbecoming liberalism: Liberal-local hybridity via the everyday as a response to the paradoxes of liberal peacebuilding. *Journal of Intervention and state building*, 3(3), pp. 324–44.

Richmond, O. P. 2010. Resistance and the post-liberal Peace. *Millennium*, 38(3), pp. 665–92.

Richmond, O. P. 2011. Critical agency, resistance and a post-colonial civil society. *Cooperation and Conflict*, 46(4), pp. 419–40.

Richmond, O. P. 2013. Peace formation and local infrastructures for peace. *Alternatives*, 38(4), pp. 271–87.

Richmond, O. P. 2016. *Peace formation and political order in conflict affected societies*. Oxford: Oxford University Press.

Richmond, O. P. and Pogodda, S. 2016. Introduction: The contradictions of peace, international architecture, the state, and local agency. In Richmond, O. P. (ed.), *Post-liberal peace transitions: Between peace formation and state formation*. Edinburgh: Edinburgh University Press, pp. 1–17.

Richmond, O. P. and Mitchell, A. 2011. Peacebuilding and critical forms of agency: From resistance to subsistence. *Alternatives*, 36(4), pp. 326–44.

Ritchie, D. A. (ed.) 2011. *The Oxford handbook of oral history*. Oxford: Oxford University Press.

Sacranie, N. K. 2013. Image politics and the art of resistance in Syria. *State Crime Journal*, 2(2), pp. 135–48.

Sandoval, C. and Latorre, G. 2008. Chicana/o artivism: Judy Baca's digital work with youth of color. MacArthur Foundation Digital Media and Learning Initiative.

Silva, A. S. Guerra, P. and Santos, H. 2018. When art meets crisis: The Portuguese story and beyond. *Sociologia, Problemas e Práticas*, 86, pp. 27–43.

Syrian Revolution: A History from Below (2020) Webinar 11: Where Next for the Syrian Struggle? [Online] https://www.youtube.com/watch?v=yJ0N7MewlFY (accessed 20 November 2022).

Tolan, S. 2015. *Children of the stone: The power of music in a hard land*. New York: Bloomsbury Publishing.

Ugurlu, N., Akca, L. and Acarturk, C. 2016. An art therapy intervention for symptoms of post-traumatic stress, depression and anxiety among Syrian refugee children. *Vulnerable Children and Youth Studies*, 11(2), pp. 89–102.

UNRWA. 2022. UNRWA Lebanon https://www.unrwa.org/where-we-work/lebanon (accessed 20 November 2022).

Varea, R. G. 2011. Fire in the memory: Theatre, truth, and justice in Argentina and Peru. In Cohen, C. E., Varea, R. G., & Walker, P. O. (eds). *Acting Together I: Performance and the Creative Transformation of Conflict: Resistance and Reconciliation in Regions of Violence*. New York: NYU Press, pp. 153–77. https://doi.org/10.2307/j.ctt21pxmd8.15 (accessed 23 August 2022).

Zelizer, C. M. 2004. *The role of artistic processes in peacebuilding in Bosnia-Herzegovina*. PhD Thesis. George Mason University. https://www.proquest.com/openview/59f36a702f69f2e654a695e314c3ff7c/1?pq-origsite=gscholar&cbl=18750&diss=y (accessed 21 November 2022).

Interviews

Abdur Rahman, Shafiq. Interview. Conducted by Azadeh Sobout, Tripoli, 29 April, 2019.

AlKafri, Abdullah. Interview. Conducted by Azadeh Sobout, Beirut, 11 June, 2019.

Alshawa, Zorba. Interview. Conducted by Azadeh Sobout, Beirut, 7 May, 2019.

Amin, Milad. Interview. Conducted by Azadeh Sobout, Beirut, 15 June, 2019.

Assi, Salim. Interview. Conducted by Azadeh Sobout, online, 11 May, 2019.

Chahine, Rami. Interview. Conducted by Azadeh Sobout, online, 17 March, 2021.

Dajani, Moataz. Interview. Conducted by Azadeh Sobout, Beirut, 21 Apr, 2019.

Dardari, Serene. Interview. Conducted by Azadeh Sobout, Beirut, 16 May, 2019.

Nachawi, Dima. Interview. Conducted by Azadeh Sobout, Beirut, 25 April, 2019.

Nahle, Ayman. Interview. Conducted by Azadeh Sobout, Beirut, 13 May, 2019.

Nachabe, Chadi. Interview. Conducted by Azadeh Sobout, Tripoli, 29 April, 2019.

Twigg, Stephanie. Interview. Conducted by Azadeh Sobout, Beirut, 24 April, 2019.

Wardani, Farah. Interview. Conducted by Azadeh Sobout, online, 20 January, 2020.

Yehya, Mehdi. Interview. Interview. Conducted by Azadeh Sobout, Fakiha, Beqaa Valley, 22 Apr, 2019.

EIGHT

Of Graffitology: Graffiti as Fugitive Practices in the Streets of Mdantsane

Zingisa Nkosinkulu

What seems to be common to all people who have experienced the negative side of modernity and its violent systems is the quest to seek ways of peace. To seek peace would mean there is evidence of disruption from the violent aspects of life. As such, different forms of peace formation (Richmond 2019) are evoked by various modes of violence that are led by 'structural violence' (Galtung and Hoivik 1971; Farmer 2009). Structural violence is violence that is designed and maintained by the colonial system to keep the poor people poor, or the colonised colonised in order to create and maintain a western-ised world. By understanding structural violence, it becomes clear that there is no single model of violence as the apparatus of the empire and state. The physical violence that includes political strike action, war and segregationist racism is only one mode of violence. Beyond that violence, violence becomes structural by being organised and normalised as a catalyst for the construc-tion and moderation of modernity. This means there is no modernity with-out violence as modernity is itself a 'paradigm of war' (Maldonado-Torres 2008). Thus, the life of those who are at the receiving end of structural vio-lence is always placed in a position where they must constantly seek ways of peace formation.

Yet, in the modern and colonial globalising world it can be argued that peace formation 'cannot be built where there is no peace to start with' (Cutter 2005, 783). Structural violence is manifested through the political technolo-gies of the empire, informed by poverty, police brutality, epistemic violence and political violence, all of which are forms of violence that result in con-flicting realities. In these conflicting realities, there is always a side that will receive the opposite side of the other reality. In other words, the centre of western modernity benefits from the violence and the conflict that is inflicted upon the periphery at the cost of building the empire for the sovereign and imperial subject. In these realities, the respective other side is being con-structed from the suffering and pain of the other. It is from this point that it becomes evident that, to exist in the 'empire' (Hardt and Negri 2000) is to exist in a zone of 'fratricidal wars, devastating "development," cruel "civilisation," and previously unimagined violence' (Hardt and Negri 2000, 46). The modern colonial world is a world of constant conflict and violence, in which one is always forced to refuse the colonially altered reality by seeking a peaceful reality. This is because 'in reality empire is the creation of a world capitalist coalition under American bourgeois hegemony' (Ndlovu-Gatsheni 2013, 21). Peace formation is common in the states of the modern world as it is a world that is founded on the 'paradigm of war' (Maldonado-Torres 2008)—a world that insists on colonised subjects seeking ways of making peace because of war and structured conflicts that are designed to fuel modernity no matter the cost. The different ways the negative side of western modernity is experienced by those who feel violated by its hidden side effect are always challenged and resisted. Coloniality is software within a program of modernity: a program such as modernity is designed to create a world for particular people while violating the worlds of others. The notion of worlds here embraces the decolonial notion of a 'rather trans-pluri-versal' and 'pluriverse' world (Maldonado-Torres 2008; Mignolo 2000), a world that is made of many worlds. Coloniality is a way of destroying other worlds while building a world of the other, the other who is a sovereign subject of the empire, to whom the empire is built and belongs. On this side of the colonial story of modernity, everything in the world including the colonised subject becomes the property of the empire. Being property of the empire means to be represented and be spoken for by the empire, it means being violated and killed at will. This position of being represented and spoken for in absentia by the systems of the empire is something that comes with extreme forms of political disruption of peace. The paradigm of war is a political affair that politicises everything local and international, its political paradigm is the one that politicises 'peacebuilding' (Cutter 2005, 781) as a political repercussion, thus leading to art being deployed as a cry for and symbol of peace formation.

Peace formation is intended to open up a discussion of how local but well-networked actors intervene in more traditional and 'realist' state formation processes, in addition to reshaping or influencing the goals of international intervention, liberal peacebuilding or statebuilding, often along the lines suggested by concepts of social and global justice. It extends the arguments made by those working in the areas of conflict transformation or peacebuilding into a newer, interdisciplinary and more comparative, trans-scalar and networked conceptual framework. It tends to be a bottom-up, intensely networked and mobile phenomenon, as opposed to peacebuilding or statebuilding, which are centred on intervention, states and institutions (Richmond 2018, 86). Peace formation is one means by which those who have suffered from the 'dark side of western modernity' (Mignolo 2011) are refusing to be captured by structural violence and political hidden intentions exercised but not publicly declared. In this chapter, graffiti will paint a picture that suggests peace formation cannot be reduced to political capture or peace that is reached after war and conflict. Rather, peace is extended to mean different things, namely peace of mind, peace of ontology, peace of knowledge, peace of being who you want to be, economic peace and political peace. However, this chapter is mostly invested in a different form of peace formation—a formation of what I will term 'ontological peace'. Ontological peace is peace of being, it is peace of being able to resist the paradigm of war that made us realise the veil of modernity. Maldonado-Torres (2008, 4) suggests 'the idea that the paradigm of war is deeply connected with the production of race and colonialism as well as by the perpetuation, expansion, and transformation of patriarchy'. In the modern world, space is mapped as a battlefield principally through colonialism, race and dehumanising ways of differentiating genders. War, in turn, is no longer solely found in extraordinary moments of conflict, but rather becomes a central feature of modern life-worlds (Maldonado-Torres 2008, 4). The effects of western colonisation have been challenged and engaged by scholars throughout different disciplines and methods. Graffiti is one of these tools that should be taken seriously as a site of thinking about peace formation. In this chapter a graffiti mural project is used to reconsider peace and peace formation. The chapter seeks to shed light on how peace formation can be communicated and represented through graffiti by discussing our Kala Brothers Crew graffiti project called African Intellectuals.[1]

This chapter is divided into four sections. The first section will distil peace formation from the underside of modernity to provide a brief contextual background on peace formation where the violence of modernity has been experienced as a normal way of life, and violence is subliminal. The second section of the chapter theorises graffiti by adopting the thematics of 'fugitive practices' (Moten and Harney 2013). These two thematics will be interwoven with other thinkers' thoughts and concepts that will contribute to the argument that graffiti is an epistemic and ontological tool, technology and weapon of 'epistemic disobedience' (Mignolo 2008) in the interest of peace. The third section engages the principles of hip hop to explore the definition of peace from the street because peace, love and happiness are elements that define the objectives of hip hop culture. This theorisation from the street about the street situates a graffiti project from Mdanstane township in Eastern Cape South Africa as a beacon and gesture of giving peace and seeking peace. The fourth section provides empirical analysis and theorisation of this graffiti project to locate how peace can be found through violence—as what is peace for one might be violence for another. This will include a brief discussion (incorporating visuals) on how graffiti murals allow different thinking and approaches to epistemic peace and ontological peace. Finally, in the conclusion, the chapter argues that graffiti as a fugitive practice can foster new opportunities to discuss and form peace.

Locating Peace Formation from the Underside

Perhaps the main problem with pursuing peace is the question as to whether peace is so colonised that its pursuit would always constitute some form of perpetual violence instead of peace formation. This problem is not from the historical development of peace and peace formation structures, but to do with formulating a theoretical and visual engagement of its meaning, because 'peace-building should be a relatively civilized process' (Bowden 2009, 303). According to Friedrich Nietzsche (2006), the understanding of the titular word—peace, has been a feature of discussions of conflict resolution and post-war reconstruction policy-making, which according to Barakat (2005) is what has been approached as peacebuilding and peace formation. Peace formation is a relatively new concept; most traditional literature is about peacemaking, peacekeeping and peacebuilding. The negative side of peacebuilding compared to peace formation is that it is engaged and approached but only post-ceasefire as a process to civilise a conflict (Richmond 2019). To civilise a conflict or any form of violent situation is to seek peace and reconstruction. Nevertheless, 'what we call peacebuilding tends to take place in conflict or post-conflict zones, which are not always the most civilized of settings' and constitute the 'zone of nonbeing' (Fanon [1952] 2008, 10). Another developing part of the literature on peacebuilding deals with the impact of peacebuilding policy and policy transfer (Barakat 2005; Ramanna 2007) that are set in place to deal with the absence of peace in a 'colonial situation' (Fanon [1961] 1990, 73; Grosfoguel 2007, 220). Approaching peacebuilding post-ceasefire reduces peacebuilding to something that can only be called for after a physical conflict and or violence has ended. However, '[e]verything necessary for normal human life starts with the absence of violence', because the 'core tasks of any government are to provide physical peace, public security and basic freedoms to its citizens' (Voorhoeve 2007, 19). This approach to peace is a way of situating peace within the project of modernity, as something that is yet to come after violent acts. Yet, the modern world has proven to be unpredictable. Decolonising peace means introducing a world that does not need peacebuilding in any form.

It becomes unclear what will come, violence or peace, because peacebuilding has been operated within a 'chronological history or archaeology of European ideas' (Mignolo 2011, 46) that feeds from war, conflict and violence. Peace in this sense is often left for when an external intervention is offered by a different government. Most of the time, it is peace offered by the government from the first world to the third world (Yilmaz 2009) under the gesture of peacebuilding. However, peacebuilding usually refers to a western-centric project focused on civil society and institution building. Peacebuilding always comes from the centre to the violent periphery. And as such, 'peace-building activities in post-conflict countries include strengthening the institutional base; making a constitution, or a new one, and establishing the rule of law; strengthening security; economic reconstruction; as well as national reconciliation' (Yilmaz 2009, 240). In this regard, for the centre to exist, the periphery must exist, and for the periphery to exist, violence must be deployed. This is because,

> [p]eace is to be desired, as Nietzsche's Zarathustra proclaimed, but only as a means to war: "Warriors, my brothers, I love you from the depth of my heart. . . . Desire peace as a means for new wars, and let the peace be short rather than long. War and courage accomplish many more great things than the love of the neighbor". (Maldonado-Torres 2008, 32–3)

Peace formation, *qua* violence required and applied to archive peace, is often not seen as the same. To show peace as something present in modern society, I chose to borrow Joris Voorhoeve's (2007) 'chronological overview' of peacebuilding in the table below, which presents cases of peacekeeping based on three points understood as something that is 1) 'post-conflict resolution'; 2) 'influenced by external actors'; and 3) focusing on 'reform of the rule of law'. This is to say that peacebuilding in the modern world is perpetual, as such it becomes implemented in some cases as military peacekeeping measures. In addition, the table reveals that '[p]eace, in this light, represents a futile idea, since "the normal state of things is war"' (Maldonado-Torres 2008, 32). Although the table does not capture all the colonial wars and peacebuilding interventions that shaped the modern world its importance lies more in its revelation:

This perpetuity of peacekeeping set the world as a crime scene, a ground upon which structural violence is the rule of war. This genealogy of peacebuilding shows that the

> paradigm of war can be characterised in terms of the privilege of conflict or the celebration of the reduction of the singularity of individual entities and subjects to the generality of the concept, to Being, to an ethnos, or a totality in philosophical reflections. (Maldonado-Torres 2008)

This constitutes the paradigm of peace as the paradigm of peace and war alike. By the paradigm of peace and war, I refer to violence as the scandal of modernity and as something that contains some precarious values of

Table 8.1 Peace Operations since 1960 based on Voorhoeve, 2007

Geographical location	Period of operations	Executing agency
Congo	1960–4	United Nations (MONUC)
Dominican Republic	1965–6	United Nations (DOMREP)
Lebanon	1978–present	United Nations (UNIFIL)
Angola	1988–99	United Nations (several missions)
Namibia	1989–90	United Nations (UNTAG)
Cambodia	1991–3	United Nations (various missions)
El Salvador	1991–5	United Nations (ONUSAL)
Mozambique	1992–4	United Nations (ONUMOZ)
Somalia	1992–5	United Nations (UNOSOM) initially under American lead
Bosnia-Herzegovina	1992–present	United Nations (UNPROFOR), later NATO (IFOR/SFOR) and EU in concordance with OSCE and the Council of Europe
Rwanda	1993–6	United Nations (UNOMUR/UNAMIR)
Haiti	1993–present	United Nations (various missions) and OAS, USA and France
Liberia	1993–1997	United Nations (UNOMIL) and ECOWAS (ECOMOG)
Liberia	2003–present	Initially ECOWAS (ECOMIL), followed by United Nations (UNMIL)
Tajikistan (ceasefire monitoring)	1994–2000	United Nations (UNMOT), OSCE, CIS
Croatia	1994–8	United Nations (various missions), EU, NATO
Sri Lanka	1987–90	India unilateral
FRY Macedonia	1995–present	UN (UNPREDEP), NATO (Amber Fox and Essential Harvest) EU (Proxima) with OSCE and the Council of Europe
Croatia (Eastern Slavonia)	1996–8	UN (UNTAES)
Guatemala	1997	United Nations (MINUGUA)
Sierra Leone	1998–present	UN (UNOMSIL/UNAMSIL), ECOWAS and British forces
Central African Republic	1998–2000	United Nations (MINURCA and BONUCA) regional states joint in MISAB
East Timor	1999–2005	UN (various missions), initially under Australian lead
Kosovo	1999–present	UN (UNMIK), NATO (KFOR) and EU, supported by OSCE and COE
Dem. Rep. of Congo	1999–present	UN (MONUC)
Albania	1997–2002	Italian-led multinational force with EU and OSCE
Lesotho	1998–9	South African (lead nation) and Botswana forces
Afghanistan	2001–present	NATO and UN
Iraq	2003–present	Mainly American, British and other coalition forces

Table 8.1 (continued)

Geographical location	Period of operations	Executing agency
Solomon Islands	2003–present	Regional Assistance Mission, under Australian lead
Burundi	2003–present	Initially African Union (AMIB), as of June 2004 UN (ONUB)
Ivory Coast	2004–present	ECOWAS (ECOMICI), UN (UNOCI), AU
Sudan (North-South)	2005–present	UN (UNMIS), AU
Sudan (Darfur)	2004–present	AU (AMIS), expansion of role of UN under discussion

peace. Its value is limited because it is designed this way. It means being able to live a life in the perpetual chase of peace, a temporary peace of waiting for something to happen. This form of peace 'will prove pertinent to the challenges found by subjects who live in contexts wherein domination operates behind the alleged tranquility of ordinary life' (Maldonado-Torres 2008, 58). Table 8.1 highlights some of the ways this alleged tranquillity has been disrupted through peace operations. Peace is something that is hidden behind violence, just like coloniality is hidden behind modernity (Maldonado-Torres 2008). This prompts the very important question, where is the colonised subject in the paradigm of peace? This question has to do with peace and existence in the colonial world, which demands a decolonial treatment of peace as a shadow of the colonial violence. This question concerns peace and existence in the colonial world. It calls for a decolonial approach to peace, viewing it as a consequence of past colonial violence. This approach seeks to understand how those who endured historical colonial violence, contributing to modernity, are now experiencing its aftermath and how these experiences inform peace-building, encompassing security and aid considerations.

In what is presented as peacebuilding, security and aid by the government of the state, whose political operations are in service of the empire, from the position of the colonised subjects who are on the negative side of modernity, it is important to then register that art and peace formation cannot be considered as separate. Also, peace formation is viewed here as shaping ontology through a particular aspect of art—graffiti murals. It is here that its darker side is explored and located around the living experience of being outside the centre of the empire. In the centre life is to be lived only by those who can authorise and exercise violence over others. The violence is hidden behind peace, makes it possible for peace to be temporary in its metaphysical sense, but only as something permanent in the realm of politics. As Öjendal et al. (2021, 275–6) argue:

Persisting expressions of violence, such as networked political violence, violence in organized crime, gender-based violence, class-driven violence, various forms of depravation, or rural and urban unrest as a result of economic marginalization remain however seemingly irrelevant for peacebuilding if we follow the latter's institutionalized lexicon.

The world that is under political rule is governed by violence, one of the defining factors. Peacebuilding, then, is what marks the caring hand of the empire. The hand of the empire that seems to create problems as well as the solutions to the problem to sustain itself, clearly marks the colonial entanglement in the development and the politics that justify the construction of the empire through violence.

The Hip Hop Way: Love, Peace and Happiness

At this point, where hip hop music is situated in the politics of *artpeace* formation, it is a subculture that can initiate self-generativity, institutional critique and work as a means of deconstruction, situating it as a tool of decolonising peace. As established, hip hop 'consists of at least four fundamental elements: Disc jockeying (Djing), break dancing, graffiti art, and rapping (emceeing)' (Alridge and Stewart 2005, 190). Graffiti, as one of these elements, signifies an act of peace formation in responding to different kinds of social ills which are caused by the government of the state. As such, 'graffiti can provide a form of socio-political commentary at the local level, and is a valuable, yet often overlooked, resource for scholars and policymakers in conflict-affected societies' (Vogel et al. 2020, 2148). Graffiti, as one of the hip hop elements, was first rejected and branded as illegal, but now is legally accepted in some parts of the world, as such:

> Since Hip Hop's birth about 35 years ago, very few academic historical studies have examined the phenomenon. It has been over a decade since the publication in 1994 of Tricia Rose's now classic, *Black Noise: Rap Music and Black Culture in Contemporary America* and Robin D.G. Kelley's *Race Rebels: Culture, Politics, and the Black Working Class*. (Alridge and Stewart 2005, 190)

Reiland Rabaka published books to engage hip hop, titled *Hip Hop's Inheritance: From the Harlem Renaissance to the Hip Hop Feminist Movement* (2011), *Hip hop's amnesia: From blues and the black women's club movement to rap and the hip hop movement* (2012) and *The Hip Hop Movement: From R&B and the Civil Rights Movement to Rap and the Hip Hop Generation* (2013). Rabaka's academic engagement with hip hop links to the American black lived experience, resistance movements and black spirituality. For Rabaka, hip hop is not a standalone signifier, it is interconnected to the construction of blackness as a site of critique and resistance through its elements—including graffiti. Thus, so far, 'other disciplines have studied graffiti from various methodological backgrounds and gained insights into past and present dynamics of societies that would greatly benefit the field' of peace formation (Vogel et al. 2020, 2148). The hip hop ways of peace formation are the testimony of violence, charting the path of reaching a peaceful new world. The focal point here is a form of radical resistance that is grounded in the element of words and language, where language becomes the centre of the combative action of rebuilding a world of many people. This is a street project that has provided a way of taking matters into one's own hands, gives weight to limited voices and as such is constructed in the form of the autobiography of the street. As a culture of peace, hip hop will have to be recognised through the channels of peace formation and security in the future. There is a way of challenging the violent rhetoric of modernity through graffiti as an arm of hip hop. Hip hop's fourth element 'graffiti, directly caters to at least four of these multiple intelligences; linguistic, musical, bodily kinesthetic and spatial' (Abe 2009, 265). It is a command of its own that demands its own authority of understanding; hip hop is a register that is outside the system, and can be considered part of a decolonial regime of peace. It is bigger than any form of system. It is deconstructive and reconstructive. Its decolonial articulation is testimony to the fact that the streets can speak and have been speaking. Graffiti here constitutes the street apparatus that comes to haunt the violent world. Also, this apparatus, in a multitude of ways, challenges the order of that violent world by bending alphabets to create autobiographical fonts that disturb the colonial structures. Thus, graffiti as part of

> Hip Hop must be [perceived] seriously as a cultural, political, economic, and intellectual phenomenon deserving of scholarly study, similar to previous African American artistic and cultural movements such as the Blues, Jazz, the New Negro Renaissance, and the Civil Rights, Black Power, and Black Arts Movements. (Alridge and Stewart 2005; 190; Abe 2009)

It is essential to register hip hop as a site of study and as a fugitive practice that operates to bring love, peace and happiness, as its principles suggest. The ability to pose existential critical questions is interconnected to the questions of being at peace. Graffiti, as a hip-hop element, positioned itself in an opposing position to stand for the struggle for peace: to be at peace, to be who one wants to be. The power of graffiti lies in its ability to mobilise and disrupt the system while constructing avatars of infiltrating the system. The subculture of hip hop contains some poetics of street ontology—graffitology. These existential poetics of love, peace and happiness are here to expose the drama of coloniality and its violent naturalised logic. These are the logics of ontological wars that must be interrogated even if it means creating a war for those who want to keep the paradigm of war in existence. Graffiti that is written in the streets is a mirror of this paradigm of resistance. These paradigms deconstruct the status quo of subliminal war by exposing its ways of terror. Hip hop brings peace to terror, brings comfort to those who are socially disturbed. This is because the quest for peace is more likely what the question of hip hop principles is instigating. The ability to love, and be at peace which will result in happiness is what is at risk at this point. Although hip hop can be denied it is through offering at the higher table of the order of modernity and academia to some extent, its elements—namely, emceeing, deejaying, break dancing and graffiti art (as well, sometimes, as beatboxing)—culminate in another element: knowledge of the self and its will to build a peaceful world. This is the element that inspires self-reconfiguration, individual free-thinking and refusal of any form of confining logic and oppressing violent systems. Means of finding ways to express the need for a peaceful and long happy healthy life are often recognised as some form of violence—like strike action. Graffiti artists strike the system literally and figuratively with their names.

Theorising Graffiti as Fugitivity

Through graffiti's combative nature against the dominating colonial culture, its element of disobedience creates not only self-authorisation, but its stolen moments also provide moments of being and becoming. This way of being and becoming is what constitutes graffiti as self-ontological-authorisation through the poetics' peace formation. Graffiti as the street apparatus emanates from the language of the street that cannot be captured as the 'repressive state apparatus' (Althusser 1971). It is a symbol of those who are seeking some form of peace against the system, as such graffiti has become a tool of resistance. Though despite 'recognition of its value by various social science disciplines, graffiti has yet to be considered seriously within scholarship on conflict and peace' (Vogel et al. 2020, 2149). Graffiti should be approached as inscriptions of peace formation that border on disobedience, delinking, disruption of the system, reconfiguration of space and absolute rejection of the colonial systems that are represented by the concrete grey wall of the state. Modernity operates like a chameleon because it poses tactics of camouflaging and blending in with the environment and appears as long overdue. As the face of the state, modernity is grey: the bridges are grey, the road is grey, the walls that hold rivers are grey and almost all the government buildings are grey. This is to say that the system is grey. For some graffiti artists/writers, a grey wall is a sign of a capitalist system, and a capitalist system is a representation and presence of the empire, but this is not something that encourages vandalism (Green 2014). Since to be a graffiti writer is to engage in the reconfiguration and re-writing of one's identity, this is not to say all graffiti is a symbol of identity or vandalism but rather a sign of acting outside the system.

What graffiti writers make us pay attention to is the use of violence to gain peace. By assuming the position of street poetry and street thinking, graffiti takes the position of a surrogate fugitive act. This is perfect in the project that is combating a particular time, the time of the state, the time of modernity. It is from these constraints that by way of Moten and Harney's (2013) study

[f]ugitivity is not only escape, "exit" as Paolo Virno might put it, or "exodus" in the terms offered by Hardt and Negri, fugitivity is being separate from settling. It is a being in motion that has learned that "organizations are obstacles to organising ourselves" ... and that there are spaces and modalities that exist separate from the logical, logistical, the housed and the positioned.

Graffiti writing is where fugitivity is exercised and as such, the:

[e]xuberantly metacritical hope has always exceeded every immediate circumstance in its incalculably varied everyday enactments of the fugitive art of social life. This art is practiced on and over the edge of politics, beneath its ground, in the animative and improvisatory decomposition of its inert body. It emerges as an ensemblic stand, a kinetic set of positions, but also takes the form of embodied notation, study, score. (Moten and Harney 2013, 72–3)

Graffiti as fugitive art is not a forced practice, it is the metacritical hope that has been challenging the immediate presence of the colonial system of the state. It rises over the edge of the silent violence to take a kinetic set position. Graffiti, just like fugitivity, is having to come to terms with the violent colonial world, inserting into it, colouring it and philosophising about it from the position of the self. Graffiti is performed through the body, not only by the nozzle. Graffiti writers write their names and messages on every surface or wall they see fit for their artwork, they have to use their body to measure the size and proportion of a piece, they have to use their colours skilfully, and they have to cover their faces and sometimes their hands to avoid fingerprints, they have to understand their environment and its surrounding like a military soldier and they must use both their hands to make their mark. Of course, the body always plays an important part in the process of any form of artmaking, presentation and performance.

Graffiti is an artform that has been closed out of the European aesthetics register, deemed an artform of the gutter because it originated from the street to depict the street. From this colonial perspective, graffiti becomes a form of violence against the system that intends to maintain a particular logic and politic. By inserting their body through their artmaking, graffiti writers are engaged in disobedience by which they get to question things including the colonial system, their existence and their being. It is through their graffiti performance that graffiti writers get to embody Fanon's words: 'My final prayer: O my body, make of me always a man who questions!' (Fanon [1952] 2008, 85–6). The body of the graffiti artist becomes a text of disobedience while seeking peace, it becomes chaos and results in disorder. Similarly, the peace that is normally offered as aid, security and conflict resolution is not an accident. The modern colonial world often offers solutions to the problem it has created, it offers a prison to the delinquent it has produced, it offers medicine to diseases it has created and it often offers aid to places it has made to be vulnerable. As an act of disobedience, graffiti as a radical tool is not deterministic concerning its language, and it does not say it is a solution or innocent, but when deployed, graffiti as a voice of the street reflects street thinking concerning the colonial order of things, becoming an act of fugitivity.

This means the lines between language and vision become blurred. Text and words cease to be just text and words but become an embodiment of something else. 'The grammatological critique performed by graffiti aims, in part, to locate the archaic, despotic, or colonial wall buried within the new smooth walls of capital' (Fieni 2012, 77). This something else is a grammar of being that graffiti becomes—a language of peace. This change is triggered because peace is being recaptured and redefended by those affected by its need. Peace in this sense will embody decoloniality of knowledge, decoloniality of being and decoloniality of power as opposed to coloniality of knowledge, coloniality of being and coloniality of power that justifies violence. What binds graffiti and the pursuit of peace is fugitivity, aspects 'pertaining to graffiti that are relevant to conflict-affected societies, namely resistance, communication and expression, memorialisation, commemoration, and inspiration or division' (Vogel et al. 2020, 2150). Both graffiti making and peace formation as fugitive practices demand a certain level of discretion and infiltration, resisting a certain condition while taking the position of being an outsider concerning the laws of the state. Graffiti as a way to claim peace is performed through ways of thinking, living, being and doing that are outside the violence that comes with the negative side of modernity. Gomez discusses the type of graffiti that contributes to peace formation, one that 'differed from simple vandalism because it had territorial significance and because it represented a powerful youth subculture which cared little about the values and laws of society, developing a language, aesthetic values, and standards all its own' (Gómez 1993, 637).

Peace formation is practised directly and indirectly; it is a formation of peace in contrast and against the systematic violence of the political state employing different means. Graffiti is a way of different means. To deploy graffiti in the name of seeking peace and in the name of subjectivity is to articulate ontological registers that have to do with this peace being absent. The will to engage in graffiti and peace is in the name of fugitivity. Fugitivity is in the name of the streets and the quest for freedom—freedom to be. So, in some cases graffiti can equal peace. That is to say, the grey walls of the empire are symbolic of the epistemic violence whose logic is to monitor enough violence to keep the machinery of modernity operational and, thus, linked to the police system. The streets in this regard become the point of departure. The link that interconnects them is the element of self-positioning, self-writing and self-authorisation that become critical to the continuous reconfiguration of broken structures and forming of new forms. Of course, this is not to forget how graffiti is criminalised publicly but commercialised in private spaces to the point it feeds the art industry economically (Green 2014; Haupt 2012). But at the level of its meaning and context, it is ignored. Graffiti art is combative art, it is a claim on the opportune—an ontological opportune that has been long-awaited and had to be stolen back. Graffiti art is fugitivity that constitutes disobedience as peacebuilding.

What does it mean then to look at a graffiti piece? Although this question might seem general, it might require some serious thought and different treatment: what does it mean to write graffiti for *artpeace* formation? What form of testimony does graffiti as fugitivity inscribe and how are these testimonies heard or perceived? The dubious manner in which graffiti autobiographical testimonies are formulated is depicted by the fact that the letter-scape of graffiti compositions is abstract; their interlocking arrows and fill-ins are the very suggestion of peace in disobedience; and is an artform that transcends Eurocentric aesthetics sensibilities and its red tapes. To stretch the question of what seeing and being seen, known and being unknown means, and specifically, under the concealing logic of the state that does not want to see anything that does not stand for its ways, that conform to the way the system wants people to operate and live their lives, what is the meaning of visibility that has nothing to do with visibility but its meaning? In graffiti art, the aim of the game is fame (Halsey and Pederick 2010). It is through this prism that images of graffiti get to be received and be seen, as something that represents the gutter and the hieroglyphics of the ghetto, an ontological text that is placed under the index of vandalism because it depicts a different world. Difference disrupts the peace. It matters not how much graffiti is seen as the voice and the image of the gutter and ghetto, its existence never shaped any meaningless adventure but itself is a necessary military street act of resistance and decolonisation. Sometimes states deploy the violence of the military to bring peace. It is no accident that graffiti employs and deploys tactics and militancy to execute the craft by way of studying the surroundings. This would be different from the military way of peacekeeping because it is defined by those who do graffiti.

Craft is one of the other words used in modernity and its colonised taste makes it appear to hold less value. Yet, sometimes it is a value looked at from the other end. Graffiti as fugitivity is a practice of seeking value in peace; a value that values many things but most importantly peace. Even though fugitivity graffiti is mostly done at night, its nocturnal element does not mean it doesn't reflect everyday social life. The everyday social life in the modern colonial world revolves around seeking and keeping your peace. The night is a moment of escaping the system, it is the time to become the one who you cannot be during the day. It is a secret moment of being and becoming while being on the lookout for being captured by the security guards or the police. Most importantly, it resists being captured by the system. Graffiti pieces can be autobiographical. This is one aspect of graffiti, though it has many dimensions and autobiography is only one of them (Vogel et al. 2020). As such these pieces tell or do something personal for the writer, whatever their reason for writing graffiti might be. This goes beyond its textuality, actuality and perpetual nature that keeps it incomplete without the complex story in its semiotic sense, but the relation of language to peace formation. This also speaks beyond the postmodern, alter-modern and colonial hybridisation of the art world, visual culture and epistemic institutional arrest. What graffiti as a fugitive practice accounts for is an agency, thought and place. Graffiti is an artform that is constructed through violence. Sometimes it is just sublime. Even though graffiti is seen as vandalism by those who valorise the law of property, it can be a way of giving beauty, and its functions extend to political language. What graffiti accounts for is peace formation articulated in and from the streets. The violence of the world is approached with a creative violence that is designed to seek peace. Of course, violence is not the same. To say that is to say violence can be negative and positive, rigid and creative, loud and/or silent. The articulation of peace, where the modern colonial world is the crime scene, is the manifestation of violence itself, even though it is concealed and denied. The graffiti letter-scape is provoking and suggests a new perspective, and so are the politics that inform part of the space that graffiti should take in society. When graffiti spreads across the world, doubt, fear and suspicion are going on. This is the nature of the peace that overwrites violence. Fugitivity is the ethos of graffiti—violence creates a world of violence, and the world of colonial domination and erasure—it is the stance of combative breathing and lasting. Through graffiti, graffiti artists are letting the quest for peace reign. All things that are located here about graffiti as the fugitive practice of peace mean resistance. Resistance is a way of getting things done by resisting other things that are insisting on being done, which might feel like violence to those who are forced to constantly pursue peace. The resistant nature of graffiti is constructed on fugitivity which insists on a disobedience that informs the formulation of peace through the tool and language of the street. Graffiti is a language that needs to be understood from the position of the street to give insights into peacebuilding. It is a tool that must be deployed and theorised from different positions. From this position, graffiti as a fugitive practice is theorised from the position of decolonial epistemic perspective and street thinking. It cannot be captured by the state apparatus and its colonial machinery, it is a fugitive way out.

The Ugly Peace: Our Graffiti Murals as Epistemic Peace

Peace is not just what it seems, it becomes a government dependence factor while it embraces the benefits of conflict. Peace becomes dependent because those who are conflicted and needing external intervention often become indebted to what it is supposed to be—peace of mind so to speak. Seeking peace becomes a perpetual agenda, where the one who is helped will constantly be needing peace from the violence that the coloniality of peace brings. This violence in many situations is pinned behind help and what is called aid. The form of peace formation or peace that graffiti offers comes from the position of the uncertain—the dubious positionality that approaches the world differently.

African Intellectuals is a graffiti project we completed in our township of birth Mdantsane, Eastern Cape, inspired by a book of the same name—*African Intellectuals in 19th and Early 20th Century: South Africa* (2008) by Mcedisi Ndletyane. Ndletyane focused on Xhosa African intellectuals who were based in the Eastern Cape Province and wrote against apartheid during apartheid while recording and reminding Xhosa people about the importance and beauty of their tradition, by challenging the apartheid and colonial ways. These intellectuals support the fact that the master's tool can be deployed to dismantle the master's house as they utilised the printing press, an item introduced through modernity, to create literature exposing modernity's violence. The book made it clear that the names that were used to name schools and some local buildings in the township were names of those who can be considered local heroes. For instance, S. E. K. Mqhayi High School is named after Samuel Edward Krune Mqhayi (1875–1945), and Dr W. B. Rhubusana Building for Eastern Cape Department of Education District Offices is named after Dr Rhubusana (1858–1936). Jabavu, a place located in Gqeberha, formally known as Port Elizabeth in the Eastern Cape Province, was named after John Tengo Jabavu (1859–1921) and is one of the names that inspired the graffiti project. These African intellectuals, even though they are being monumentalised, are still largely unknown. Our project was funded by the Eastern Cape Provincial Arts and Culture Council (ECPACC) to paint graffiti murals around the East London area and Mdantsane township where the names of these intellectuals are used for streets and buildings. The aim was to find suitable walls and paint a portrait of each intellectual in between two pieces of graffiti. We were a crew of three friends, which meant that, while one was painting the face, two of us would be painting their names. For instance, when Xeno painted a face, Ziggy and I (Zang) painted our names on the sides of the face, which was followed by names and quotes of the intellectuals. Eventually, we painted four graffiti murals. During the process, people would stop and ask questions about graffiti and the faces we were painting. The idea was to paint these murals to inspire the public to think about the names and the people behind the names. We believed that in this way we would be fighting 'epistemic racism/sexism' (Grosfoguel 2013). It becomes obvious that epistemic violence in 'this reality is easily missed if the genealogy of the modern world order is analysed from the centre of the empire' (Ndlovu-Gatsheni 2013, 7) where it has been initiated and orchestrated in the first place. The names of the African intellectuals were just names that were given to streets and buildings without being concerned about the epistemic violence that they still had to endure posthumously. To think about these intellectuals and their contribution when it comes to peace is imperative and constitutes a 'positive peace' position (Galtung 1969, 190). This is because, by definition, '"positive peace" implies going beyond ending violence, toward greater social, gender, class, and inter-group justice. Within the "positive peace" framework, musical expression, whatever the context, potentially facilitates a wide range of emotionally-informed interactions' (Hintjens and Ubaldo 2020, 286). By way of their intellectual contributions, these intellectuals can be seen as positive peace actors. However, it might not be obvious what these thinkers have to do with peace. Or, how can peace be linked to these thinkers, who are no longer alive? From the position of those who have suffered under any form of colonial violence and its manifested terror, these thinkers can and have a lot to do with peace formation. They might have advocated for peace in their intellectual contribution and social actions but indirectly. Peace is among all the other things these thinkers invite us to reflect deeply on, thus making the project a project of *artpeace*. These reflections reveal that '[c]onflict and conciliation dynamics puts the accent on obstacles to peace making in civil wars and insurgencies. The end of hostilities finds the adversaries and the society more divided than before violent conflict' (Oberschall 2007, 186). Those who are offered means to realise peace are often left owing a huge dept which shifts things to be different or even worse. Where the project started and ended are two different epistemic positions, for the artists and for the public that sees the graffiti pieces every day.

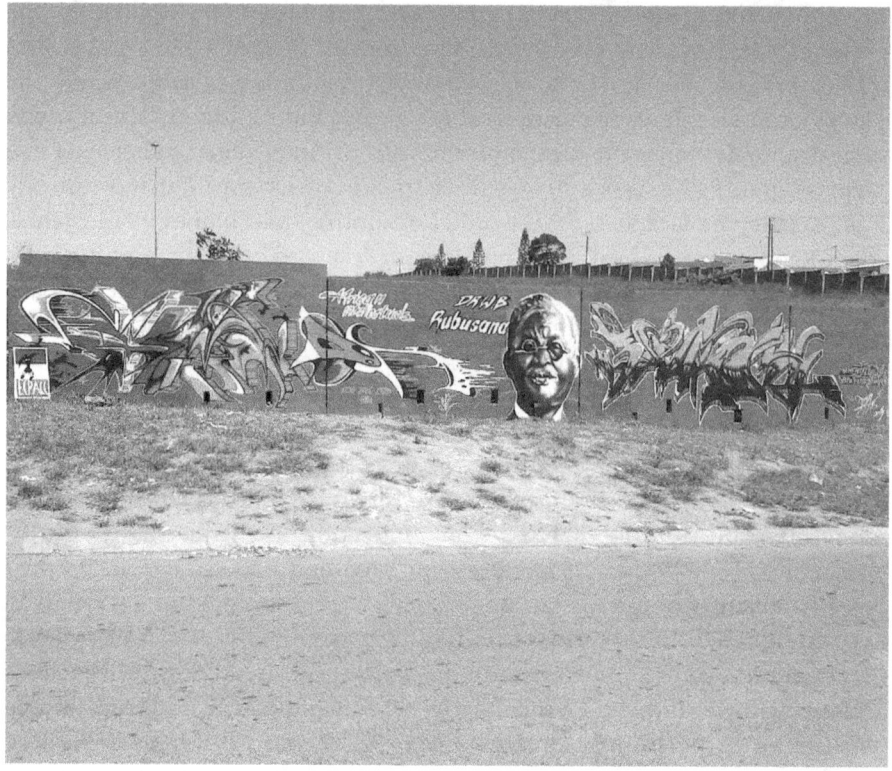

Figure 8.1 Xeno, Dr W. B. Rubusana by Zang, Ziggy at NU. 10 Soccer Field.

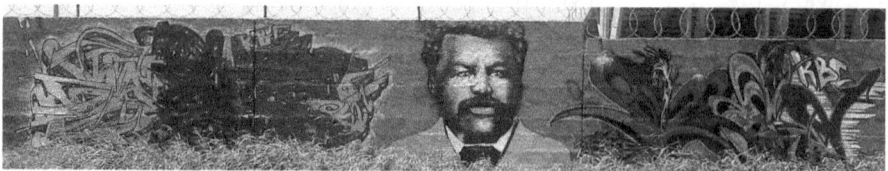

Figure 8.2 Zang, Jabavu by Ziggy, Xeno at NU. 2 Sisa Dukashe Studium.

The project was painted on the public walls by three artists. The aim, of course, was to monumentalise and provoke interest in the local public—specifically children—about these intellectuals. The project was also intended to turn the streets into museum spaces where people can stop and reflect—gaining peace of mind. The role African thinkers often play in the intellectual constellation is neglected or rendered as something that is mirroring European standards and its highly praised intellectuals, which always leads to their resistance. This also always places those who are outside the centre at the receiving end of epistemic violence. However, this project places these intellectuals as decolonial peace activists. The original contribution of this

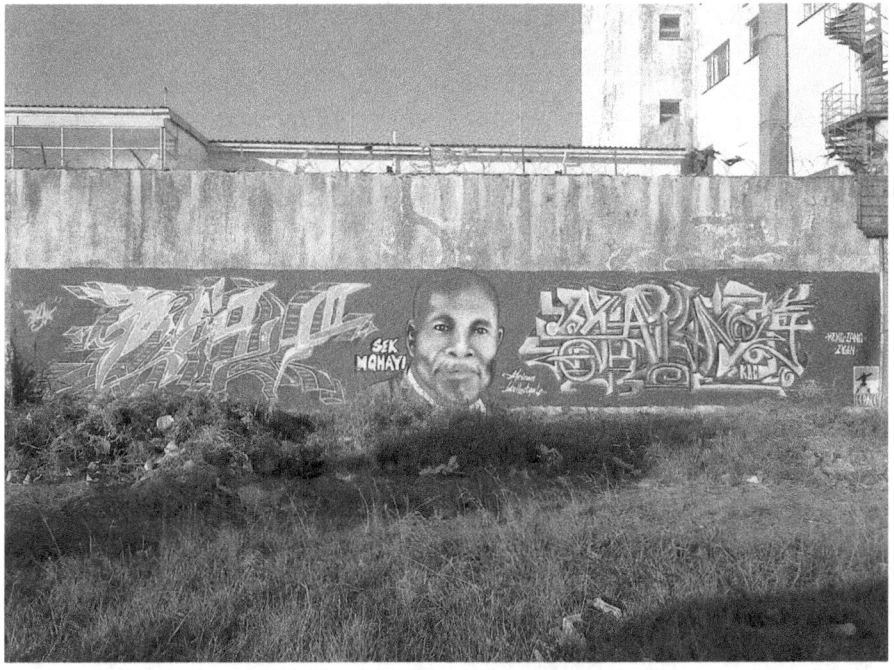

Figure 8.3 Ziggy, S. E. K. Mqhayi by Xeno, Zang at NU. 2 High-Way Taxi Rank.

project and these intellectuals becomes extended to something that cannot be neglected at the level of the piece. The place of peace formation is in the work of these thinkers and the graffiti project that depicted their faces transcended the realm of just being a street tagging project, but an activist moment of 'epistemic awakening' (Ndlovu-Gatsheni 2011). Graffiti as a form of epistemic awakening becomes graffiti that transcends other definitions and interpretations of graffiti (Wilson 1987; Kindynis 2018; Oliver and Neal 2010; Bushnell 1990; Bloch 2019a, 2019b; Cresswell 1992; Haworth et al. 2013). Their intellectual contribution, the peace formation techniques and the graffiti are intertwined. This chapter situates these thinkers through the graffiti murals in the realm of peace and decolonial declarations. This is to argue for the case of peace formation from the streets. Also, at a deeper level, it can be argued that the streets can offer peace in as much as they can offer violence. In this sense, *artpeace* is being highlighted when these thinkers are situated outside the archive, an archive which only reduces them to figures of heritage and history. It is a matter of what kind of peace is being engaged and what kind of engagement techniques are being deployed. There seems to be something ignored when it comes to the places of conflict that are seeking peace. Their position to deserve unconditional peace is always overlooked.

This chapter, by exploring these intellectuals through the graffiti project also demonstrated their engagement with content that depicted their environment while seeking epistemic freedom and political peace. This showed that peace formation will come from the environment and the people who feel violated in different ways. This happens in different ways that might have nothing to do with graffiti or peace formation. There has been no clear engagement of peace formation that has to do with ontological liberation, economic freedom and epistemic freedom. This leads to art-based methods including graffiti being overlooked and seen as disconnected from formal peace work; such work overlooks it as a vehicle for mobilising peace formation and decolonisation. But with the engagement of these intellectuals, there is *artpeace* formation. What would be the status of things, if they are not about peace? These intellectuals are therefore in the position of provoking thoughts about these matters, and it is from a place of being violated. In the point of searching, the graffiti murals of this project instigated something ongoing that cannot be measured the way success is normally defined. These kinds of projects inspire, and so do the African intellectuals that the book depicted, with the idea of peace formation renewed in the process. Where peace is reduced to post-conflict activity, the idea of ceasing fire and offering help, or dropping bombs followed by food parcels, the rhetoric of modernity dominates. *Artpeace* programmes that take the form of artistic interventions carry a call for a different kind of peace —an ontological peace.

Conclusion

Graffiti and its element of resisting the system introduces a different way of facing systematic violence and peace formation. The African Intellectuals graffiti project is a good testament that art-based projects lead to new ways of peace formation. The graffiti project was further necessitated by the fact that epistemic violence is another form of violence that needs to be challenged. Violence has been inflected throughout the modern world, and as such, it proves that the negative side of modernity is a continuous state of terror. This naturalised form of violence keeps demanding precarious peace formation that constitutes a form of perpetual political violence. This violence influences the ontology of the subject, therefore making it structural terror. Peace formation is necessary to fight against violence that proves to be the catalyst that renders the world under the paradigm of war. The graffiti project we did was a way of rethinking, reshaping and reconfiguring the epistemic violence that concealed the names of local heritage while inserting ourselves. Different forms of violence demand various ways of action and reconstruction. Peace formation in the modern colonial world means dealing with the past and the present. The colonial definition of peace makes any peace-seeking project a superfluous agenda. As such, projects of resistance and peace formation in a world that operates under the paradigm of war become irrelevant. Their irrelevance is justified because they get swallowed by the perpetual forms of violence in the world. Yet by allowing graffiti to speak for peace and peace formation, the project becomes a decolonial intervention of an art-based project. The mural of this project stands to remind people of the violence that came, distorted and erased their ways of life, but also highlights the figures' deserved intellectual recognition. The hope is to inspire more peace activists to trust their decolonial ways of thinking, seeking and dealing with the absence of peace within modernity.

Note

1. The graffiti project executed in Mdantsane was a way of dealing with and engaging with peace. Kala Brothers Crew is a creative collective officially led by me, Zingisa [Zang] Nkosinkulu (visual/graffiti artist, art historian, and curator), Xolela [Xeno] Sogoni (print-maker and graffiti artist) and Xolani [Ziggy] Nkuta (multimedia artist and graffiti artist).

References

Abe, D. 2009. Hip-hop and the academic canon. *Education, Citizenship and Social Justice*, 4(3), pp. 263–72.

Alridge, D. P. and Stewart, J. B. 2005. Introduction: Hip Hop in history: past, present, and future. *The Journal of African American History*, 90(3), pp. 190–5.

Barakat, S. 2010. *After the conflict: Reconstruction and development in the aftermath of war.* London: I. B. Tauris and Co Ltd.

Bloch, S. 2019a. Broken Windows Ideology and the (Mis)Reading of Graffiti. *Critical Criminology*, 28, pp. 703–720.

Bloch, S. 2019b. An on-the-ground challenge to uses of spatial big data in assessing neighborhood character. *Geographical Review* 110(1–2), pp. 210–14.

Bowden, B. 2009. Wendy M. Sargent: Civilizing peace building: Twenty-first century global politics. *Democracy and Security*, 5, pp. 303–5.

Bushnell, J. 1990. *Moscow Graffiti: Language and Subculture.* Boston: Unwin Hyman.

Cresswell, T. 1992. The crucial 'where' of graffiti: A geographical analysis of reactions to graffiti in New York. *Environment and Planning D: Society and Space* 10(3), pp. 329–44.

Cutter, A. 2005. Peace building: A literature review. *Development in Practice* 15(6), pp. 778–84.

Fanon, F. [1952] 2008. *Black skin, white masks.* Translated by C. L. Markmann. London: Pluto Press.

Fanon, F. [1961] 1990. *The wretched of the earth.* Translated by C. Farrington. London: Penguin Books.

Farmer, P. 2009. On suffering and structural violence: A view from below. *Race/Ethnicity: Multidisciplinary Global Contexts*, 3(1), pp. 11–28.

Fieni, D. 2012. What a wall wants, or how graffiti thinks: Nomad grammatology in the French Banlieue. *Diacritics*, 40, pp. 72–93.

Galtung, J., & Höivik, T. 1971. Structural and Direct Violence: A Note on Operationalization. *Journal of Peace Research*, 8(1), 73–6. https://doi.org/10.1177/002234337100800108

Gómez, M. A. 1993. The Writing on Our Walls: Finding Solutions Through Distinguishing Graffiti Art from Graffiti Vandalism. *U. Mich. J. L. Reform*, 633 (26). https://repository.law.umich.edu/mjlr/vol26/iss3/5 (accessed 6 September 2023).

Green, M. 2014. A beautiful mess: The evolution of political graffiti in the contemporary city. *Cornell International Affairs Review*, 8(1), pp. 7–17.

Grosfoguel, R. 2007. The epistemic decolonial turn: Beyond political-economy paradigms. *Cultural Studies*, 21(2–3), 211–23.

Grosfoguel, R. 2013. The structure of knowledge in westernised universities: Epistemic racism/sexism and the four genocides/epistemicides. *Human Architecture: Journal of the sociology of self-knowledge*, 1(1), 73–90.

Halsey, M. and Pederick, B. 2010. The game of fame: Mural, graffiti, erasure, *City: Analysis of Urban Trends, Culture, Theory, Policy, Action*, 14(1–2), pp. 82–98.

Hardt, M and Negri, A. 2000. *Empire*. Cambridge, MA: Harvard University Press.

Haupt, A. 2012. *Static: Race and representation in post-apartheid music, media, and film*. Cape Town: HSRC Press.

Haworth, B., Bruce, E. and Iveson, K. 2013. Spatio-temporal analysis of graffiti occurrence in an inner-city urban environment. *Applied Geography*, 38, pp. 53–63.

Hintjens, H. and Ubaldo R. 2020. Music, violence, and peace-building, *Peace Review*, 31(3), pp. 279–88.

Kindynis, T. 2018. Bomb alert: Graffiti writing and urban space in London. *British Journal of Criminology*, 58(3), pp. 511–28.

Maldonado-Torres, N. 2008. *Against war: Views from the underside of modernity*. Durham, NC: Duke University Press.

Mignolo, W. 2000. *Local histories/global designs: Coloniality, subaltern knowledges, and border thinking*. Princeton, NJ: Princeton University Press.

Mignolo, W. D. 2008. Epistemic disobedience, independent thought and de-colonial freedom. *Theory, Culture and Society*, 26(7–8), pp. 1–23.

Mignolo, W. D. 2011. Epistemic disobedience and the decolonial option: A manifesto. *Transmodernity: Journal of Peripheral Cultural Production of the Luso-Hispanic World*, 1(2), (Fall), pp. 44–66.

Mignolo, W. D. 2011. *The Darker Side of Western Modernity: Global Futures, Decolonial Options*. Durham, NC: Duke University Press.

Moten, F. and Harney, S. 2013. *The undercommons: Fugitive planning and black study*. New York: Minor Compositions.

Ndlovu-Gatsheni, Sabelo.J. 2013. *Empire, global coloniality, and African objection*. New York: Berghahn Books.

Nietzsche, F. W. 2006 [1883–92]. *Thus spoke Zarathustra: a book for all and none*. Cambridge: Cambridge University Press.

Öjendal, J., Bachmann J., Stern, M. and Leonardsson, H. 2021. Introduction – peacebuilding amidst violence. *Journal of Intervention and Statebuilding*, 15(3), pp. 269–88.

Oberschall, A. 2007. *Conflict and peace building in divided societies: Responses to ethnic violence*. London and New York: Routledge.

Oliver, J. and T. Neal. 2010. *Wild signs: Graffiti in archaeology and history*. Oxford: Archaeopress.

Rabaka, R. 2012. *Hip hop's amnesia: From blues and the black women's club movement to rap and the hip hop movement*. New York: Lexington Books.

Ramanna, A. 2007. Peace building in post-conflict societies: A study of the process in Nicaragua. *The IUP Journal of Governance and Public Policy*, IUP Publications, vol. 0(3), September, pp. 19–34.

Richmond, O. P. 2019. Peace and the formation of political order. *International Peacekeeping*, 26(1), pp. 85–110.

Vogel, B., C. Arthur, E. Lepp, D. O'Driscoll and B. T. Haworth. 2020. Reading socio-political and spatial dynamics through graffiti in conflict-affected societies, *Third World Quarterly*. 41(12), pp. 2148–68.

Voorhoeve, J. 2007. *From war to the rule of law: Peace building after violent conflicts*. Amsterdam: Amsterdam University Press.

Wilson, P. and Healy, P. 1987. Graffiti and vandalism on public transport. *Trends & issues in crime and criminal justice*, 6. Research Brief. Canberra: Australian Institute of Criminology.

Yilmaz, E. M. 2009. Peace-building in war-torn societies. *Peace Review*, 21(2), pp. 238–48.

NINE

Through the Ballads: Remembering the Past as *Artpeace* Formation

Primitivo III Cabanes Ragandang

Growing up in the outskirts of Northern Mindanao in the Philippines, *agulô* is a Bisayan term associated with the sobbing of a restless soul. According to my grandmother, *agulô* is akin to a sad ballad which can be heard when a person dies and leaves unhealed 'wounds' on earth. Grandmother said that the soul would never rest in peace and will continue to *agulô* if concerns on earth are left unsettled. My grandmother's reflections connect well to debates in peace and conflict studies, in that the foundational comparison between positive and negative peace paved the way for conceptualising peace beyond the absence of violence (Galtung 1964). In this juxtaposition, the recognition of structural violence is key. Structural violence refers to the 'injustice built into social structures...that leads to unjust treatment or discrimination of particular social groups' (Kappler 2017, 2). Structural violence is recognised as no lesser than any form of violence. As Galtung (1985, 146) puts it, 'violence is violence... regardless of how it is exercised... intended or not'.

But what happens when the healing of the past is missed, either intended or otherwise? In this chapter, I advance the concept of 'hypernegative peace' as a foundational component for the workings of peace formation. At the outset, I argue that 'hypernegative peace' occurs when a peace project fails to include the healing of generational wounds caused by past violence and trauma in its framework, including those traumata caused by and during the colonial era. I also argue that the recognition and reconciliation of hypernegative peace is an essential prerequisite for successful peace formation. Specifically, the current and future peace projects—in larger and general terms—will only be successful if peace actors recognise and reconcile the past.

Ballads are one of the mechanisms by which local communities express their unhealed wounds of the past. In southern Philippines, this artistic form of remembering the past is 'homegrown' and organic. It is an oral form of recalling the community's traumatic history and a vehicle of memory passed across generations (Yerushalmi 1996). While it is a non-violent mechanism of expressing unhealed wounds, local communities have been experiencing obstacles that impede the ballads' capacity to create change. These obstacles include basic translation issues, subaltern treatment of the 'wounded' community and memory discrepancy between and among actors. As a result, the artistic means of spotlighting hypernegative peace remain in the margins of existing modes of power and politics.

Drawing from the case of the Tausugs' ballad called *parang sabil kissa*, this chapter explores the intersection between peace formation and ballads to underscore how hypernegative peace plays out. The Tausug tribe is one of the 13 Islamised indigenous tribes in Mindanao in the Philippines. After the end of the Second World War, the Americans left and a Filipino-led government took over. It created what is now known as the Republic of the Philippines. The Moros continued their struggle for self-determination because they were annexed as part of the republic (Hashim 1998), despite the protest and petition of the Moro leaders for their exclusion and subsequent independence (Wadi 2008). Instead, the Philippine government negotiated with the Moros not to separate from the republic. The negotiation resulted in the creation of an autonomous region for the Moros in Mindanao. Alongside the peace negotiation are various peace projects. In terms of aid, USD 40 million per year is poured into Mindanao projects (see Adriano and Parks 2013), which comes in the form of absolute loans, soft loans, tied and untied loans, grants and mixed credit (Abas 2004).

In this chapter, I explore how the Tausugs utilised *parang sabil kissa* in expressing their unhealed wounds from the former American colonisers. The case study investigates the events of 2002 when the Americans returned to Sulu for a military exercise to support the Philippine government in an anti-terrorism project, locally known as Balikatan. Learning about the American's return, the Tausugs resisted and constantly performed their *parang sabil kissa* in radio stations and government centres (De Guzman 2003). The performance was a way of expressing their resistance against the Americans' return and their means of reminding everyone that their colonial wounds are yet unhealed.

The aims of this chapter are three-fold. First, the concept of hypernegative peace is introduced in the context of the positive-negative peace dyad. Second, I explore why healing of the past should be a core component to peace formation, and analyse the role that ballads play in this process. I argue that the unhealed wounds are cultural in nature, and thus are expressed through cultural ballads. The third part of this paper illustrates the concept through the case study of the aforementioned Tausugs' *parang sabil kissa*. Remote interviews were conducted to gather the primary data of this chapter. Due to the travel limitations brought by the COVID-19 pandemic, the online space became my fieldwork site, where I conducted phone and Zoom interviews between February and July 2021.

The selection of the participants occurred through snowball sampling and were contacted directly through email, their phone numbers or Facebook messenger. Nine primary interviews were conducted, with all of the interviewees being either Tausugs or Moros who have first-hand knowledge of *parang sabil kissa*. Primary-sourced data are also used; they constitute those from the narratives of individuals who have first-hand experience of the case. Secondary data from online sources are also used to triangulate the primary data. The interview results and the reflection of the researcher form part of the limitation of the findings. Thus, this chapter does not necessarily reflect the case of other contexts but may serve as a baseline for future research. It can, however, contribute to the existing studies that investigate the role of arts, specifically of ballads, in peace formation and forms of remembering the past.

What is Hypernegative Peace?

In one of her bedtime stories, my grandmother told us that the *agulôic* ballads of the restless soul signify the unfinished 'business' of a dead person. Such business is mostly akin to an injustice (for example, the person was killed and the convict is still at large). In my grandmother's words, 'regardless of how elegant the funeral is, there will never be a "rest in peace" and the *agulô* will continue if the injustice is left unaddressed'. Congruent to her words, I argue that no matter how cutting edge a peace project is, there will never be peace if wounds from the past are left unhealed. It is part of a 'hyper' form of negative peace because a peace project concurrently happens even if traumatic pasts are left unaddressed. Hypernegative peace is described in more detail in this section, a concept which I built from the classical juxtaposition of positive and negative peace. I first review positive and negative peace and then introduce the characteristics of hypernegative peace.

One of the early concepts that contributed to the development of peace research is the distinction that Galtung made between positive and negative peace (Grewal 2003). Galtung (1964, 2) argued that positive peace occurs only when there is 'integration of human society' and structural violence is addressed. Positive peace goes beyond the idea of 'absence of violence', a concept which has been widespread and well-accommodated in peace research (Galtung 1985, 145). It means that beyond the absence of war, positive peace refers to a situation where there is 'a state of social justice' (Kappler 2017, 2). It is positive peace because the target is on the root causes of violence. Galtung (1985, 145) compares it to health:

> [W]here health can be seen as the absence of disease (meaning absence of symptoms of disease), but also as something more positive: as the building of a healthy body capable of resisting diseases, relying on its own health forces or health sources.

A healthy body cannot be determined by the body's skin alone. It is also not a healthy practice when one simply puts a bandage over the sick part of the body. It is beneficial when the patient's history is considered in diagnosing the current symptoms. Negative peace refers to the absence of violence without necessarily eliminating its root causes. It makes peace temporary; it is a band-aid solution that does not offer long-lasting peace. Negative peace thus emanates from structural and agential limitations.

As a structural limitation, negative peace manifests the limited capacity of the structure to address violence and achieve peace. It is the best available option for the structure to halt the violence, address immediate symptoms and mitigate the possible effects of force (Herath 2016, 107). For instance, a ceasefire is the structure's best option to limit violence caused by armed conflict. A ceasefire may not be addressing the root causes of armed confrontation but it temporarily prevents the occurrence of violence (cf. Dijkema 2007).

As an agential limitation, negative peace pertains to the maximum capacity of the agency to halt violence. When two people refuse a dialogue to resolve a misunderstanding, it is negative peace. While not talking failed to address misunderstandings, there are times that avoidance is the best option possible. Avoidance may not ensure addressing the root causes of violence, but it is the agency's best option (Georgakopoulos 2004; cf. Tjosvold and Sun 2002). In this case, negative peace offers a lesser form of violence. It is negative because it temporarily achieves peace without addressing the root causes (cf. Leung 1988). But while it is too 'negative' to describe, negative peace as a structural and agential limitation still aims to achieve peace. Both positive and negative peace recognise that violence, no matter what it is, is detrimental to peace. But what happens when a peace framework fails to recognise and reconcile the past?

If negative peace aims to halt violence temporarily, hypernegative peace is the deliberate or unintentional disremembering of the past in the peace framework. Forgetting past wounds, in the course of doing peace in the present, is a worse (that is, 'hyper') form of negative peace. As Yerushalmi (1996, 108) puts it, 'forgetting, the obverse of memory, is always negative, the cardinal sin from which all others will flow'. When a peace project fails to listen, recognise, and address the *agulôic* past, it is like putting a bandage over an unhealed wound without fully treating the root causes of the wound.

As mentioned, hypernegative peace is characterised by forgetting as a deliberate act. The colonised uninterrupted remembering of their trauma in colonial times is hard to decouple with the colonisers themselves.

For instance, the conflict in Muslim Mindanao is rooted in the colonial era when the Spaniards tried to subjugate them and introduced Christianity. It happened at a time when Islam was already a well-practised religion in the region (Caballero and Hairullah 2015; Gowing 1979; Majul 1988). Over a hundred years after the colonisation, former colonisers returned as international peacebuilding 'partners' bringing with them aid and expertise in post-conflict reconstruction (Abas 2004).

Later, the concept of hybrid peace gained a spotlight in the literature where local agency partnered with the international. In Mindanao, international partners are now seen in two ways: as a former coloniser and a present peacebuilding partner. But between the two is the altruistic image of the international actors that appear and never as an apologetic former coloniser aiming to heal the colonial past (cf. Estremera 2016). Atrocities committed against the Mindanao Muslims in the colonial past are not discussed. In fact, it is the locals who tend to express gratitude for the aid that the international 'partners' (their former colonisers) provide them.

I argue that the act of remembering and healing the past (that is, addressing hypernegative peace) is a foundational component of any peace project, without which other components of peace cannot be worked on. It can also serve as a preventive tool so that a past injustice will not happen again (Björkdahl and Kappler 2019; see also Helmreich 1992). It can also encourage the current generation prevent the reoccurrence of past injustices (Soltes 2010) and leave them a lesson to learn (Cohen, Meek and Lieberman 2010, 527).

Peace Formation and Expressing Hypernegative Peace through Ballads

Central to this book project is the concept of peace formation, which refers to localised peace practices (Richmond 2016) involving local actors, mechanisms, and strategies. As mentioned in the introduction of this chapter, one element of peace formation is that it carries the community's narratives of their accumulated memory (cf. Lopera, Vicente and Adzhari 2013). These narratives are never forgotten but carried in what Yerushalmi (1996) refers to as 'vehicles of memory', such as written, oral, symbolic and artistic forms. Ballads are one of the artistic forms through which local communities express their unhealed wounds of the past and thereby expose hypernegative peace. They represent a cultural and artistic mechanism that embodies the voice of the local community. But why ballads?

Ballads, as well as other forms of music are not always peaceful. They can also provoke violence (Dean 2019; cf. Pruitt 2013). This section unpacks the characteristics of ballads. At the outset, the argument is that most of the unhealed wounds are neither economic nor political. Rather, they are cultural and addressing them is better expressed through cultural means and the ballad is one of those means (Remollino 2008). The first characteristic of ballads is that they are a means to preserve and remember memories. This represents a remembering process which travels through emotions and is transmitted transgenerationally (Dobbin and Ross 2018; cf. D'Costa 2013). During the transmission process, emotions serve as the receptor making historical ballads valuable to those who hear them. Ballads can be so powerful that they 'touch[...] the soul' (Mutero and Kaye 2019, 295). As Hintjens and Ubaldo (2019, 279) put it:

> Although human beings have played music for a very long time to promote peaceful outcomes (perhaps even before they could talk), they can use the same sounds, tones, and rhythms to stir up emotions that promote violence and send humans... into battle.

The remembering process occurs when there is a transgenerational tie that connects the past to the present. These transgenerational ties allow for ballads to transmission even in a different time and post-conflict space (cf. Björkdahl and Kappler 2019). These transgenerational ties can be either personal or communal in nature. As a personal tie, ballads may contain narratives that tell a story—heroic or traumatic–of a family or ancestor related to a person in the present (Saada 2021; cf. Baddiri 2007). Because of these ties, the current generation becomes too invested in the ballads (Saada 2021), developing a sense of ownership and indigeneity. This process solidifies the veracity of the stories contained in such ballads, making them an artistic authority of an unhealed past.

As a communal tie, ballads tell a collective narrative of the community and may identify the individual's connection to the community. As Assmann (2006, 13) stressed, collective narratives are an accumulation of individual memories; after all, individuals 'do not only live in the first person singular but also in various formats of the first-person plural.' In this case, ballads create a sense of belonging within the community. Such belonging paves the way for respect to each other and thereby contributing to the community's betterment (Risal 2019, 299).

The second characteristic of ballads is that they can be a mechanism of remembering a traumatic past and therefore a means of non-violent resistance. No one dies by listening to the ballad per se. In fact, understanding the message from ballads may prevent violence and heal the past wounds. As Dean (2019, 308) puts it:

> Music in the form of resistance brings out hidden truths and often musical expression becomes the center for change in a community. This in turn brings awareness, evokes

empathy, and induces action from those who do not suffer. In this way, music as resistance works to create more equal conditions and relations in society by eliciting transformative change.

By remembering a traumatic past, ballads are, in a way, a form of expressing resistance, a first step to addressing hypernegative peace. However, they are a 'subtle form' of resistance (Remollino 2008, 179), an indirect approach of dropping hints to imply and refer to something unsolved (see Ragandang 2020). They do not directly confront the former transgressor but require active listening so that meaning is understood beyond what lyrics convey. Within the colonised and coloniser dyad, for instance, the former colony's ballads do not directly address its former colonisers to heal their traumas during the colonial era, though they still allow for tis trauma to be articulated in a safe and artistic space. This observation correlates to the contention of Stavrevska et al. (2016, 8) that 'some acts of resistance are observable, but fail to be recognised as resistance'.

The third characteristic of the ballads refer to their transgenerationality and shared gender role. Transgenerationally, a ballad requires interest and commitment from the current younger generation to keep it alive. In most post-conflict contexts, ballads are orally remembered and are rarely written down. This oral tradition does not only require listening for transmission but also memorisation. Every time a ballad is transferred from one generation to another, new stories are added, making some ballads too long and complex. The transgenerational transmission of ballads possesses a shared responsibility between two generations. For the elders, the responsibility is to pass on such ballads as comprehensively as possible in order to preserve the events and feelings of the past to teach the next generation about their roots. For the younger generation, the responsibility is to ensure that the transmitted ballads are kept in the generation and transferred to the generation to come.

Such intergenerational sharing of responsibility deviates from the saying: 'youth is the hope of the land' that Philippine national hero Jose Rizal[1] popularised (see Campoamor 2019). While the younger generation holds the responsibility of being the next custodians of their communities, such responsibility will only be well-fulfilled if the current generation of elders is training and transmitting their wisdom to the youths (Mawallil 2021). In this case, there is a need for harmony between the wisdom of the elders and the energy of the youths. Entrusting all the responsibilities to one generation will hurt the transmission process.

As mentioned above, ballads are also characterised with a shared gender role. In the Bangsamoro, for instance, men and women share responsibility in performing the ballads: it is the women who usually memorise and perform the ballads while men are their partners playing the instruments

(Asain 2006; Remollino 2008). While there is no strict gender requirement as to who memorises and who plays the accompaniment, this shared gender role signifies value and equality afforded to women and men. The women's leadership in keeping, memorising and performing the ballads entails that women share a distinct and equally important role to men in this aspect of what could be called *artpeace* formation. This aspect is important to highlight as Moro women are historically prone to unequal treatment (cf. Saleeby 1905).

Alongside these three characteristics of the ballads, it is possible to identify obstacles that impede the process of highlighting hypernegative peace, something which will be addressed in the next section. Local communities are challenged on how to creatively navigate their approach in a way that such blockages are addressed and navigated. As long as these obstacles exist, ballads as an artistic mechanism will remain in the margins of power and politics.

Obstacles that Impede Ballads' Ability to Create Change

My grandmother said:

> It is possible that everyone has the ability to hear the *agulô* of a restless soul, but not many are gifted to understand the message it wants to convey. In this case, not everyone can help resolve the soul's unfinished business and help the soul to eventually rest in eternal peace.

This is echoed in the *agulô*. Ballads do not automatically offer a space to highlight hypernegative peace and contribute to peace formation as different obstacles can impede the process. The first obstacle that impedes the reach of ballads and their ability to create peace-related change refers to the basic translation process. The lyrics are usually in the local language and are therefore not intelligible to external listeners who do not speak the language. There are some scholars who focus on transcribing them into English. Without English transcription, it is impossible for the 'outsiders' to understand the ballads even if the message is intended for them. Failure to get the message will also impede the process of healing the traumata. Even for me who grew up and studied in Mindanao, I cannot understand the ballads played in the local language because I do not speak Tausug.[2] Yet, these transcription efforts are vital especially because ballads are mainly based on oral tradition and thus might get lost between generations as discussed above.

The second obstacle refers to memory discrepancy or the contrasting versions of what really happened in the past (Fraile-Marcos and Noguerol 2019; cf. D'Costa 2013). As mentioned above, the first characteristic of ballads is that they require memory. At its core, hypernegative negative peace is disconnected from the past, the site the lyrics of the ballads are based upon. For the colonised-coloniser dyad, for instance, this conflicting memory is evident when the colonised memory of their colonial past is trauma-driven while the former colonisers look at the colonial memory as a victorious past. For instance, the Moros look at the former colonisers as the cause of their trauma. Colonisers are villains that continue to be remembered in their stories and songs as such.

However, for the colonisers, the colonial era reflects their victories past, part of their economic strategy as a country (cf. Hawkins 2011). Thus, there exists a discrepancy in how history is remembered between two competing actors. When these two actors work together in the name of peace, the memories of the past between the two do not connect. They even collide. In this case, remembering is a devalued currency in hypernegative peace. Related to this, current technological platforms (for example, televisions, computers, cellular phones) increasingly capture the attention of the younger generation. Instead, in the past, ballads had no competition in capturing the attention of both old and young; they used to be one of the core platforms to mobilise people.

Now, gadgets have also captured people's attention, especially the younger generation's—both men and women. The divided attention of the younger generation could be detrimental to the continuity of the ballads: youths are expected to be the next custodians of ballads as an artistic mechanism of highlighting hypernegative peace. If the youths' interest in the ballads declines, it is possible that the ballads will eventually disappear (Asain 2021; Saada 2021, personal communication).

The third obstacle refers to a subaltern treatment of the 'wounded' group (the owners of the ballads) by those in the circle of power and politics. Subalterns constitute an unrecognised and marginalised group in a society which does not share the same spectrum with the popular. As Spivak (2004) puts it, 'subalterns are not in the currency', that is, they are not valued. In the colonial past, the coloniser was the popular who treated the colonised as subalterns and the communication lines for the latter to express their wounds was disconnected. As Spivak (1995) argued, broken communication lines between the popular and the subalterns is one of the manifestations of this subaltern treatment. It is for this reason that communication alternatives, such as the ballad, transpire. I argue that ballads became a subaltern's tool of expressing a traumatic past, the healing of which is a foundation in peace formation and vital in the larger peace project. Failure to recognise the past makes peace projects akin to an unhealed wound of a restless soul who would repeatedly chant the *agulô*.

Treating a group like a subaltern does not automatically make them subalterns, however. In fact, the ability to develop and transmit narratives through artistic ballads manifests a collective agency. The subalternised group can express itself (cf. Chow 2014). However, the subalterns' narratives are often overpowered by the more modulated narratives of the powerful, a case of power dynamics in hybrid peacebuilding (Dinnen and Allen 2018; Mac Ginty and Richmond 2016). This also correlates with the contention of Lederach and Lederach (as cited in Dean 2019, 306) 'that without spaces where people can experience and interact with others, they will feel disconnected from the peace process'. The ballads can provide such a space for the local community.

As mentioned at the beginning of this chapter, peace formation highlights and affords value to people's experience. A peace project that is disconnected from the people on the ground is less likely to succeed (Arviola 2008; Paffenholz 2014; Richmond 2016), regardless of how noble the intention of the peace project is. By being noble, it can focus on countering terrorism and other forms of violence (negative peace) to eventually integrate human society (positive peace). Hypernegative peace comes in when, in the course of ending violence and integrating the human society, wounds of the past are left unaddressed.

In this vein, I will now zoom in on the Tausug's *parang sabil kissa* where the Tausug's unhealed wounds during the American colonial era re-emerged a century later, and were expressed through ballads. This re-emergence happened when the Americans returned to the Tausug's land for a proposed joint military exercise (called *Balikatan*) in 2002 to counter the looming terrorism in the region. The goal of the case study is to show how an unaddressed past will continue to haunt the present's peace project. The case study also helps the reader understand why healing the past is not only crucial but foundational in *artpeace* formation processes.

Hypernegative Peace and the Tausug's *Parang Sabil Kissa*

This section will now illustrate the intersection of hypernegative peace and ballads in peace formation. Mindanao is the Philippine archipelago's second-largest island, known as the home to the second-oldest conflict in the world (Schiavo-Campo and Judd 2005). The conflict is driven by the quest for self-determination of the Moros, the 13 ethnolinguistic tribes who are indigenous in the islands of Mindanao, Sulu and Palawan. One of these tribes are the Tausugs who predominantly occupy Sulu, a place known 'historically [as] a symbol of U.S. imperialist aggression in the Philippines' (Remollino 2008, 177). The Moros' struggle for self-determination is rooted in the colonial era. Colonisation in the Philippines lasted for over four centuries. The Spanish colonised the Philippines for over three centuries (1565–1898). When they tried to subjugate and introduce Christianity in the Islamised Moro lands in Mindanao, the Moros resisted (Gowing 1979; Majul 1988). When the Spanish left and the Americans took over in 1898, the Moros still resisted. As Ingilan (2018, 41) stressed:

> For the Tausugs, Lupah Sug wherein...the space of peace exists, is an ideal environ-
> ment; however, once the...space of corruption and unjustness...takes over the terri-
> tory, the Muslims are obligated to fight the enemy that has pushed the Dar'al harb
> in their homeland.

In their effort to control the Tausugs of Sulu (and of the Moros in Mindanao in general), the Americans mounted a series of 'pacification' efforts which at times were conducted via violent armed strategies prone to killings. Silva (2002) stressed that it was the fierce Moro resistance that led the Americans to develop what is now known as a .45 calibre pistol. One of the armed encounters of the Americans with the Tausugs resulted in the infamous Bud Dajo massacre in 1906. This American-led atrocity killed over a thousand Tausugs, including women and children (Majul 1988; cf. Hawkins 2011). But it is disputed as to whether the Bud Dajo clash be categorised as a 'battle' or a 'massacre' (Remollino 2008, 177). It constitutes a case of memory discrepancy as discussed in the previous section.

A century after the Bud Dajo massacre, the Americans returned to Sulu for the Balikatan in 2002. Balikatan is a joint Filipino-American military exercise aimed to suppress the looming of terrorism in Sulu, especially of the Abu Sayyaf Group.[3] In the bilateral agreement between the Philippine and American governments, the Tausug community of Sulu was not consulted about the military exercise which involves American soldiers coming to Sulu. As a result, the Balikatan military exercise faced opposition from the local community (Araneta 2003).

Because of this, anti-American sentiments among the Tausugs of Sulu revitalised their unhealed colonial wounds, especially of the American-led Bud Dajo massacre. There was no healing; the Americans did not apologise (Taylor 2016) even with some reminders from the Philippine government to do so (Estremera 2016; cf. Lind 2011). The Bud Dajo case is even considered part of the American colonial victories in the Moroland and has been justified as a military tactic of winning a battle (cf. Hawkins 2011). In fact, it is often mentioned in contemporary debates concerning American foreign policy in the Philippines (cf. Estremera 2016).

There are also sentiments which revolved around the issue of the Tausugs' trust of the Americans, describing the former colonisers as 'untrustworthy... (who) have a secret plan that can destroy the area' and that 'no matter how great and important their help is, there will always be a cost' (Lopera, Vicente and Adzhari 2013, 46). Radics (cited in Lopera, Vicente and Adzhari 2013) argued that the US military presence through Balikatan in the Tausug homeland of Sulu is a new form of colonisation. As Ingilan (2018) argued, the American colonial interest in Sulu is an insult to Tausug's ideology of space. One of the Tausugs' mechanisms of expressing their protest against the Americans, and concurrently to remember the atrocities the Americans caused to their tribe, is through their ballads called *parang sabil kissa*. The Bangsamoro Commission for the Preservation of Cultural Heritage (2020) described the *parang sabil kissa* as the iconic semblance of bravery and history of the marginalised and often misunderstood Muslims of southern Philippines. The melodic accompaniment of the Tausug ethnic narrative song transmitted across generations epitomises the struggle and resistance for identity and freedom. They are performed solo and accompanied by Moro musical instruments such as the *gabbang* (native xylophone), *suling* (native flute), and the *biyula* (native violin) (Ingilan 2018). These ballads suggest a story and history of the Tausugs.

De Guzman (2003) recalled that when the Tausugs learned about the Balikatan, they were surprised and thus went to the streets and radio stations and played their *parang sabil kissa*. The announcement of the Balikatan revitalised their American colonial trauma that had been left unhealed even during the years of peace efforts in the region, a case of hypernegative peace. As De Guzman (2003) wrote:

> (Jolo) Residents are reminded of the United States' past atrocities almost daily. The local radio station plays mesmerizing ballads known as "kissa": songs that recollect how Jolo's Tausug warriors fought the Americans in Bud Dahu at the turn of the previous century.

The lyrics of *parang sabil kissa* are based on the events that occur in the present and are connected to the events that occurred in the past. Asain (2013) wrote that as an introduction, the singers of *parang sabil kissa* would usually start the performance with *'hi tarasul ta hi kissa, in manga waktu masa....'* ('let's compose it in poems or ballads, a time long past...'). A century after the Bud Dajo massacre, its memory remains an unhealed wound among the Tausugs. As De Guzman (2003) noted, some of its lyrics are as follows:

> "We heard the Americans are coming," the lyrics will go, the singer's voice rising with the melody of two violins, "and we are getting ready. We are sharpening our swords to slaughter them when they come ... our ancestors are calling for revenge."

The Tausug's *parang sabil kissa* tells the narratives of how the tribe fearlessly 'fight to their deaths because of an insult on their persons with historical, political and romantic undertones and steeped in Islamic religious beliefs' (Ortega 2020). Asain (2013) further described the *parang sabil kissa* as follows:

> Ballads are handed down by word of mouth. Ballads in the Muslim cultural communities rhyme. When we speak of ballads in the various Muslim cultural communities, we refer to the traditional ones, which are handed down from one generation to the next by word of mouth.

The Tausug's artistic expression of their struggle through the ballads is expected 'as theirs is a struggle that has a strong cultural aspect to it' (Remollino 2008, 175). In fact, Sakili (as cited in Remollino 2008) argued that the Moro struggle is neither economic nor political; it is cultural. These ballads were not only expressing resistance but are also tales of pride among the Moros. Moro writer and scholar Noor Saada (2021, personal communication) also added that the Moros are an oral-based culture, so there is active dissemination. Unlike in others which are written-based, there is a need to engage in oral transmission before it is lost. After all, that was the only primary mode.

Secondly, and related to what was mentioned earlier, oral transmission was so active because of the absence of TV, newspapers, and other mediums in the past. Saada and Asain (2021, personal communication) also argued that this is worrying because of the mushrooming of multi-media that divides the attention of the younger generation (cf. Ragandang 2020). In the past, everyone's attention was focused on the *parang sabil kissa*; now, attention is divided given the presence of technological platforms such as computers and cell phones.

In addition to the technological platforms that divide the attention of the younger Tausugs, another apparent challenge for the *parang sabil kissa* refers to the basic translation processes discussed above. *Parang sabil kissa* are performed by the Tausugs using the Tausug language. They require a translator for non-Tausug speakers to understand the message, without which it would fail to be transmitted to the larger audience. Despite the vibrancy of their oral tradition, the Tausugs also have a written-based tradition. Like most non-Arab communities that practised Islam, the Muslims in Mindanao also have an Arabic-based Jawi system (Abubakar 2013). But 'like many orphans and widows of war, (it) is in dire need of attention and support'. The forces of nature over time destroyed those documents written on ordinary paper (Saada 2016). Since the colonial era, *parang sabil kissa* has served as a way to resist external control. Now, it also 'serves as an avenue to reveal the richness and prominence of an overlooked culture' (Landasan 2009, 1).

To express resistance to the Balikatan, several rallies, public debates and a few petitions took place alongside the singing of the *parang sabil kissa*. The Philippine government acknowledge the resistance of the local community and even thought of cancelling the military exercise (Araneta et al. 2003). But even then, there are members of the local community, including local government executives, who supported the military exercise on the argument that it would help curb terrorism (Pareño and Villa 2003). Eventually, the military exercise took place, and the Americans gained re-entry to the Tausug's soil in Sulu, and the Tausug's unhealed wounds are left unaddressed.

Hypernegative peace occurs when, in the course of peace intervention, narratives of the past are not included in the peace framework. When the Americans supported the peace effort in the Tausug's land (and generally in Mindanao), they failed to include the healing of the past atrocities that the American soldiers in the colonial era had committed. Whether it is deliberate or not, the failure to heal the past and the exclusion of these memories in the current peace project is damaging to the peace project's success (cf. D'Costa 2013; Yerushalmi 1996). Such failure transcends transgenerationally as the narratives of the past are transmitted across generations.

Conclusion

As my grandmother said, 'the soul will continue the *agulô* if the concerns are left unsettled. It must be addressed. Addressing them can be scary and difficult but not addressing them will continue to haunt the peace of both the living and the dead.' The Tausug's ballads are the *agulôic* memories of their unhealed past wounds. Leaving them unaddressed will haunt peace not only in Sulu but also in Mindanao as a whole. Thus, recognising and reconciling with the past is an essential prerequisite towards a successful peace project and is foundational in peace formation. But while healing the past is essential for peace formation, it is apparent that the healing process—along with the mechanisms of expressing it—is undermined by those in power and politics in the Philippines.

This chapter has shown that the Balikatan military exercise in Sulu constitutes a form of hypernegative peace: the intention of the intervention was noble because it aimed to suppress terrorism and works towards social integration, but it failed to reconcile and heal the *agulôic* memory of the Tausugs. The former keep remembering the Americans as murderers of their ancestors who returned to their land yet again without permission. The military exercise was prepared by the actors holding power in the government without consulting the local community or understanding what implication the military exercise would have on their trauma.

As a foundational component in the *artpeace* formation process, local communities remember the unhealed trauma of the past through the ballads. As this chapter has shown, ballads are a cultural way of expressing an unhealed past which is largely cultural in nature. It is where trauma is remembered and is akin to a wound that never heals every time the ballad is played. Its purpose is twofold: first, it is the group's way of remembering and expressing an *agulôic* past that the peacebuilding framework excludes. By expressing them in the ballads, they are able to create a collective memory of agony, which becomes a space for dialogue (cf. Pruitt 2013). Like the soul that annoys the peaceful night with its *agulô*, another purpose of the ballad is for peace formation to repeatedly remind those in power and politics that there are neglected wounds left unhealed.

But despite the ballads' repetitive reminder, the *parang sabil kissa* failed to create change at the macro-level. There are a range of reasons for that. From the outset, they have been performed in a language foreign to those in politics and power. Building from this basic translation obstacle, another layer that impedes the ballad's purpose to create wider change is the subaltern treatment of the local community by those who hold power. With this subaltern treatment, the communication lines between the popular and the subalterns are disconnected. With such a disconnect, transmitting messages between the two is not possible. It is also subaltern treatment when the local community's voices are not considered in the decisions that largely affect their lives. The case of the Tausugs shows that there is a lack of local consultation.

But while a disconnect of the communication line entails a classical characteristic of subaltern treatment, I argue that the Tausugs themselves are not subalterns. They possess agency and are aware of their cultural identity. One of Spivak's inspirations in her subalternity work is that of Karl Marx's remark that 'the poor cannot represent themselves, so they must be represented' (quoted in Spivak 2004). Spivak (2004) also stressed the role of agency as a way towards the subaltern's institutional validation. While the Moros have the agency to express and represent themselves, the structure's treatment of them as subalterns broke such representation lines.

With the foregoing, I conclude that a transformative approach to peace formation means building a strategic connection with those holding power and politics. Emphasising localised, artistic and everyday peace practices is better positioned if geared towards communicating them to the actors of the larger peace project. Likewise, it is noble when there is recognition and effort to reconcile the past in any peace project and ballads can be one way of recognising what matters to local communities if those in power learn to listen.

Notes

1. Jose Rizal (1861–96) is known for his writings that contributed to the Filipino struggle for independence from the Spaniards. One of his writings is the *A la juventud filipina* (To the Philippine Youth) where he describes young Filipinos as the hope of the country.

2. I speak Binisaya and Tagalog. These languages are completely different from that of the Tausug.
3. The Abu Sayyaf Group was established in 1990 as a splinter group which resorted to terrorist tactics, such as kidnap for ransom, executions of civilians, and bombings (Niksch 2007).

References

Abas, S. 2004. *Foreign aid, assistance and investments in Mindanao*. PhD Thesis, Ateneo De Davao University, Davao City.

Abubakar, C. A. 2013. *Surat Sug: Jawi tradition in Southern Philippines*. Cuaderno Internacional de Estudios Humanísticos y Literatura (CIEHL), (19), pp. 31–7.

Adriano, F. and Parks, T. 2013. *The contested corners of Asia: Subnational conflict and international development assistance (the case of Mindanao, Philippines)*. California: The Asia Foundation.

Araneta, S., Frialde, M., Echeminada, P., Bagares, R., Villanueva, M., Calica, A. Rodel Clapano, J., Pareño, R. and AFP. 2003. Balikatan may no longer be held in Sulu. *Philstar*. https://www.philstar.com/headlines/2003/03/04/197587/balikatan-may-no-longer-be-held-sulu (accessed 15 September 2021).

Arviola, Jr., S. 2008. Community-based lifelong education in the Philippines: a proposed model in grassroots participatory democracy in Southeast Asia. *EDUCARE: International Journal for Educational Studies*, 1(1), pp. 1–16.

Asain, C. 2006. The Tausug Parang Sabil kissa as literary, cultural, and historical materials. *The Journal of History*, 52(1).

Asain, C., 2013. Folk literation of the Muslim cultural communities. https://ncca.gov.ph/about-ncca-3/subcommissions/subcommission-on-cultural-communities-and-traditional-arts-sccta/central-cultural-communities/folk-literature-of-the-muslim-cultural-communities/ (accessed 24 August 2021).

Assmann, A. 2006. Memory, Individual and Collective. In Goodin, R. and Tilly, C. (eds), *The Oxford Handbook of Contextual Political Analysis*. New York: Oxford University Press, pp. 210–24.

Baddiri, E., 2007. Personal reflections on the Bangsamoro struggle. Online: January 10, 2021. https://www.beyondintractability.org/reflection/baddiri-personal (accessed 20 September 2021).

Bangsamoro Commission for the Preservation of Cultural Heritage. 2020. *Parang sabil*. https://m.facebook.com/BCPCHBARMM/photos/a.595195487226209/3224573180955080/?type=3&source=57 (accessed 16 June 2021).

Björkdahl, A. and Kappler, S. 2019. The creation of transnational memory spaces: Professionalization and commercialization. *International Journal of Politics, Culture, and Society*, 32(4), pp. 383–401.

Caballero, J. and Hairullah, M. 2015. Islam in Moro history. In Caballero, J. (ed.), *History of the Filipino Muslims and other indigenous peoples of MINSUPALA*. Iligan City: MSU-Iligan Institute of Technology, pp. 19–34.

Campoamor, G. 2019. Rizal's future today: Jose Rizal's ideals and their relevance to the youth. *PhilStar Global*, 28 July. https://www.philstar.com/lifestyle/arts-and-culture/2019/07/28/1938619/rizals-future-today-jose-rizals-ideals-and-their-relevance-youth (accessed 14 August 2021).

Chow, R. 2014. *Not like a native speaker: On languaging as a postcolonial experience*. New York: Columbia University Press.

Cohen, H., Meek, K., and Lieberman, M. 2010. Memory and resilience. *Journal of Human Behavior in the Social Environment*, 20(4), pp. 525–41.

D'Costa, B. 2013. *War crimes, justice and the politics of memory*. Mumbai: Athena Information Solutions Pvt. Ltd.

De Guzman, O. 2003. Songs of resistance: History repeats itself. *Frontline*. https://www.pbs.org/frontlineworld/stories/philippines/guzman02.html (accessed 17 August 2021).

Dean, C., 2019. Using music-based programs to improve peacebuilding initiatives. *Peace Review*, 31(3), pp. 302–11.

Dijkema, C. 2007. Negative versus positive peace. http://www.irenees.net/bdf_fiche-notions-186_es.html (accessed 5 July 2021).

Dinnen, S. and Allen, M. 2018. Reflections on hybridity as an analytical lens on state formation: The case of Solomon Islands. In Wallis, J., Kent, L., Forsyth, M., Dinnen, S. and Bose, S. (eds), *Hybridity on the ground in peacebuilding and development: critical conversations*. Canberra: The Australian National University Press, pp. 129–44.

Dobbin, A. and Ross, S. 2018. Memory matters: how recall can build resilience. *The British Journal of General Practice: The Journal of the Royal College of General Practitioners*, 68(669), pp. 198–9.

Estremera, S., 2016. Duterte reminds US of Bud Dajo massacre. *SunStar*, 6 September. https://www.sunstar.com.ph/article/96464/Business/Duterte-reminds-US-of-Bud-Dajo-massacre (accessed 26 January 2021).

Fraile-Marcos, A. and Noguerol, F. 2019. Critical dystopias in Spanish memory as an act of resilience. In Fraile-Marcos, A. (ed.), *Glocal narratives of resilience*. New York: Taylor and Francis Group, pp. 148–62.

Galtung, J. 1964. A structural theory of aggression. *Journal of peace research*, 1(2), pp. 95–119.

Galtung, J. 1985. Twenty-five years of peace research: Ten challenges and some responses. *Journal of Peace Research* 22(2), pp. 141–58.

Georgakopoulos, A. 2004. The role of silence and avoidance in interpersonal conflict. *Peace and Conflict Studies*, 11(2), pp. 85–95.

Gowing, P. 1979. *Muslim Filipinos: Heritage and horizon*. Quezon City: New Day Publishers.

Grewal, B. S. 2003. *Johan Galtung: Positive and negative peace*. School of social science, Auckland University of technology, 30, pp. 23–6.

Hashim, S. 1998. Interview with Sheikh Salamat Hashim by Nida'ul Islam magazine. https://fas.org/irp/world/para/docs/ph2.htm (accessed 24 August 2023).

Hawkins, M. 2011. Managing a massacre savagery, civility, and gender in Moro province in the wake of Bud Dajo. *Philippine Studies*, 59(1), pp. 83–105.

Helmreich, W. 1992. *Against all odds: Holocaust survivors and the successful lives they made in America*. New York: Simon and Schuster.

Herath, O., 2016. *A critical analysis of Positive and Negative Peace*. 20(281), pp. 29–104.

Hintjens, H. and Ubaldo, R. 2019. Music, violence, and peace-building, *Peace Review*, 31(3), pp. 279–88.

Kappler, S. (2017). Positive Peace. In F. M. Moghaddam (Ed.), *The SAGE encyclopedia of political behavior* (640-641). SAGE Publications.

Ingilan, S. 2018. Tausug's identity in Parang Sabil: A critical discourse analysis. *CMU Journal of Science*, 22(1), pp. 39–45.

Landasan, R. 2009. *Literary symbol of my ethnic culture: parang sabil kissa*. http://ridwan89landasan.blogspot.com/2009/08/literary-symbol-of-filipinos.html (accessed 14 September 2021).

Leung, K. 1988. Some determinants of conflict avoidance. *Journal of Cross-Cultural Psychology*, 19(1), pp. 125–36.

Lind, J. 2011. *Sorry states*. New York: Cornell University Press.

Lopera, R., Vicente, H. and Adzhari, N. 2013. The American military in Sulu: peacekeepers or occupiers? In Inson, C., Ofreneo, M. and De Vela, T. (eds), *Meaning-making in Mindanao*. Cotabato City: Notre Dame of Jolo College, pp. 40–7.

Mac Ginty, R. and Richmond, O. P. 2016. The fallacy of constructing hybrid political orders: A reappraisal of the hybrid turn in peacebuilding. *International Peacekeeping*, 23(2), pp. 219–39.

Majul, C., 1988. The Moro struggle in the Philippines. *Third World Quarterly*, 10(2), pp. 897–922.

Mawallil, A. 2021. Online interview via Zoom with the author. 24 February.

Mutero, T. and Kaye, S. 2019. Music and conflict transformation in Zimbabwe, *Peace Review*, 31(3), pp. 289–96.

Niksch, L. 2007. *Abu Sayyaf: Target of Philippine-US anti-terrorism cooperation*. Washington DC: Library of Congress Washington DC, Congressional Research Service.

Ortega, C. 2020. Demystifying the Tausug through literature. *The Daily Ttibune*, 20 January. https://tribune.net.ph/index.php/2020/01/24/demystifying-the-tausug-through-litera ture/ (accessed 21 July 2021).

Paffenholz, T. 2014. International peacebuilding goes local: Analysing Lederach's conflict trans-formation theory and its ambivalent encounter with 20 years of practice. *Peacebuilding*, 2 (1), pp. 11–27.

Pareño, R. and Villa, B. 2003. Majority of Sulu residents welcome Balikatan 03-1. *PhilStar Global*, April 11. https://www.philstar.com/headlines/2003/04/11/202303/majority-sulu-resi dents-welcome-balikatan-03-1 (accessed 18 June 2021).

Pruitt, L. 2013. *Youth peacebuilding music, gender, and Change*. New York: SUNY Press.

Ragandang, P. 2020. Filipino students use 'padungog-dungog' to resist educational inequal-ity. https://www.newmandala.org/filipino-students-use-padungog-dungog-to-resist-educa tional-inequality/ (accessed 9 August 2021).

Ragandang, P. 2020. Social media and youth peacebuilding agency: A case from Muslim Mindanao. *Journal of Peacebuilding & Development*, 15(3), pp. 348–61.

Remollino, A. 2008. Songs of resistance, tales of pride in Moroland. In Tuazon, B. (ed.), *The Moro reader history and contemporary struggles of the Bangsamoro people*. Quezon City: Center for People Empowerment in Governance, pp. 175–9.

Richmond, O. P. 2015. The dilemmas of a hybrid peace: Negative or positive? *Cooperation and Conflict*, 50(1), pp. 50–68.

Richmond, O. P. 2016. *Peace formation and political order in conflict affected societies*. Oxford: Oxford University Press.

Risal, S., 2019. Music for peacebuilding and conflict resolution in Nepal. *Peace Review*, 31(3), pp. 297–301.

Saada, N., 2016. Kissa and dawat: The continuing story-telling tradition of the Moro people. *Minda News*, December 10. https://www.mindanews.com/mindaviews/2016/12/kissa-and-dawat-the-continuing-story-telling-tradition-of-the-moro-people/ (accessed 10 December 2016).

Saada, N. 2021. Online interview with the author via Zoom, 27 March.

Saleeby, N. 1905. *Studies in Moro history, law, and religion*. Manila: Bureau of Public Printing.

Schiavo-Campo, S. and Judd, M. 2005. *The Mindanao conflict in the Philippines: Roots, costs, and potential peace dividend*. Washington DC: World Bank, Conflict Prevention & Reconstruction Social Development Department.

Silva, J. 2002. *Fr. Eliseo "Jun" Mercado, Jr., OMI*. New York: Synergos Institute.

Spivak, G. 1995. Can the Subaltern Speak? In Ashcroft, B., Griffiths, G., and Tiffin, A. (eds), *Post-Colonial Studies Reader*. London and New York: Routledge, pp. 24–8.

Spivak, G. 2004. Gayatri Spivak: The Trajectory of the Subaltern in My Work. University of California Television (UCTV). *YouTube*, uploaded 8 February 2008. youtube.com/ watch?v=2ZHH4ALRFHw (accessed 15 June 2021).

Stavrevska, E. B., DasGupta, S., Vogel, B. and Chadha Behera N. 2016. Agency, autonomy and compliance in (post-)conflict situations: Perspectives from Jammu and Kashmir, Cyprus and Bosnia-Herzegovina. In Burgess, P. J., Richmond, O. P. and Samaddar, R. (eds), *Cultures of governance and peace*. Manchester: Manchester University Press, pp. 88–112.

Soltes, O. 2010. Memory, tradition, and revival: Who, then, speaks for the Jews? In E. Langenbacher and Y. Shain (eds), *Power and the past: collective memory and international relations*. Washington DC: Georgetown University Press, pp. 121–46.

Taylor, A. 2016. It's not just Hiroshima: The many other things America hasn't apologized for. *The Washington Post*, May 26. https://www.washingtonpost.com/news/worldviews/wp/2016/05/26/the-things-america-hasnt-apologized-for/ (accessed 2 September 2021).

Tjosvold, D. and Sun, H. F. 2002. Understanding conflict avoidance: Relationship, motivations, actions, and consequences. *International Journal of Conflict Management*, 13(2), pp. 142–64.

University of California Television. 2004. Gayatri Spivak: The trajectory of the subaltern in my work. [Online Video]. www.youtube.com/watch?v=2ZHH4ALRFHw&t=430s (accessed 15 June 2021).

Wadi, J. 2008. Multiple colonialism in Moroland. In Tuazon, B. (ed.), *The Moro reader history and contemporary struggles of the Bangsamoro people*. Quezon City: Center for People Empowerment in Governance, pp. 28–37.

Yerushalmi, Y. 1996. *Zakhor Jewish history and Jewish memory*. Seattle, WA: University of Washington Press.

Acknowledgments

I would like to thank and remember my late mother, Mama Melina, and late grandmother, Nanay Tening, for their stories on *agulôic* ballads diffused through this chapter. I dedicate this work to them. My gratitude also to Professor Bina D'Costa for introducing me to the importance of the politics of memory. I also thank Stefanie Kappler and Birte Vogel for their comments on earlier versions of the chapter. All errors remain mine.

CONCLUSION

Artpeace and its Potential for Peacemaking

Stefanie Kappler and Oliver P. Richmond

New Directions

When we first set out to investigate the role that art can play in relation to formal and informal peace processes in Sudan, the DRC, Syria/Lebanon, the Philippines, Bosnia-Herzegovina, South Africa and Colombia, we assumed that the creative synthesis of subaltern political claim-making in conflict-affected societies with peacemaking would offer critical insights into how grassroots movements might envision emancipatory forms of peace. We expected substantive, critical potential but were also aware that most of the contributions of *artpeace* might be therapeutic in nature. We also expected to be able to explore blockages to *artpeace*, which would probably be limited by its inability (along with social and local agency more broadly) to have a substantive influence on larger-scale political and geopolitical dynamics, on internationally or elite-driven peace processes within the state and social structure, or at the regional and international level. Indeed, how often do we see artwork referenced in peace negotiations? Where are artists included by default in the design and implementation of peace-related agendas? These rhetorical questions are perhaps at the root of the legitimacy crisis that western and liberal models of peacemaking face.

The constituencies included in peace processes tend to be narrow, and even the inclusion of civil society remains controversial. Even in instances where artists are included, they often have little room for critical engagement and risk being instrumentalised. Yet, we were also aware, through our collaboration with artists and activists in this project, that the arts were seen in different locales as well as by some state and international actors as sites of potential dialogue and reconciliation. They may also have the potential to develop or access wider, indeed global, networks interested in peace as a local practice, and help influence a conceptual framework for critical global politics also influenced by aesthetics (Bleiker 2009).

New Categories and Tools for Peacemaking

With this in mind, the editors of this volume have produced a set of categories based upon a general understanding of the broad relationship between the ethical, political, civil and aesthetic parameters of *artpeace*. These categories (*artpeace* formation, artivism, *artpeace*building, arttransformation, artmediation, artpacification and everyday *artpeace*) try to capture the objectives, agency, politics, capacities, audience and impact of the relationship between artistic endeavours on the one hand, and peace processes in our different cases on the other hand. They were developed through a synergy between theory and practice in the arts and peacemaking, connecting the evolution of peace and conflict studies conceptualisations (drawing on international relations theory, anthropology and ethnography) (Millar 2015; Richmond 2011 and 2016; Vrasti 2008) with social movements, networks and related agency in the terrain of the arts (Mitchell et al. 2020). In our cases, we found most arts-related peace activities were gathered around *artpeace* formation, artivism and everyday *artpeace*. These categories were deployed in the case studies represented in the preceding chapters, and in what follows we offer some brief, concluding thoughts about the salience of our categorisations of *artpeace*, and the potential we see for *artpeace* in practice, drawing on the empirical contributions of our collaborators.

In a nutshell, in theoretical and conceptual terms, *artpeace* is a praxis that represents political agency, creativity and critique, as well as legitimacy in peacemaking contexts, but its operation is little understood in relation to actual practices of peacemaking. The question of whether, and if so how, it influences peacemaking and peacebuilding remains open. However, we do see traction in our categories.

Empirical Observations

Upon empirical testing these categorisations reflect how the degree of entanglement between art and the politics of peace varies with the nature of their relationship. This has a number of different dynamics. Firstly, where art serves as a mere tool to legitimise or implement a hegemonic, top-down, one-sided version of peace, it is rather limited in its transgressive and emancipatory potential and remains primarily therapeutic in nature, even consolidating the status quo. This is primarily the case with the categories of artpacification, *artpeace*building, artmediation and, to a certain extent, arttransformation.

Secondly, in relationships where (community) artists tend to be in the driving seat of the creative agenda—to different degrees in the categories of *artpeace* formation, artivism and everyday *artpeace*—we discover more potential for political change, if only at local levels and with limited impact on national and regional peace processes.

Thirdly, the relationship between art and politics, as we have seen in our case studies, is never a natural given, but is shaped by the political landscape in which it is situated and the levels to which communities are mobilised to challenge potentially harmful political dynamics which authorise direct, structural or cultural violence. These indicate the ease with which small-scale practices of mobilisation for creative solutions to entrenched conflicts, even though they may connect with global networks and receive widespread attention, are blocked, impeded, undermined, censored and even erased.

This is an important—and negative—lesson from this study. Blockages are widely understood in *artpeace* movements, and they represent powerful means of curbing *artpeace* agency through their control of existing institutions, and their impact on funding, infrastructures and censorship practices. All of the case study chapters in this book have demonstrated various such obstacles to a meaningful relationship between art and peace and the risk of the former being instrumentalised by the latter. However, where there are multitrack processes at play (Sudan), politically mobilised structures (Lebanon) or engaged arts-based subcultures (Colombia, South Africa), *artpeace* seems to develop in less one-sided and more politically relevant ways.

As Richmond's initial and exploratory chapter suggests, the starting point for the evolution of *artpeace* was often taken to be an imperial, state-centric, elite and Eurocentric view of the arts. This tends to differentiate art as separate from social dynamics, craft and folklore, and thus elevates it to an aesthetic experience that sits above people's everyday lives. This also means it tends to be controlled by elites to authorise power-relations and war, primarily used as a way of consolidating and legitimising the political status quo, even where wars occur or indeed where war and violence are used as political tools. Artwork, in this understanding, is elite-oriented, staged, separated from people's lived experiences, used to consolidate certain forms of politics, interests and norms over alternatives and, in peace terms, following a logic of counter-insurgency or pacification at best. However, Richmond's chapter outlines how resistance to war, and thus to the power-structures that authorise war, emerge in the more hidden corners of artistic development, and how this provides a platform for the early development of and experimentation in *artpeace*.

There is clearly little that is revolutionary about art situated in a contemporary, elite-oriented social order, where some of the energy for change may be tamed, museum-ised and curated away. Additonally, international actors, by ignoring, underfunding or co-opting *artpeace* dynamics in conflict-affected contexts may be playing into the hands of venal national elites who prefer to profit from or maintain conflict and block peace. Sometimes *artpeace* has to work within such limitations and find clever tactics to take on power in its own ways. Yet, artists benefitting from this social order tend to be predominantly middle-class, white and male—not least helped through the precariousness of labour that freelance-based artwork brings with it, which is hardly affordable for those without additional economic safety nets behind them, or those with caring responsibilities. These factors limit the potential of art to mobilise against hegemony and power. Art's willingness and ability to contest engrained structures of dominance, coloniality and injustice may be performative at best and only deployed when politically convenient. Yet, as Richmond's chapter suggests, even such limitations have the capacity to produce change and may evolve in wider, if not global, society.

Against this background, this book and its conceptual framing have attempted a somewhat broader yet more specific perspective, challenging a narrow, Eurocentric and convenient view on the arts. This is not to argue that non-European art, for instance, is diametrically opposed to the European tradition and instead to acknowledge the aesthetic interlinkages between different artforms (Huyssen 2022). Still, different expressions of art and aesthetics can be seen as embedded in diverse political traditions and are shaped accordingly—vulnerable to erasure on the one hand, but remarkably resilient on the other hand. Yet, our findings suggest only very small-scale micro-impacts emerge in very specific conflict-affected societies, with a rare but broad-brush international scale of potential influence, which is nearly impossible to quantify. Our broad range of case studies investigated by scholars and activists from different backgrounds, disciplines and institutions has demonstrated that art may, after all, be in the position to occupy a meaningful political position in the micro-renegotiation of social orders after and during conflict and violence, with very occasional large-scale impact. Indeed, there have been historical examples, and wider representations are now starting to emerge, as our cases studies have illustrated.

Possibilities and Pathways for Peace Formation and Arts in the Face of Blockages

How can the arts become an integral, rather than a marginal, sphere contributing to our understanding of the complex ways in which peace organically emerges, and what difference does it make for peace at large? How do we understand the phenomenon of *artpeace*, how it creates, resists, mobilises, envisions emancipation and moves into more agential areas of political engagement? How does *artpeace* assist in the various elements of peacemaking, mediation, peacebuilding and conflict transformation, while expressing local political claims in the context of a formal peace process?

It is important to problematise the role of the arts as agential in cementing prevailing social relations and power structures on the one hand, and as a potential progressive force for change on the other, shedding light on a range of local to global dynamics related to violence and to peace. We can clearly see how formal and informal political struggles, conflict and violence are reflected in *artpeace*. Does it indicate a way forward, given its ability to maintain and develop ideas, promote cooperation, reconciliation and justice through more empathetic forms of communication, which in turn influence social perceptions and international dialogue? Our case studies indicate much potential here, but potential that has to be understood in creative and social terms, as opposed to directly political. So how can arts-based work realise its potential as an essential part of peacemaking, sensitive to the needs of the communities it serves but offering creative progress, and what are the obstacles preventing it from fulfilling this function? Specifically, if we are to investigate the role of the arts in the field of peace formation and to create new lines of praxis, we need to ask under what conditions the arts can serve as a platform of resistance against oppressive power structures, when they contribute subversive politics on their own (creative) terms, and when they are blocked from doing so. This requires an understanding of subaltern politics in conflict-affected societies as well as a capacity to engage with the way such claims travel across the state and international system (if they do).

According to our case studies, *artpeace* incorporates creative, critical agency and resistance which is subtle, highly developed, easily networked, but only marginally effective. We find that critical, subversive and creative ideas about promoting peace and justice are likely to emerge, however, and percolate into wider society, with some undetermined impact on formal political debates, though not usually in the fora of peacemaking (which is often closely stage managed and associated with elite power-based politics). *Artpeace*building, mediation and pacification, are however, not suited to the varieties of *artpeace* we observe, so *artpeace* formation and arttransformation are its more common, low key, bottom-up characteristics, with everyday *artpeace* being extremely common but widely ignored by policymakers. Being marginalised provokes creative experimentation and raises problems for the legitimacy of formal political order, reform and dialogues, something of which *artpeace*'s proponents are aware, even if only in the long term.

This means that the epistemological boundaries that shape our understanding of political authority in conflict-affected societies are too narrow and reductionist; too focused on power, law and institutions; and misunderstand the agencies that they are comprised of. It makes only limited sense to dichotomise artist methodologies in opposition to more formal politics, however. Instead, we need to understand the ways in which creativity, innovation, expression and representation related to marginalisation on the grounds of gender, race, generational and class stratifications that are present in the public sphere are reproduced, challenged and/or transformed by *artpeace*, while recognising that art itself is embedded in a highly politicised social terrain. This means that it may not be sufficient for the arts to challenge such intersectional inequalities aesthetically, but they also need to reconstruct the very system of political reform and peacemaking which they are embedded in. Given this paradox, can the arts ever drive peaceful political reform given they would be challenging the very structures that have given rise to their existence in the first place? Is *artpeace* evolutionary or revolutionary? Given that it operates in a social context, with no direct power, and in the long term, it would appear to be primarily the former, being focused on challenging exclusionary and violent rationalities and creative and intellectual resistance rather than effective, direct political action.

Part of the problem is that, if the arts have traction and are subversive, then power will silence them before they even start being active. Blockages abound against *artpeace* and have become very sophisticated. We have found evidence that current powerholders try to prevent *artpeace* actors from emerging in the first place through practices such as censorship, deprivation of funding and refusing to grant authorisation or access to public spaces. In that sense, political blockages can be deliberately constructed, especially in contexts where artists seek to address wider structural inequalities and challenge the status quo and embedded power relations. Such blockages may emerge from a language of liberal rationality or modernity that shapes the political legacies of imperial politics and the structural violence they carry (see Nkosinkulu's chapter), or the marginalisation of art forms that are hard to translate into the commonly used languages of peacebuilding. Ragandang's chapter, for instance, shows how community ballads in the Philippines point to unaddressed grievances and, thus, how communities sing about the way they wish the peace process to develop. However, their message remains unheard and cannot be understood by those designing such processes because of cultural and linguistic blockages. We find politically engineered blockages such as the NGO-isation of art in the DRC (as with Schouten's chapter) or the appropriation of travelling arts into static peacebuilding frameworks (see Sobout's chapter). Verjee's chapter in turn focuses on an international system governed by powerful states that are at times ignorant of the complex interactions between multiple levels of governance within countries. He shows how some artistic interventions in South Sudan can contribute to elite peace processes while others deliberately aim at different audiences. Not only are such blockages engineered by state-based actors, but as the chapter on Medellín, Colombia, shows with reference to gang violence, blockages can emerge from powerful non-state actors, too, if they feel it threatens their objectives (see Ó Brádaigh Bean's chapter).

These dynamics, though at least partially domestically-driven, also capture an internationally driven, status-quo oriented peace process, as the chapter on Mostar, Bosnia-Herzegovina, illustrates (see Cole's chapter).

Importantly, and connected to Cole's chapter, the literature that deals with the process of curating as a social practice has illustrated the ways in which art is subject to a political filtering during the course of its wider institutionalisation, whether that is in public spaces (such as cityscapes) or semi-public spaces (such as museums) (cf. Douglas 2017; Kappler and McKane 2019; Smith 2006). The institutionalisation of the arts through curatorial processes is certainly one way for them to gain formal traction through increased accessibility for larger audiences and presentation in public fora. At the same time, the process of translation from creative to political praxis can be subtler and start with the artwork itself, that is, an *artpeace* sensitivity is inherently part of its genesis. Yet, either way, the extent to which art is political can never be generalised but is subject to the surrounding power relations and how they are mediated.

Some Caveats, Gaps and Omissions in *Artpeace*

Interestingly, almost none of the case studies discussed by our contributing authors reference artwork hosted in powerful or national museums. Instead, they focus on art as an everyday, activist practice, conducted in public spaces and for broad publics. Art, as discussed in many of the chapters, is an inherently political expression of basic needs as much as political demands, ranging from poverty alleviation and pedagogics to some larger-scale mobilisation against situations of injustice and discrimination. The artists discussed are rarely isolated individuals, but tend to be deeply embedded in the communities they claim to represent—albeit to different degrees.

A further dynamic that emerges from our cases, is that the artificial distinction between art and craft or folklore (predominantly a colonial distinction) makes little sense for our authors, though there clearly is a hierarchy in terms of political agency. Rather, community-based work feeds the very arts that the different artists create, mostly of a DIY, self-taught, youth-oriented and informal nature. Ballads, graffiti and hip hop, for instance, are more than popular culture items; they are fed by and inform the very politics that make the negotiation of a new social order tangible to those at its receiving ends. Thus, *artpeace* may not be an end in itself, but represents a grass-roots, bottom-up connection between creativity, empathy, mobilisation, agency, resistance and the politics of peacemaking (in particular its need for local legitimacy). This also leads to reactive dynamics, however, in terms of more traditional and reactive notions of political power and their representation, which may seek to censor *artpeace* and its attempt to form a viable peace process from below where elites have failed to address political issues from above—either at the state or international level.

It would be naïve to suggest that non-Europeanised understandings and practices of art are therefore the uncritical answer to our question of whether and how art can positively influence peace formation, locally and globally. The book has illustrated how, even in more limited methodological and epistemological settings, *artpeace* emerged slowly and has broadened its engagement to challenge—discursively—entrenched power structures and their founding assumptions. *Artpeace* fundamentally, but discursively, questions iniquitous power relations and social injustice, and seeks to challenge violence as a political tool by highlighting its injustice and contradictions. It points to emotional, cultural and social concerns and where possible it imagines or projects solutions. It sometimes reaches for common international norms, and often proposes that local mobilisation, resistance and reconciliation is plausible, as well as offering pertinent tools that engage with how people think about pluralist politics.

However, we can also see from the case studies in this volume that even recent, local articulations of *artpeace* are not immune from in-built inequalities and they, too, can even act as carriers of cultural and structural forms of violence. In the case studies of South Sudan, Bosnia-Herzegovina and the DRC, the authors indeed observed varying degrees of commercialisation and instrumentalisation of artworks for elite-oriented processes. Artists may be co-opted into promoting liberal peace agendas in their work—facilitated by the fact that such political agendas tend to enjoy much better funding infrastructures than the arts themselves, and the search for income through the sale of art or even conflict tourism makes art additionally vulnerable to such processes of co-optation. Those processes create their own patterns of exclusion, favouring globally marketable and politically convenient artforms over those who might shake the global peace architecture to its very core. This may also be part of the subtle erasure of emancipatory perspectives that do not conform to the liberal, neoliberal, authoritarian or nationalist rationalities of the modern state. We think, having observed the salience of *artpeace* as a political sensibility, if not representative of direct agency, that the erasure of such expressions has been a long-standing reaction of power-structures invested in war. In other words, the resonance of *artpeace* is significant and political even without direct agency, but so is its erasure, co-optation or absence.

What is also striking in many of the case studies discussed in the book is the gendered nature of the artwork at play. In fact, most of the individual artists referenced in the different chapters tend to be male, which demonstrates the increased visibility of their artwork in public spaces, which in turn also has an impact on who we, as researchers, see, discuss and curate in books like this. Importantly, we see the public-private binary reproduced in the artworld: while, for instance, the African intellectuals portrayed in Nkosinkulu's chapter and given a presence in *public* space are all male, Ragandang's grandmother plays an important role in translating the function of the ballads to the *private* space of the household. Certainly, when we look to achieve gender-just peace (Björkdahl 2012) and assess the potential contribution of the arts in this endeavour, this reads as a note of caution. Are the demands articulated by women primarily articulated as community-based representations (as our Lebanon case study seems to suggest), while men's art tends to be viewed as individual achievement and thus, unlike art conceptualised by women, worthy of individual compensation? Similar exclusions can certainly also be said to be true with respect to the LGBTQI community, though it might also open spaces. Haworth et al (2022, 41), for instance, argue that LGBTQ+ voices have found a space to contribute to the cultural and public debates through graffiti work in Cyprus, despite being otherwise marginalised in public discourses.

These are only two axes of intersectional exclusion that we need to be mindful of when investigating the power relations inherent in *artpeace*. Participation is at risk of differentiation based on gender, race, class, ability and generation, to name but a few. Our case studies indeed do reflect a strong presence of youth-oriented work and, perhaps with the exception of Ragandang's analysis, risk overlooking older generations' contributions to *artpeace*. It is therefore clear from our conceptualisation and cases that art is not immune to the inequalities shaping politics in the wider sense. Art is embedded in a political landscape that empowers some and disempowers others. In this landscape, the politics of gatekeeping must not be underestimated. Gatekeeping can be sustained by powerful political actors (through forms of censorship), economic agents (by funding some artwork and withdrawing resources from other work) or by curators themselves. The latter play an important role in deciding which artwork is worthy of exhibition and deserves a public space. Where curatorial roles are distributed in communities (see Sobout's chapter), this may produce different political results from a situation where privileged individuals act as curators of artwork. Investigating the ways in which art is archived, staged, tamed and presented is therefore crucial in understanding the frictional relationship between art and politics, art and peace and, thus, *artpeace*. This specifically raises questions of how publicly marginal or even erased art might be curated, and how the political ecosystem shapes sensitive curatorial decisions. In that sense, *artpeace* is not a binary phenomenon. It cannot be neatly categorised into western versus non-western art, art versus craft, or power versus resistance. Instead, the politics of *artpeace* lie in the nuances through which it is negotiated: who creates art, who consumes it (or engages with its political rather than material capacities), who curates it and for whom?

Conclusion and the Future of *Artpeace*

All of the above is not to say that aesthetics themselves do not have a role to play in the ways in which communities mobilise and network. Art can be the rare catalyst of potentially explosive energies, destabilising unjust political orders and bringing people together around an agenda that centres their views on peace, justice and social order. In the individual chapters of this book, we have found such pockets of mobilisation, where *artpeace* is articulated and discussed in marginalised communities, setting the scene for political action. Such dynamics are mirrored across all conflict zones, it appears. The art projects discussed in this book do respond to everyday needs, articulate subaltern politics, resist power and create new links within communities. They show that the reordering of social relations is possible through aesthetic engagement—or artivism, as some chapters frame this process. At the same time, it appears that, despite being linked to wider global movements and trends, these processes tend to be locally secluded, concentrated in smaller communities, and often struggle with translating their political energy into the wider politics of peace. They encounter various blockages when trying to upscale to a bigger level, ranging from political pressure to financial disincentives of doing so. This also means that their power is limited in challenging a system in which violence, conflict and injustice are largely global in nature and transcend the immediate locality in which art is produced and consumed.

The future issue this book raises then is whether and how such powerful pockets of political energy, as articulated through the arts, can be connected more broadly, especially given the rise of digital networks, technologies and capacities? How can solidarities and links emerge that allow for these seemingly localised processes to have a sustainable and meaningful impact upon the "hard politics" of peace as we shift from an analogue to a digital era?

Essentially, what this book has shown is that there is a need to redefine the role of the arts in politics away from their definition as an apolitical phenomenon, unconnected with practices of peacemaking (often promoted in Eurocentric understandings of art), in favour of a view of the arts as essential, political, networked and globally connected. This touches on the big political and philosophical issues of peacemaking, and provides a medium for critical mobilisation and resistance, reimagining relations between enemies, for reconciliation, and social reconstruction as a preliminary to cultural, political and structural peace agreements. Yet, rather than viewing art as a panacea for political and social problems uncritically, we suggest there needs to be a multi-dimensional understanding of politics, internal power relations and inequalities, which *artpeace* often provides a critical intuition about. This may be in terms of the interpretation of historical wrongs, the imagining of solutions to open, entrenched and hidden war, conflict and violence. There is much more that can be developed around this nexus, we would argue. We hope to have shown that non-traditional approaches to political mobilisation, activism and curation are thus a key area of political innovation and legitimisation in the realms of peacemaking. This is globally and locally hinted at through the creative, inclusive, resonant and critical participation of the arts, communities and activists as well as the inclusion of broader publics than most traditional arts, or indeed political venues, have thus-far been able to achieve.

References

Björkdahl A. 2012. A Gender-Just Peace? Exploring the Post-Dayton Peace Process in Bosnia: A Gender-Just Peace? *Peace & Change*, 37(2), pp. 286–317.

Bleiker, R. 2009. *Aesthetics and World Politics*. Houndmills, Basingstoke: Palgrave Macmillan.

Douglas, S. 2017 *Curating community. Museums, constitutionalism, and the taming of the political*. Ann Arbor, MI: University of Michigan Press.

Haworth, B. T., Lepp, E., Arthur, C., and Vogel, B. 2022. "Your wall cannot divide us": Graffiti in Cyprus and insights into conflict-affected landscapes. SAUC-Street Art and Urban Creativity, 8(2), pp. 35–49. https://sauc.website/index.php/sauc/article/view/584 (accessed 24 August 2023).

Huyssen, A. 2022. *Memory Art in the Contemporary World: Confronting Violence in the Global South. New directions in contemporary art*. London: Lund Humphries.

Kappler, S. and McKane, A. 2019. "Post-conflict Curating": The Arts and Politics of Belfast's Peace Walls *De Arte*, 54(2), pp.4–21.

Millar, G. 2015. Ethnographic Approach to Peacebuilding: Understanding Local Experiences in Transitional States. London: Routledge.

Mitchell, J. P., Vincett, G., and Hawksley, T. (eds). 2020. *Peacebuilding and the Arts*. Cham: Palgrave Macmillan.

Richmond, O. P. 2011. *A Post-Liberal Peace*. Abingdon: Routledge.

Richmond, O. P. 2016. *Peace Formation and Political Order in Conflict Affected Societies*. Oxford: Oxford University Press.

Smith, L. 2006. *The Uses of Heritage*. Abingdon: Routledge.

Vrasti, W. 2008. The Strange Case of Ethnography and International Relations. *Millennium*, 37(2), pp. 279–301.

EU representative:
Easy Access System Europe
Mustamäe tee 50, 10621 Tallinn, Estonia
Gpsr.requests@easproject.com

www.ingramcontent.com/pod-product-compliance
Lightning Source LLC
Chambersburg PA
CBHW070415290526
45791CB00005B/1716